The Commons in Transition

A volume in the Fontana Studies in Politics.

Also published:

Governing Britain
A. H. Hanson and Malcolm Walles

In preparation:

Understanding Local Government
Jeffrey Stanyer

GW00707788

Contributors

Norman Chester *Warden of Nuffield College, Oxford*
Bernard Crick *Professor of Political Theory and Institutions,*
  University of Sheffield
Sir Edward Fellowes *Formerly The Clerk of the House of Commons*
J. A. G. Griffith *Professor of English Law, University of London*
A. H. Hanson *Professor of Politics, University of Leeds*
Nevil Johnson *Nuffield Reader in the Comparative Study of*
  Institutions in the University of Oxford, and Professorial Fellow
  of Nuffield College
Geoffrey Lock *Deputy Assistant Librarian, House of Commons*
Geoffrey Marshall *Fellow of Queen's College, Oxford*
S. A. Walkland *Senior Lecturer in Political Theory and Institutions,*
  University of Sheffield
H. Victor Wiseman *Formerly Professor of Politics, University of*
  Exeter

The Commons in Transition

By Members of the Study of Parliament Group

Edited by A. H. Hanson
and Bernard Crick

 Fontana/Collins

First published 1970
Second Impression October 1970
Third Impression September 1973

Printed in Great Britain
Collins Clear-Type Press London and Glasgow

*In memory of our friend and Colleague,
Victor Wiseman (1909-1969)*

Contents

Introduction

In a sense, these essays are a collective product. Their authors, all members of the Study of Parliament Group, have been meeting regularly during the last five years to exchange views about the working of Parliament and—occasionally—to formulate agreed proposals for its improvement. Each, we think, would readily recognise that if the Group did not exist his knowledge of Parliament would be poorer and his views lack the degree of maturity that comes from regular exposure to constructive criticism.

The Group is a small body, consisting of some academics, some Clerks of both Houses and some officers of the House of Commons Library. But while this present volume emerges from discussions in the Group as a whole over the last five years, yet it should be emphasised, however, that the Group collectively accept no responsibility for the opinions here expressed—still less for any factual error that may have crept in.

Indeed, the Group is seldom unanimous, except in its belief that parliamentary government in Britain is a valuable institution which should be studied more intensively with the object of preserving and improving it. We stress this fact because those interested in the Group's activities have sometimes ascribed to it a 'monolithic' character which it does not and cannot possess. Although from time to time it has given evidence to Select Committees on Procedure and issued publications in its own name, it has never claimed to speak on behalf of all its members, some of whom, displaying the tolerance which should be the hallmark of citizens of a parliamentary democracy, have agreed to the public expression of majority opinions about which they have had reservations.

That the Group is no unified pressure group will be evident from a reading of these essays. It is clear, for instance, that there is considerable difference of opinion about the proper role and organisation of committees, both standing and select; and one may reliably surmise that Professor Griffith's views on legislation and Sir Edward Fellowes's on Standing Orders would not find unanimous support. The essayists, in fact, are not attempting to present a common point of view but contributing as individuals to a continuing discussion.

Nor should the reader expect from this volume a coverage of every important aspect of the working of Parliament, or even of every procedural matter that is currently a matter of controversy. Each contributor has dealt with a subject that he finds particularly interesting. The coverage, therefore, reflects the preoccupations of those who volunteered or were persuaded to write, rather than an ideal scheme in the minds of the editors. We have limited ourselves, moreover, to the House of Commons—which reflects both the main interests of our members and the state of uncertainty surrounding the 'Lords Question'. Thus this book makes no claim whatever to be the fully comprehensive and realistic general book on Parliament which is needed to replace the out-of-date and rather out-moded *Parliament* of the late Sir W. Ivor Jennings. If there is a plan, it has not been to attempt a balanced coverage—we say nothing, for instance, about the changing character of Members themselves, nor about the conduct of debate on the Floor—but rather to fill in huge gaps in existing accounts: to provide, in fact, an essential supplement to, not a self-contained replacement of, the existing literature. If there is, however, a rather heavy emphasis on committees, this is because so many of the Group's members have found in them the most significant growth-point of the House.

In this connection we should make clear, as editors, that all these essays were completed and were in the press, except our own, before the publication of the First Report of the Select Committee on Procedure, 1968–69, on 'Scrutiny of Public Expenditure and Administration', which contains important recommendations about the work of the Estimates Committee in relation to the new specialised committees.

Our collective thanks are due to many Frontbench and Backbench Members for the interest they have shown in the Group's work; and also to Mr Michael Turnbull for his friendly assistance in preparing this symposium for publication.

A.H.H. B.R.C.
September 1969

Chapter 1

Legislation

J. A. G. Griffith

It may seem strange that a lawyer should be asked to write about legislation. For lawmaking is a function partly of Governments (and therefore more apt to be commented on by political scientists) and partly of private corporations (and therefore more apt to be commented on by industrialists). Lawyers are handmaidens only, recruited—with whatever result—to introduce precision.

But one of the earliest writers to comment on the part played in modern times by Governments was a lawyer who left practice to become an academic:

When in the summer of last year, I mentioned, among some individuals of my own circle, my intention of sending in testimonials for this chair, I found a general disposition among professional men (and, among them, men of the most superior understandings), to dissuade me from so doing, on one or other of the following grounds:
1. That the office of a Law Professor was undesirable for a practising lawyer; for any one, in short, but those who had nothing else to do.
2. That it was one of doubtful utility to the public.[1]

So, J. J. Park, Esquire, in the first lecture of a course on the theory and practice of the constitution 'delivered at King's College, London, in the commencement term of that institution', that is, 1832. Mr Park was none of your Blackstonian legal philosophers. He put on his title page the statement by Comte: 'Les savans doivent aujourd'hui élever la politique au rang des sciences d'observation.' Avoiding the liberal democratic fallacies which John Stuart Mill and, especially, Bagehot were to propound (they were respectively 26 and 6 years of age at the time), he had no illusions about the seat of the lawmaking power. His views are worthy of resurrection, partly because of their clarity and partly because it is com-

1. J. J. Park, *The Dogmas of the Constitution* (1832), pp. 1–2.

monly believed that those views were not current until much later:

We shall be told (as we are by Blackstone and others) of an executive or *law-executing* government, whose business is to carry into effect the behests of the legislature, or *law-making* government; but who, by some strange misconception of their functions, if those be they, do invariably throw up their offices as soon as that law-making government manifests an unequivocal difference of opinion with themselves, as to *what is to be legislated*. We shall be told that the legislative power of the crown resides solely in its veto, or power of dissenting to the resolutions of the other two estates; and we should then recollect that no such power has ever been exercised for 140 years, namely, since the bill for triennial parliaments; so that a fundamental part of the constitution should appear to have been surrendered.[2]

The mind of the modern reader may jump a little when subtracting 140 from 1832. But our author corrects his dates in an addendum thus: 'I have since observed that the royal veto was once exercised in the reign of Queen Anne; but I cannot now remember upon what occasion';[3] and, he seems to add, this splendid man, 'I am not going to spend any of my valuable time looking for the damn'd thing just to satisfy you pedants.' He goes on:

We shall be told, that (with the exception at least of bills of grace) the crown has no *initiative*, or power of proposing laws to the other two estates, but a power of rejection only; yet we shall find every bill of any great importance introduced by the immediate servants of the crown, *in their official characters*; and not only that, but (as it is currently admitted in debate) on their responsibility too; responsibility which only belongs to them as *officers of the crown*, and which, *as members of parliament*, they do not possess. We shall be told that the king, as a branch of the legislature, can know nothing of any resolution of parliament, till it has passed both houses of the legislature; and, that it is when the bill, embodying the resolution, is presented to him, that his function for the first time accrues of acceptance or of rejection: and yet we shall hear the first minister of the crown broadly admitting, that the pre-assent of the king is implied to a bill brought in by his own confidential servants.[4]

And again:

2. Op. cit. pp. 9–10.   3. Op. cit. p. 126.   4. Op. cit. pp. 10–11.

We find, that no sooner is an administration formed, than it immediately takes upon itself not only what is properly called the *executive* government, but another and much more important function, not recognised by the theory of the constitution—the management, control, and direction, of the whole mass of political legislation, according to its own views of political science and civil economy: that, although some scattered portions of legislation are gladly left by this over-burdened administration to private individuals, who are desirous, either through vanity or public spirit, of signalising themselves as legislators,—yet that even this is done, as it were, by the connivance of the administration, or *government*, as it is emphatically called; and that it follows, as a necessary consequence, from government being always in the majority of the House of Commons, that no private individual could carry any measure through parliament which government should see reason to oppose, —so that a single intimation of such intention at once compels the private legislator to drop or withdraw his measure:—that even this connivance at private legislation is not considered constitutional or becoming, when the measure is one of political importance, as it is deemed not merely the *right*, but the *duty* of government, to take upon itself the responsibility of introducing such measures into parliament; and government has even been severely reprimanded, by leaders in opposition, for abandoning that duty to others;— finally, that as soon as, from any circumstances whatever, government, or the administration, shall be deprived of the power of so managing, controlling, and directing the course of political legislation, by a change of the majority into the minority, or find sufficient reason to apprehend that they *shall* be deprived of that power, they do, according to the actual course of the constitution, resign office, upon the express grounds that *they* can no longer carry on the government *advantageously to the country*;—and that, so far from doing that as an act of offending greatness, it would be esteemed politically *dishonourable* and *improper*, if they were to *retain* office after the support and adhesion of a majority in the House of Commons should have been unequivocally withdrawn from them. Now, gentlemen, there is not one word of all this in the standard history of the constitution, although it has been going on ever since you and I were born; it was going on all the time that Mr Justice Blackstone was living, and for a long time before that; and although, if we were to go far enough back to lose sight of this system of *parliamentary* government, we should lose it in a system, if it be possible, still more unlike that of the theory;—*prerogative government*, or government carried on *out* of parliament, by the Court, or the *Privy Council*, or the great *officers of state*, amenable rather to parliament for their misdeeds, when grievous, than sharing with them the business of political management.[5]

And finally:

Gentlemen, is it possible to give an ontological definition of *legislative* function? To put this to the test we must make this inquiry. Suppose the whole power of law-making, and of ruling, to be vested in one individual, and not distributed among different estates of the realm, can we distinguish between acts or functions which are legislative, and acts or functions which are governmental, or politic only? Because I apprehend that if functions have no ontological distinction when united in one person, or body politic, their separation and distribution between two or more such, constitutes an accidental, and not an ontological, distinction between them. Now, if we take the matter in this position, and thus strip it of all adventitious or conventional elements, we must, I think, admit that, to give an ontological meaning to the term *legislative*, we must confine it to those acts and proceedings of the sovereign power which either directly or indirectly, either *in rem* or *in personam*, constitute a rule, or create an obligation, binding on any class or number of the governed community. Thus the making of a tax is legislative, because it imposes the obligation of payment; but the disposal of the produce is governmental or administrative, because it only indirectly, and by its consequences, affects the community.[6]

I am not, as I shall say later, wholly persuaded that we clarify the matter completely by insisting that both the sovereign power and general application are necessary to a useful definition of what is legislation. Mr Park's word is not so deep as a well nor so wide as a church door; but 'tis enough, 'twill serve.

The British constitution, like every other, defines the terms of the relationship between Governments and the governed. The political history shaping it was of a strong royal power which, after some initial success, failed to absorb other political groups challenging its authority and fell. Power passed in the early eighteenth century from the person of the sovereign and his circle to Ministers because of the nature of the revolutionary settlement and because the sovereign withdrew from the conflict. But the power of government itself cannot die and, as the constitution changed, and Parliamentary

5. Op. cit. pp. 39–41.   6. Op. cit. 116–17.

and other influences waxed and waned, this power persisted. It persisted and developed most rapidly throughout the middle years of the nineteenth century, revealing a characteristic vitality which was only slightly tempered by the comparative weakness of individual Governments. For the river of government runs more deeply than the waters of particular Administrations, and is not greatly affected by surface changes of persons or franchises.

The political changes of the nineteenth century, the movement for reform of institutions, the weakness of parties between 1840 and 1870, the great arguments which moved around 'the condition of the people', all helped to conceal, though some of them in fact fostered, the fast developing drive of governmental power. And the battle of philosophies was won by the forces of state intervention before the opposing army was properly in the field. In 1816 the skirmishes began. By the middle of the century, the outcome was clear. By 1870 it was all over and a great body of legislation was on the statute book. Much of it was inefficient, all of it was incomplete. But the idea of state intervention in domestic affairs as a considerable part of the answer to the economic, industrial and social problems of the time had been accepted in so many different spheres for limited purposes that the general philosophy was there to be induced. The Fabians and the Labour Party were heirs before they were progenitors; and Herbert Spencer was a general without an army.

The authority of British Governments is original not derived. It does not rest on electors or Parliament. The Government is sovereign and omnipotent. The electorate appoints the Government and cannot remove it during its period of office.

The Government is authoritarian in decision and in action. It makes up its own mind; it puts into effect its own policy. Only if it seeks to acquire new powers by legislation must it first obtain the approval of any other body. In the whole vast field of current administration it is supreme. The basis of the system is the power of the Government to govern as it pleases and to present the action as something accomplished. In the most vital and dangerous sphere of all—that of foreign policy —the determinants are unknown, the information is largely hidden, and the details of action are seldom divulged until they have been put into effect. The history of foreign affairs from 1930 to 1939 and during the post-war period has been one of a series of momentous and sometimes catastrophic decisions subsequently revealed in part to the interested public. Constitutional lawyers here make a distinction. The conclusion of treaties and the making of war and peace are, they say, the exercise of prerogative powers. But how, in this, do they differ from the confirmation of a compulsory purchase order, the amalgamation of water undertakings, the approval of a development plan, the settlement of teachers' salaries, the construction of trunk roads, the reduction of purchase tax, the supervision of capital investment in the coal industry, the administration of the health service, the fixing of national insurance benefits, or any other governmental function? All these, it is replied, depend on statute, whereas the prerogative powers, do not. Why the need for statutory powers in one case and not in the other? Not because one is more important than the other but because a statute is needed before private rights are interfered with. And private rights here mean rights enforceable in courts of law. A minor military campaign may quickly reduce the value of my possessions because of heavier taxation or inflation but these are not rights I can protect at law. The distinction between prerogative and statutory powers, then, is in this sense largely historical. And the prerogative may be used where no enforceable private rights are to be infringed. So it has no relevance to the authoritarian character of the conduct of foreign affairs. If so, then where statutory powers are used, the conduct of affairs might be equally authoritarian. And so it is. For an Act of Parliament does not pretend to be concerned with the merits of particular actions but only with the general principles of decision: who should decide, to what purpose, and with what effect on private rights. An Act does not empower a Minister to confirm a compulsory purchase order made by the London County Council on one acre of land lying between Chancery Lane and the Strand. It knows nothing of this land. It passes no judgment on the merits of the case. The Act merely empowers the local authority to make and the Minister to confirm compulsory purchase orders on land required for stated purposes. The administration of this Act, its actual application, the details of decisions, the timing, the instructions from superior to inferior, the drawing of plans, the allocation of money—all these actions are based not on the statute but on the authority of the institution of government. We recognise that these are the functions of the institution. A Government Department needs no more statutory authority to administer its affairs than does a private person to administer his. Only when private enforceable rights are infringed is the statute necessary. And Acts which provide for more than this contingency are declaratory merely.

To this argument there is one apparent objection. For many government institutions are not natural but artificial persons. They are corporate bodies owing their existence to statutes. And the law, it is said, recognises as their acts only those for which there is statutory authority. This objection, however, is not valid, for it relates only to the creation of the institution. There inheres in the Queen the constitutional right and power to govern. Much of government is carried on in her name and by her servants— by, for example, the individuals called Secretary of State. Other parts of government are carried on by other bodies, some created by statute. Where a new body is created to perform functions previously performed by the Queen's personal servants or previously performed by no one, the device of corporation with its perpetual existence is most valuable. But it is only because a new, previously non-existent, thing—called a corporation—is to be created that special powers are necessary. It is not because of what it will do—for that, special powers will be necessary only so far as it infringes private rights—but because of what it will be (a new person created, as nature cannot create, out of nothing at all) that the statute is used. Nor indeed, is a statute essential, though it is convenient. For these new creations for the purpose of government, and for other purposes, can be made by the Queen's own act, by the conferring of a charter. A borough is recognised as an institution of government but is not a creature of statute. Its previous incarnation as an urban district council has terminated. Its soul has migrated to a higher form of existence and has been liberated to a mayor, alderman and burgesses where before it was constrained in the arid impersonality of a council. The fiction of corporate identity is retained. But once the corporation, whether statutory or chartered in origin, is created, its authority as an institution of government depends not on its statute or charter but on the fact that it is recognised as part of the organised power of government of which the Queen is the head. For other bodies are frequently being created by statute and charter to which this recognition is not accorded. They may be social or cultural or professional bodies; they may or may not have associations with government institutions; but they are not part of government. For they do not perform that function.

The need for statutory authority if private, legally enforceable, rights are to be interfered with does indicate one of the limitations to be attached to the omnipotence of Governments. Governments are constrained by the framework of the law until they change it. The changing of it is in their hands and every piece of legislation put before Parliament by the Government is to effect some change, usually to give more power to the Government. But until the Bill is enacted, the Government is limited in what it may do.

We speak of the sovereignty of Parliament but less confusion would be caused if we spoke of the sovereignty of the Government. For by the sovereignty of Parliament we mean that of the Queen in Parliament and by the sovereignty of the Queen in Parliament we mean the legislative sovereignty: that a Bill which receives the threefold Assent is law and that there is no limit to what may be so enacted. It is necessary to determine where lies this sort of sovereignty and, in particular, whether the Judiciary has any authority to set such a law aside. But it is only one aspect of sovereign power, this power to make laws. There is also the wider power of government itself—the power to take decisions, the authority to administer, the recognised executive force. This executive force is not merely the right to put into execution Acts of Parliament. A Government which had to find statutory authority for each one of its actions, whether large or small, whether touching private rights or not, would be quickly hamstrung. Its existence would be suspect—for that part of the constitution which creates Governments is unwritten; so would be its right to advise the Queen and all its great powers over Parliament. Statutory authority is but a part of its power—and the most recent part. The executive force of Governments derives from the power of the Queen to govern through her Ministers and that power is ultimate. Beyond it lies nothing but the barricades.

Sovereignty then in this wider sense is an attribute of the Government. That is its origin and its only resting place. That part of Sovereignty which is the making of laws is not wholly with the Government. The process of legislating is indeed a Governmental process but the assent of the Houses of Parliament must be obtained. But the strength of the Government's position lies in its power to command that assent. And where its sovereignty seems partial, it is made whole again. For the Government is the Government because it controls Parliament. If it had not that control, it would not be the Government. The essential distinction between Government and Parliament must be emphasised. These two great institutions fulfil contrasting and complementary functions. But, as institutions and for those functions, neither is subordinate to the other. The Report of the Select Committee on Delegated Legislation in 1953 is a mine of misinformation about the constitution. One of its statements when speaking of the purposes of delegated legislation is this: 'Parliament lays down the policy and general principles of the new legislation and then empowers a subordinate authority to fill in the details which enable the Executive to carry out administratively that policy.'[7] I am not concerned with the unreality of saying that Parliament lays down policy in an Act, as contrasted with the Executive which carries it out. The interesting phrase is 'a subordinate authority'. This can only mean either the Queen (for Orders in Council) or a Minister or Government Department (for other types of statutory instrument). Let us assume that the Select Committee did not mean to call the Queen in Council a subordinate. What of a Minister? To whom is he subordinate? He is called a Minister because he is a principal servant of the Queen. He is certainly not a servant of Parliament; nor is the Executive; nor is a Government Department; nor, for that matter, is a civil servant. An Act may authorise a Minister to make regulations—'to fill in the details'—and to

7. H.C. 310–I, para. 100.

take administrative action. Surely the Select Committee was not trying to suggest that, in its executive function, the Government is subordinate to Parliament? If not, then how is the making of regulations to be distinguished? Perhaps by this: that Parliament normally has the right to examine and must approve the Government's legislative proposals before they become law but has no such right to examine its administrative proposals; that therefore we speak, not very accurately, of Parliament 'delegating' its legislative function when we should speak of Parliament waiving its right of examination and approval; and so the making of regulations (at least those which are not laid before Parliament or are made before they are laid) can be said to be with the permission of Parliament. But even if this somewhat tenuous distinction is accepted, it does nothing to turn the Minister into a subordinate authority.

The right of the Government to govern is part of the constitution. No one disputes it. Parliament—a separate institution —has acquired powers and functions of its own. But they are not powers of government. That the Government can command a majority in the House of Commons no more affects the relative status of the two institutions than the constitutional incapacity of the judiciary to set aside a statute makes the judges subordinate to Parliament. All these institutions have their functions. Each of them has emerged against the background of the others. Each of them has taken its present form because of the way the others have developed. None can be understood save by reference to the others. Yet each is a distinct institution and knows that its continued existence depends on the maintenance of this distinction. Its own functions must be separately and jealously preserved. And the function of the Government is to govern.

This separateness of function has long been the characteristic of the judiciary. The limited view of their functions adopted by judges is sometimes the despair of laymen (and of some lawyers) by whom it is called legalism. Judicial 'ignorance' of facts widely known is almost a music-hall joke but their general judicial attitude of the irrelevance of governmental policy to their interpretation of statutory powers reflects a deep reluctance to overstep their constitutional function. Sometimes it leads to absurdity, to the virtual nullifying of legislation; and an amending statute sooner or later—according to the importance of the subject and the state of the legislative programme—is passed to nullify the decision in its turn. But, while it is true that certain judges take a more 'liberal' view of their task and are willing to look beyond the apparent meaning of the words before them, the traditional self-limitation remains firm.

The lines of distinction between parliamentary and governmental function are less clearly marked and less appreciated. This is partly because the separateness of the judicial function is emphasised by the separateness of the personnel of the Bench and by a seemingly more obvious difference between adjudication on the one hand and legislation and administration on the other. Adjudication in the courts is set apart by its formal characteristics and its procedure. It is normally a dispute between two parties and the dispute is heard and settled in recognisable courts with special names and sitting in one of a number of specific places. So what judges do is superficially more clearly separate from what Parliament or the Government does. These latter two institutions are indeed physically separate; for Parliament has its palace at Westminster while the Government lives in Whitehall and elsewhere. But all members of the Government are also members of one or other of the Houses of parliament and this overlapping of membership smudges the outline of their separateness of function. More importantly, the function of Parliament, while not that of government, is concerned with the function of government. Parliament came into existence because of the function of government whereas the judiciary came into existence because of the need to resolve disputes between private individuals as well as disputes—crimes—to which the State was party. So again the separateness of the functions of the Government and Parliament is made less clear. But this is only in appearance not in reality. For in reality the functions are distinct.

All this begins to look like a new version of the doctrine of the separation of powers. But powers are variously classifiable into different categories. The old doctrine was concerned with the categories of legislative, judicial and executive powers, and thought to find a parallel between these three and the three institutions of Parliament, the Courts and the Government. Bagehot, in well-worn words, refutes the doctrine:

No doubt by the traditional theory, as it exists in all the books, the goodness of our constitution consists in the entire separation of the legislative and executive authorities, but in truth its merit consists in their singular approximation. The connecting link is *the cabinet* ... The efficient secret of the English Constitution may be described as the close union, the nearly complete fusion, of the executive and legislative powers. [8]

Bagehot sees the power of legislation as vested in Parliament and the power of execution as vested in the executive; then the cabinet is the link, 'a hyphen which joins, a buckle which fastens, the legislative part of the state to the executive part of the state'. [9] The weakness of this formulation, at least as an explanation of the constitution today, is that it goes only halfway in its refutation of the doctrine of the separation of powers. That doctrine had two assumptions. The first was that Parliament (contrasted with the Government) was the legislative part of the state. The second was that this part was separate from the executive part of the state. Bagehot refutes the second assumption by saying that the cabinet links, joins, fastens these two parts; that the presence of the cabinet in Parliament is of the essence of the constitution. But he left the first assumption untouched and indeed restated it. This is not surprising. It was no part of his thesis to emphasise the great power of Governments, but to emphasise the great power of Parliaments over Governments, to see cabinets as committees appointed and dismissed by Parliaments. Yet the first assumption is more fundamental than the second and is as false. For, as I have said, legislation is essentially and primarily a function of Governments. It is their most characteristic weapon, this power to make laws. Without it, Governments become mere executants in that whole great domestic field where legislation, regulation and administration are one operation. If a Government cannot legislate, cannot lay down the general principles, cannot modify its inheritance and determine for itself, where this is necessary, the conditions under which it will function, then its dynamic power is gone,

8. W. Bagehot, *The English Constitution*, pp. 10–11.
9. Op. cit. p. 14.

its positive force must quickly be dissipated and it ceases, in any real sense of the word, to govern.

The idea of the separateness of function, then, is not a modification of the doctrine of the separation of powers but its contrary. It attributes to the function of government those powers of legislation and execution which are the reason for its existence and finds in Parliament other distinct functions which must not be confused. The executive and legislative powers are not separate 'parts' of the state joined by the cabinet. The exercise of these two powers is the primary function of government.

Governments make rules, deeply affecting our lives, on domestic as well as foreign affairs, which, not being in the form of Bills or of delegated legislation, never come before Parliament of necessity. They can be said to be administrative rules though they do not always rest on statutory authority. But the distinction does not much advance the argument. I am admittedly making an assumption which is disputable: that all rules which do deeply affect our lives should pass the scrutiny of Parliament. 'Deeply affect' is an ill phrase, a vile phrase. But we must make some qualitative difference between rules of one level of importance and of another if we are to insist on parliamentary scrutiny in the one case and not in the other. The present method is to give time to the Opposition and the choice of subjects for debate. And this works well within limits. But the time which the Government takes for bills is so great and so much of their content is so unimportant that, within the strict limits of the total availability of parliamentary time, there is little assurance that the more important matters are debated, but only that the more important matters in bills are debated—and even that is a partial truth.

Take two closely connected questions. Every two years the Government enters into long negotiations with local authority associations about the amount of the rate support grant. This is surely a 'deeply affect' matter. And the decisions being made by statutory order must come before the House of Commons. But annually the Government enters into long negotiations with local authorities about the amount of capital expenditure—on schools, houses, etc.—they may be permitted to embark on. This is not grant money. No money passes at all.

Nor is there direct statutory authority for this control. There may be general statements of policy in white papers which lie behind these allocations and they may be debated. But this is fortuitous. And remote. Governmental decisions on capital expenditure by local authorities do not necessarily come before Parliament at all.

I am not competent to say how parliamentary time could be created or transferred to enable scrutiny of such matters to be undertaken. Certainly if it were agreed by all participants that the purpose of parliamentary debate was to improve the Government's legislative proposals then timetables could be set down which would maximise the opportunity for this to be done. But the House of Commons, in addition to being the main arena for debate on the merits or demerits of legislative proposals, is also the main political arena. And this means that the blocking of Governmental legislation, the embarrassment of Governmental programmes inside as well as outside the House, are proper tactics for the Opposition to employ if they think fit. Similarly, while there is much to be said for taking the committee stage on Bills outside Parliament—and enabling proposals for amendment to be made to Government Departments for their consideration and report to Parliament—this would greatly strengthen the Government at the expense of the Opposition (who would be deprived of their occasional victories and their more frequent opportunities for exerting indirect pressure towards compromise agreements). Many think the Government already has too much authority and power in the House of Commons. Almost any reform designed to improve the efficiency of parliamentary procedure means an improvement in the efficiency of the Opposition. And since the constitutional rules requiring certain policy proposals—called Bills—to be submitted to Parliament are the result of victories won by Parliamentarians over Ministers of the Crown, the Government of the day is likely to be reluctant to support such reforms. And so the lesson has been drawn most recently, from the Government's treatment of the new specialist committees, that the House of Commons can never adequately reform itself. But since the reason for this is that the Government controls the House and the Government has a limited interest in reform, to what other body can we look?

Government, as I have said, is sovereign.

The only way to persuade Governments to do something they have no wish to do is to make the political return to them of not doing less than the political return of doing. So they must, by campaign, by propaganda, by the threat to electoral prospects, be persuaded that the reform is the lesser evil. And this means that the public feeling against the Government must be considerable. And to create such a feeling about Parliamentary reform is not easy. It is technical; it is remote; it is not normally associated with the function of Government; it is for the benefit of politicians, probably with the result that they work shorter hours. And, anyway, what's in it for us?

And, finally, if parliamentary reform on legislative procedure is likely to benefit primarily the Opposition and so to be unpopular with Governments, it is also likely to be unpopular with Oppositions as alternative Governments. If so, that rules out of the campaign about one-third of the House of Commons. And the future of this reform lies, if anywhere, with an alliance of Backbenchers.

Backbench pressure produced the Select Committee on Statutory Instruments and on Nationalised Industries and the new specialist committees. But all these are limited and will be kept so. We shall not have House of Commons Committees like those in Congress until we have a system under which the Government is as weak in relation to the representative body as is the President of the United States. The two ends of a see-saw cannot both be up in the air at the same time.

Chapter 2

Standing Orders

Sir Edward Fellowes

For over 450 years the House of Commons conducted its business without any Standing Orders. By 1832, there were 4, all dealing with public money. In December 1967 the number of Standing Orders had increased to 117. Yet even so the Public Business Standing Orders are not a complete code. They are, so to speak, the statute law which restricts or enlarges the ancient practice of the House and must be read in conjunction with that practice, and Mr Speaker's interpretations of practice, Standing Orders and the relationship between them.

It has been said that if Rip van Winkle had been a Member of the Long Parliament and returned to St Stephens after his nap, he would have noticed little change in the procedure of the House of the early nineteenth century. The saying illustrates how recently (compared with the long history of the House of Commons), the great changes embodied in the Standing Orders have taken place. A Member who left the House in 1869, could he return to it, would surely be astonished and perhaps shocked by its proceedings in 1968. But the revolution of the last hundred years cannot be considered without some knowledge of the main objects of the old practice and procedure for only thus can one judge how far changes in procedure have changed those objects. It would also seem appropriate, at a time when it is alleged that the House of Commons is declining in popular esteem, to see if any deductions can be drawn from that review about what further changes might help to restore or confirm confidence in the House as an institution.

Through the centuries, consciously or unconsciously, the House of Commons had developed methods of doing business which secured two main objects:

1. to prevent the House being taken by surprise, with the result that business is transacted in the absence of interested members; and

2. to provide opportunities for members to initiate discussion on any matter of public interest.

The first may seem an odd objective. But when it is remembered that there was formerly no fixed hour either for beginning or ending a day's sitting and that the order in which the various items of business appeared upon the Order Paper could be changed without notice at the will of the Members present, it will be seen that there were opportunities for 'fiddling' the business, especially at the beginning of a sitting before many Members had arrived and towards the end when many had gone home. By multiplying the number of occasions on which matters, especially Bills, could be debated, the House guarded against the possibility that such 'fiddling' might become completely successful. A measure might slip through on one or two occasions but interested members would by then have been alerted and subsequent manoeuvres to avoid debate were less likely to prove successful. The second object was of much greater importance. It was under Queen Elizabeth I that the House of Commons finally vindicated its right to initiate discussion on any matter of public interest and to ensure that the scope of matters debated could not be limited by the will of the executive. To render this right effective, a Member must have the opportunity to initiate a debate at the time which he thinks suitable. The procedure that the House then devised secured that opportunity, since motions such as those for the Adjournment of the House or of the Debate, for the Speaker to leave the Chair (an essential preliminary to every sitting of a Committee of the Whole House) etc., could be used for the initiation of a debate on any matter regardless of its irrelevance to the day's programme or to the subject of the original business.

No fixed time for beginning or ending a sitting; an Order Paper which could be turned upside down or inside out without notice or superseded altogether by the introduction of some topic, however remote from any of those advertised for discussion, and a legislative process festooned with opportunities for repetitive debate (though in practice these were rarely abused): such were the conditions under which the first reformed House of Commons (1832) met to conduct its business. In that House was a large number of Members who had never before sat in Parliament and, as has happened since in such cases, it was not long before the question of changing the House's procedure was raised. Proposals for change took two lines: the representatives of the business community wanted a more orderly method of conducting business while the Government, committed to an enlarged legislative programme, wanted more time for the business for which they were responsible, fewer opportunities for debating Bills, and more freedom from irrelevant interruptions. But the House of Commons does not quickly abandon old procedures and it was nearly forty years before the tidying-up process was completed. Even then the amount of change was kept to a minimum.

By 1870 the Order Paper had been 'validated'. In other words, when the time for Public Business arrived, the Clerk was directed to read the Orders of the Day, which were to be disposed of in the order in which they stood upon the paper. Nevertheless, on days when Government business had precedence (i.e. on three days a week instead of one as in 1832, this could be arranged in any order the Government pleased) without giving any regard or priority to the order in which notices of business had been given. Furthermore, the number of opportunities for debate on Bills had been drastically reduced. Apart from amendments on the Report stage, such opportunities in the House stood at four or five, instead of the eleven which had been available in 1832.[1]

However, the hazards provided by the possibility of a Private Member initiating a debate on some other topic, by means of motions such as those for the Adjournment of the House or of the debate or for the Speaker to leave the Chair to enable the House to go into Committee, had been only partly reduced—and even so only in respect of the last type of motion. But here an important change had been made; since by the so-called Rule of Progress, the consideration of a Bill, once begun in Committee, could be resumed on another day with-

1. There are now (1962) only two.

out the necessity of proposing the Question 'That the Speaker do now leave the Chair'. This was a great gain to all Members sponsoring a Bill but above all, of course, to the Government.

But when an attempt was made to extend the Rule to include sittings of the Committee of Supply the Government gained only a Pyrrhic victory. The House gave them one day a week on which the Rule could be applied to Supply but in return insisted that on Fridays, which was a 'Government' day, Supply should stand as the first order of the day and the Rule of Progress was not to apply. The result was that in practice Fridays[2] became of little use to the Government, becoming to all intents and purposes a Private Members' motion day.

One change there was, however, which although facilitating public business made a mockery of the subject's traditional right to petition the House of Commons. The passage of the Reform Bill caused a great increase in the number of public petitions, and as the merits of each were open to debate, their consideration occupied an appreciable amount of time. Moreover petitions were considered before the commencement of public business, with the result that the longer proceedings lasted upon them, the later the business on the Order Paper began. In 1842 the debates on petitions occupied a disproportionate amount of the House's time and yet, so numerous had petitions become that although the House devoted special morning sittings to them, the arrears, like the modern telephone waiting list, defied all efforts to reduce them. A rather half-hearted attempt to shorten proceedings on each petition resulted in nothing more than a row with the Speaker. At last, the Government intervened and carried Standing Orders which put an end to all debate upon petitions by limiting the Member presenting a petition to a recital of the parties petitioning, a formal presentation of the 'prayer' (that is the object) of the petition, and a statement of the number of signatures. Thereafter the petition was to go to a committee whose report was similarly limited. The result was that nowhere could the merits of the petition be canvassed. Consequently, petitions to the House are now rather rare—although some publicity may be achieved in the press by the method of

2. Fridays were then a full day. Wednesdays were the short day.

presentation—and petitioners hoping for results now resort to Downing Street or to an office in Whitehall. The apparent unwillingness of the House (as opposed to its individual Members) even to listen to the complaints of the people it represents may be a contributory factor to the indifference allegedly felt towards the House of Commons.

The changes outlined above had been completed by 1870, and for the next eleven years there were no further major changes. It was not for want of trying on the Government's part, however; for their appetite for time was more voracious than ever. They found Question Time increasingly irksome as greater use was made of it; and since there was no limit on its length, it tended to trespass upon the time available for public business. But as the habit of giving written notice of Questions became usual (though not as yet compulsory), the Speaker assumed the right to edit them or refuse them altogether. Although modern practice may not be a good guide to practice at times of greater procedural freedom, Members are now willing to agree to changes in the wording of their Questions to bring it into order and get it on the paper. This may well have also been so a hundred years ago, and as the rules got stricter changes in the original draft may have become more drastic, with the result that, the real question which the Member wished to ask not having received an answer, supplementaries were used to extract the desired information. Although any supplementary in those days was treated as highly irregular, a number did in fact get asked because the Member then had a remedy no longer available, in that he could counter a call to order by the stock phrase 'Then Mr Speaker to put myself in order I will move the Adjournment of the House.' The Speaker did his best to discourage what he considered the abuse of such motions, but he was not always successful and Question Time, thus extended, often lasted for two hours or more and so made considerable inroads into the time available for Public Business. Members stuck doggedly to their rights and to get their business done the Government had to resort to morning (really early afternoon) sittings and Saturday sittings, and to the appropriation of all Private Members' time towards the end of the session.

Nevertheless, despite all these hazards, the Statute Book

for those years shows that, when it is remembered that all Bills
had to be taken in Committee of the whole House, that there
was no closure of debate or selection of amendments and no
limit to the scope of debate on dilatory motions, the proceedings of the House, provided that they were conducted
with good sense and a fitting regard for the wishes of the
majority, were not as unbusinesslike as might be now imagined.
But businesslike behaviour *did* depend on the satisfaction of
these conditions, and after the general election of 1874 they
tended to prevail less frequently than before. In the new
Parliament of 1880 things got so much worse that the House
took summary powers to suspend any member who had been
named by the Speaker 'for abusing the rules of the House by
persistently and wilfully obstructing the business of the
House'.

In the following year, the storm finally broke. After the
House had sat for forty-one and a half hours consecutively
came Mr Speaker Brand's coup d'état. The details of this are
too well known to need repetition. The Speaker was widely
acclaimed, both at the time and subsequently by authorities
such as Redlich, as the saviour of our parliamentary system.

The majority must of course ultimately prevail, for the only
alternative to counting heads is to start breaking them; but it
may still be asked whether so Cromwellian a solution was
really necessary. Why, for instance, was a comparatively new
Standing Order, giving the Speaker the power of naming
Members for abusing the rules or for persistent and wilful
obstruction never resorted to in the course of the forty-one
hour sitting? Two days later the whole of the Irish Party was
suspended under that very Order! The method adopted by
the Speaker, who certainly did not lack courage, seemed
designed not only to bring about a root and branch solution
of the problem of obstruction but to deal with situations where
the legitimate rights of an individual Member to initiate topics
of debate were in conflict with the Government's interest in
carrying through its legislative programme. His sensational
action aroused the same feeling of deliverance from imminent
danger as did the Munich agreement and must have influenced
the House to agree to the drastic restrictions which followed.
As a temporary measure the Speaker was authorised to draft

rules which would become operative when a Resolution was passed declaring that a certain item of Business was urgent. Notable amongst them was the drastic curtailment of a Member's right to move the Adjournment of the House before Public Business had begun, the introduction of the Closure and the application of the Rule of Relevance to Dilatory Motions. These were put into force immediately and also applied on two or three subsequent occasions during the session, one of them being on Supply.

In the following session (1882) the Government set about transforming Mr Speaker's rules into permanent Standing Orders but met with such resistance that they were compelled to devote an Autumn Session solely to that business. Since the Opposition front bench under Sir Stafford Northcote, a notoriously weak Leader of the Opposition, were broadly in support of the Government's proposals, the brunt of the resistance fell upon the Fourth Party led by Lord Randolph Churchill, who persistently referred to 'la Clotûre' in much the same tones as his more famous son used to refer to the 'Narzees' in the last war. It used to be said that when the two front benches are in agreement Private Members should look to their liberties. Never was this more truly illustrated than in 1882, when Private Members lost most of their opportunities of initiating debates and the whole purpose of the House was transformed. Its former role was then lost; a new one has yet to be discovered.

In 1888 the Government at last decided to delegate some of the detailed work on Bills to Standing Committees, a measure which had long been recommended by Sir Erskine May. At first all Bills on a particular subject, e.g. Trade or Agriculture, went to a specialist committee, but in 1902 this was changed. Henceforward a standing committee could consider any Bill, regardless of its subject-matter, the allocation of Bills to committees being left to Mr Speaker. These committees originally consisted of a permanent cadre nominated by the Committee of Selection, supplemented by a small number of Members who were particularly interested in the particular Bill under consideration; but over the years the permanent cadre was gradually whittled away. Today the membership of all these committees is constituted afresh for each Bill, with the result that the Committee is 'permanent' only in its designation. Although for many years all Bills except the Finance and Consolidated Fund Bills automatically stood committed to a standing committee unless the House otherwise ordered, Governments were long shy of using standing committees for major controversial Bills which were always committed to a Committee of the whole House until after 1945. Theoretically this was to preserve every Member's right to share in the Committee's deliberations, but, since a guillotine would certainly have been applied had the majority of Members attempted to exercise this right, the real explanation is probably to be found in the fact that Governments had (or thought they had) less control over standing committees than of committees of the whole House. Hence, not only were highly controversial Bills kept on the floor but also Bills exciting little interest or of a routine character, since it was quicker to deal with them in that way. Except for a short time after 1918, when the pressure of legislating was at its height, it was not until after 1945 that standing committees were fully utilised. Although this may be regarded as a form of rationalisation, it has led to the problem of finding a sufficient number of Members to man the committees.

In 1902 the Conservative Government introduced and passed a number of other important procedural changes, inspired by Mr Balfour, then Leader of the House and on the eve of becoming Prime Minister. Mr Balfour had an acute, logical and very tidy mind, which was offended by aspects of the procedure then existing. First, the Government control over the time of the House was not absolute; secondly, Private Business and Questions to Ministers could impinge upon Public Business to an uncalculable extent; and, thirdly, the Business of Supply tended to be concentrated into the last few weeks of the session, during which day after day was spent on arid debates in thinly attended sittings utterly unworthy of a sovereign legislature controlling the expenditure of a great empire.

To remedy these defects Mr Balfour proposed to give the Government all the time of the House apart from a specified number of Tuesdays and Wednesdays. To prevent interference with Public Business, moreover, he proposed to set time limits on both Private Business and Questions. For the latter, three-quarters of an hour was allowed (subsequently extended to nearly an hour in 1906). Since 1882 Questions had been the main opportunity, limited though it was, left to Private Members of showing initiative; hence the development of the practice of putting the supplementary question—which procedurally was a Question asked without notice. In 1886 the House had passed a resolution requiring written notice of all Questions unless the Speaker had given consent to any particular Question. This Resolution was converted into a Standing Order in 1888, and it was after this that the Speaker began to tighten up on Supplementaries—although he could not cut them out altogether. The increase in the number of Questions which followed the damming up of other outlets for Private Members meant more supplementaries, and as there was no limit to the time allowed for Questions, Public Business (which in practice usually meant Government business) sometimes did not get under way until dinner time. Mr Balfour's proposals to remedy this situation were carried, though his original idea of postponing Questions till after midnight (he was no admirer of Question Time) had to be dropped. Although Question Time still kept its position in the Orders of the Day, it was no longer permitted indefinitely to delay the commencement of Public Business.

In the 1950s the ingenuity of Members, together with the extraordinary desire of Ministers to make statements on matters great and small, often combined to postpone Government business to an appreciable extent; but, except by such irregular means, Question Time has not been extended since 1906, with the result that it has become of less use to the Private Member. This is due to the growth in the number of Ministers, to the growing length and complexity of Questions (in turn caused by the limit on the number of oral Questions a Member may ask on any one day), to the growing length and number of supplementaries, to the verbosity of the replies, and to the increasing use made of Question Time by Opposition frontbench Members.

The greatest change made in 1902 was in the procedure for granting Supply. Mr Balfour aimed at ending the congestion at the end of July and August by spreading financial business more evenly over the session and eliminating many tedious debates on minor votes which involved no question of principle and attracted little or no public interest. His proposals were that Supply should stand as first order of the day on Thursdays and that after a fixed number of allotted days had been spent on it all outstanding votes should be passed, without discussion, under the guillotine. Mr Balfour lived at a time when detail of proposed expenditure was what really mattered and so applied his new system to the old procedure by which the House considered how much should be spent upon a number of unrelated items. This may have been a system well suited to a time when any total government expenditure was only an infinitesimal portion of the nation's income, but is not suited to conditions in which the major question is what proportion of the gross national product the Government should take and how it should be distributed among major functions.

Since the Government were sure of getting its money in the end under a guillotine, Mr Balfour rightly established a convention that the Opposition should decide which votes they wished to debate. But by giving the Opposition a vested right in parliamentary time he riveted upon the House a system which by some strange mythological process is treasured as the ultimate assertion of the rights of the Commons, whereas in practice it renders the House, so far as control of Government spending is concerned, the most helpless assembly in the Western world. This system, of course, is also peculiarly unfair to Government backbenchers, who have no say in what aspects of expenditure shall be discussed. As for Mr Balfour's attempt to spread Supply equally over the Session, this ultimately succumbed to the constant pressure to get Government legislation to the Lords in good time. The rule about Thursdays was so constantly waived that by 1934 it had been abolished and thereafter quite a considerable number of Supply days gravitated towards the latter half of July. After 1945, moreover, the guillotine was extended to cover Supplementary Estimates. No doubt much time had been wasted, sometimes deliberately, on the detail of Supplementaries, but no Minister liked incurring one since he might have to wait many hours for his vote to be reached and then in the early hours of the morning be 'grilled' on some minute point of detail about which he knew little or nothing. Now a Minister may not even be aware that his Department is having to ask for more money. Another development was in the *use* of the days allotted to Supply. The debates that occupy these days have gradually been emancipated from the trammels first of a single vote, then of a schedule of votes, then of an Amendment 'on going into Supply' and finally of any tangible connection at all with Supply. The Opposition have won complete freedom of initiative on these days. With the abolition of the Committee of Supply itself the appearance on the Order Paper of the item 'Supply (— allotted day)' will soon carry only the fading memory of a former mystery.

Among the procedural changes made when the Liberals were returned to power in 1906 were a number relating to the times of the sittings of the House. Mr Balfour's scheme of two sittings a day, divided by an interval for dinner, was abolished and one continuous sitting from 2.45 p.m. to 11.00 p.m. instituted. In 1945 the hours of 2.30 p.m. and 10.00 p.m. were substituted, which meant that three backbench speeches a day were eliminated except on occasions when the rule was suspended.

In 1918 a number of changes aimed at speeding up the legislative process were introduced. The most important was the Standing Order giving the Chair power to select amendments to motions or to clauses in a Bill. This, on occasions, had already been applied before the war to certain specified parts of a Motion or clause. Its original aim was to cut out discussion on repetitive, frivolous or closely related amendments. Although not in theory mandatory, in practice it has developed on mandatory lines. Another change, represented at the time to be a device for cutting out a couple of stages on a Money Resolution in connection with a Bill, was put to quite expected use. In Committee on a Housing Bill, Dr Addison (subsequently Lord Addison) accepted an amendment which increased the charge upon the Exchequer. The Treasury were very angry about this and discovered that if the new Standing Order about these money resolutions was used, such an increase of the charge would, by reason of a technicality in connection with the Royal Recommendation, be out of order. So the Government announced that in future the procedure, originally intended to be used only in cases where haste was necessary, would be used in all cases. Treasury Ministers, delighted to find a method by which they could avoid detailed argument on their financial proposals, instructed that Money Resolutions should coincide more and more closely with the actual words of the Bill, until in the Distressed Areas Bill it became impossible to add to the areas specified in the Bill—and at long last the tide turned.

Ever since Mr Speaker Brand's coup in 1881, backbench Members had seen their former rights whittled away. They had seen their supposedly most potent function, that of raising grievances before granting Supply, transferred to the Opposition frontbench and their last remaining vestige of control, the Oral Question, limited by time and number. Twice only in the 50 years from the 1880s to the 1930s, had there been signs of concerted rebellion. In 1913 the Government was persuaded to set up a committee on Private Members' time—but the War of 1914 put a stop to its proceedings. After the War the Coalition Government, with its huge majority, tried to flout all precedent by carrying over an Electricity Bill (a public Bill) into the next session but were compelled to withdraw in the face of determined backbench opposition led by Edward Wood, Walter Guinness and their band of young Conservative Members known, from the seats they usually occupied in the back row below the Gangway as 'the Mountain'. Then, in the 1930s, came the rebellion that had some serious results. Although the protest against the drafting of the Money Resolution on the Distressed Areas Bill had no immediate consequence, Captain Crookshank and others mounted a campaign which eventually compelled the Government to yield. The Standing Order remained, but Mr Baldwin, then leading the House, gave an assurance that an instruction would be issued that in future financial resolutions should be drafted in terms which would not unduly prevent amendments being moved to the Bill. For a time it seemed doubtful how far this instruction would restore liberty of amendment, but by 1960 the issue was settled and financial resolutions were being drawn as widely as before the Standing Order came into use. It may seem that undue prominence has here been given to a small technicality but the contention is that this revolt represented a turning of the tide. At last a limit was being set to the Government's domination of the House, and the rights of the Commons were being reasserted. This was a consequence of a growing malaise among backbenchers which reflected the uncertainty about the worth of parliamentary institutions which at that time pervaded the country. Further instances are Churchill's successful protest against the withdrawal by the Secretary of State of a memorandum submitted to the India Joint Committee and Duncan Sandys' against being threatened with the Official Secrets Act for the draft of a parliamentary Question, which he had sent to the Secretary of State for War. His claim of Privilege was supported by a Committee of the House. However, for the second time a backbench resurgence was interrupted by a world war.

Amongst the procedural changes which followed this war was the extension to the chairmen of standing committees of the power of selecting amendments and an amelioration of the guillotine procedure by the institution of what was intended to be an unprejudiced 'business committee' to fix a detailed allocation of the overall time agreed to by the House. The official Opposition benefit from this more than do backbenchers, especially those on the Government side, since the timetable is usually arranged to meet Opposition wishes. Discussion is therefore likely to be centred more on the political aspects of the Bill than on its practical detail. But a distinct concession to backbenchers was made in the arrangements for ending a day's sitting. Before the war the arrangement had been that business (unless exempted) was interrupted at 11 o'clock and that when any decisions then pending had been taken, the remaining Orders on the paper were read through. If all this finished before 11.30 p.m. a motion for the Adjournment had to be made, but at 11.30 p.m. the House automatically stood adjourned unless there was exempted business or unless divisions on Questions outstanding at 11.00 p.m. took more than half an hour. As a result of this arrangement, debate on the adjournment, being fraught with so many uncertainties, rarely took place. During the war, as some compensation to Private Members for having all their time taken for Government business, it was arranged that half an hour would always be available each day for an adjournment debate, and this arrangement was embodied in Standing Orders in 1945. At first Mr Speaker allotted the subjects for debate from a list submitted to him, giving preference to an individual or constituency grievance, but later resort was had to the ballot for all but one of the weekly Adjournment debates.

The pre-war discontent among backbenchers, which has already been referred to as having had spasmodic results, reappeared in the new post-war Parliament. At first Members seemed more inclined to vent their sense of frustration on the Chair rather than on the rules which it was its occupant's duty to enforce, and but for the patience, good humour and innate kindliness of the post-war Speakers, the authority of the Chair might have suffered irreparable damage. For the last 15 years or so, members have been directing more of their attention to the rules and a number of Procedure Committees have been appointed and some interesting experiments tried. Most of these have entailed additions to the work of Members and difficulties have been experienced in getting enough of them to carry out duties which involve increased attendance at committees, and in finding enough time in the House to discuss the resultant Reports. But apart from a mitigation of the conditions under which an Emergency Adjournment can be obtained, nothing has been done to restore to Members their freedom to initiate debates about matters on which the Executive would prefer discussion to be avoided or postponed. It is that right of which backbench Members on both sides of the House (as distinct from the Opposition as such) have been deprived. This, it may be suggested, is at the root of the sense of frustration felt by Members and of the indifference felt by the public. Another reason for the public indifference is the greater speed with which matters of great current interest can be discussed by Members of Parliament on radio and television. At notice of an hour or even less, one of the current affairs programmes can put on a discussion which cannot be mounted in the House with anything like the same promptness.

Looking back over the history of the Standing Orders it will be seen that the two objects of giving sufficient time to the

Government for the passage of its necessary legislation and of securing that the business announced for a particular day will in fact be taken have, broadly speaking, been achieved. But in the process it appears, at least to some observers, that the life has been squeezed from the individual Member. It is true that recently committees have been set up to provide the House with more information about the activities of the executive, but so far (although admittedly it is still too early to reach a final judgment) without a great deal of success, since Members have no time to read bulky reports and hence debates upon them are largely left to the members of the relevant committees. It is not only more information but more power of initiation that is required—the power to start debates on 'hot' topics while they are still hot without having to await the assent of the executive. One further fact that seems to emerge from the study of the Standing Orders is the comparative use of opportunities for initiating debates once that 'opportunity' has been institutionalised. Compare the Private Members motions which are debated with the 'early day' motions on the paper. The latter represent the 'hot' subjects; the former are for the most part 'safe' expressions of party opinion or platitudinous expressions of pious hopes. Questions have become almost useless, for reasons already stated, and as yet the new Emergency Adjournment has not added a fresh threat to evasive ministerial replies to Questions. Even the daily debate on the Adjournment depends upon the luck of the draw and even then the lucky Member has to wait at least a week. To be any good, the initiative must be capable of being exercised spontaneously. The problem is how to reconcile this with reasonable certainty of business and with time for the Government's legislative programme.

It may be that a reformed House of Lords, recognised as a coadjutor and not as a rival of the popular chamber, may have its part to play in such a reconciliation; but the House of Commons, as the representative chamber, subject to all the whirling winds of popular opinion, will remain in imbalance until its Members regain the right to debate topics of public interest while they are still of interest to the people whom they represent.

Chapter 3

The House of Commons and Finance

A. H. Hanson

The traditional functions of the House in matters of finance are so well known that one puts them down only for the record. It grants Supply, authorises expenditure, and checks disbursements. In theory, if no longer in practice, the whole process is dominated by the time-honoured late-medieval principle of 'redress of grievances before granting supply'. In the background hovers the shadowy historical figure of a Monarch perpetually striving to extract resources from the representatives of unwilling subjects and to spend whatever he succeeds in extracting on purposes of which they disapprove.

For purposes of financial 'control', the House evolved procedures of tortuous complexity. Many of these became, in the most literal sense, meaningless, and it is to the House's credit that of recent years they have been considerably simplified, in the interests of intelligibility and commonsense. No longer, for instance, does one have to go through the pantomime of 'moving the Speaker out of the Chair' or assembling in 'Committee' of Supply to discuss practically anything under the sun *except* Supply. Despite such improvements, which have been accepted almost without opposition even from the more traditionally-minded Members, there has nevertheless been little change in the House's fundamental approach to the financial problems with which it is presented. What the House actually does is not very different from what it used to do when the essence of public finance was the raising of modest resources to meet equally modest commitments. Hence its procedures have come to look increasingly obsolete in an age which has seen not merely a phenomenal increase in public expenditure, but the development of a governmental responsibility for the overall *management* of the economy.

41

More specifically, the obsolescence of these procedures is due, as Lady Hicks puts it,

to a number of causes: first to the sheer growth in size of the public sector—in absolute terms and in relation both to population and to national product ... Secondly the content of public activity has drastically shifted in emphasis, in favour of programmes and projects which are not completed within a single budgetary exercise. The growth of public investment of a more or less commercial nature is one aspect of this change ... Finally, the assumption by the Government of responsibility for stability and growth in the economy as a whole extends its interest in control and efficiency outside its own sphere of activities, through the medium of social accounting.[1]

In the light of this veritable revolution, we need to ask not simply what changes in procedure are required, but whether Parliament should continue to *try* to discharge a distinctively financial function. Can a body of amateurs, however public spirited and industrious, express meaningful opinions about problems which the baffled experts are now trying to feed into computers? There is no lack of students who give a sceptical answer to this question. Professor Peacock, for instance, sees salvation only in 'a major change in the attitude of the electorate towards public spending', which he clearly thinks is not likely to happen[2]. Mr Anthony Barker, although more optimistic, emphasises the limits of 'human capacity to to absorb the implications and details of an overall plan for public expenditure'.[3] Such sceptics may well be right; on the other hand, experience suggests that parliamentary institutions are far more adaptable to new needs than is commonly imagined. Here, at any rate, we shall assume that an attempt at adaptation is worth making, and that something useful can come of changes in procedure, provided that they are accompanied by corresponding changes in attitudes.

According to a role-conception which now seems incredibly

1. Ursula K. Hicks, 'Epilogue', in Alan T. Peacock and D. J. Robertson (eds.). *Public Expenditure, Appraisal and Control* (Edinburgh and London, 1963), p. 149.

2. 'Economic Analysis and Government Expenditure Control', in Ibid. p. 16.

3. 'The Planning and Control of Public Expenditure'. *Moorgate and Wall Street*, Spring 1964, p. 37.

old-fashioned, the Member of Parliament, when he came to deal with financial matters, was an economy-hawk, swooping down on extravagance and defending the taxpayer against extortion. Among students of parliamentary government, almost the only remaining believer in this primitive approach to 'control' of finance is Dr Paul Einzig who, in *The Control of the Purse*, makes approving noises over *real* amendments to the estimates that were actually carried by nineteenth-century Parliaments and suggests that their twentieth-century successors might well follow suit. For instance:

The Royal Parks and Pleasure Grounds were . . . the target of . . . successful attack on July 12, 1880, when Arthur O'Connor, Member for Cork, moved the reduction of the Vote by £80, being the cost of providing food for Pheasants in Richmond Park. His argument was to the effect that, since the birds in Phoenix Park, Dublin, had not received a similar grant there was no justification for such unequal allocation of funds between England and Ireland. The Amendment was carried.[4]

Ah, brave old days!

It must be admitted, however, that this view of the M.P.'s financial role, although untenable in respect of Supply, still has *some* reality on the 'Ways and Means' side. In so far as those Members who participate in the debates on the Budget Resolutions and the Finance Bill take advantage of their opportunity to subject proposals for new taxation and for changes in old taxation to detailed criticism—which they do to a very considerable extent—the concept of the Member as the taxpayer's defender is not obsolete. At least, in Ways and Means he can propose the non-provision of the resources necessary to finance the services for which he has voted in Supply.

As, therefore, taxation *does* need to be looked at very carefully by the representatives of the electorate, criticism of Finance Bill procedure has remained rather muted. Even Mr Michael Ryle, whom no one would accuse of admiring tradition for its own sake, has written that 'no change in practice would seem to be required for improving control of total taxation, particularly following the recent simplification of procedures (centring on the abolition of the Committee of

4. (London, 1959), p. 271.

Ways and Means.)' Although he finds techniques for the scrutiny of individual taxes defective, he nevertheless concludes that 'full opportunities for criticism' of the Government's proposals 'are available in the course of the Bill's passage'.[5]

The 'control' of Supply, however, is entirely fictitious, and has now been recognised as such for many years, dating back to a period long before government had begun even to think in terms of 'economic management'. As the Select Committee on National Expenditure said in 1903:

the examination of Estimates by the House . . . leaves much to be desired from the point of view of financial scrutiny. The colour of the discussions is unavoidably partisan. Few questions are discussed with adequate knowledge or settled on their financial merits. 670 Members of Parliament, influenced by party ties, occupied with other work and interests, frequently absent from the Chamber during the 20 to 23 Supply days, are hardly the instrument to achieve a close and exhaustive examination of the immense and complex estimates now annually presented. They cannot effectively challenge the smallest item without supporting a motion hostile to the Government of the day; and divisions are nearly always decided by a majority of members who have not listened to the discussion . . . The Estimates are used in practice mainly to provide a series of convenient and useful opportunities for dealing with Policy and Administration, rather than to the criticism and review of financial method and of the details of expenditure.

This, of course, is as true today as when it was written. The only relevant difference between then and now is that the House has at last formally accepted the situation, in that it no longer even pretends to devote 'Supply Days' to consideration of supply. If the term 'Supply Day' continues to be used, future generations of M.P.s may well wonder what was its origin.

The attempt to force Parliament to direct its attention to Supply, by the establishment of a select committee for that purpose, failed almost completely. First appointed in 1912, the Select Committee on Estimates found that it could not usefully duplicate the 'vetting' work performed by the Treasury, and eventually came to occupy itself mainly with

5. 'Parliamentary Control of Expenditure and Taxation'. *Political Quarterly*, Vol. 38, No. 4, Oct.–Dec. 1967, pp. 442, 443.

questions of administrative efficiency, by choosing appropriate Votes simply as a peg on which to hang its enquiries. Although it has done very valuable work, particularly since 1946, it is not a financial committee in any real sense.[6]

The House's duty of checking the legality, propriety and wisdom of actual authorised expenditure (within the context of current Government policy) is, however, very much better provided for, through the Comptroller and Auditor General and the Public Accounts Committee. Of recent years, this most prestigious of all the House's select committees has increasingly concerned itself with the techniques of financial administration and decreasingly with questions of mere legality, which nowadays hardly present any major problems. Its work, adequately described elsewhere,[7] will occupy us very little in this essay.

Dissatisfaction with Parliament's financial role is of two kinds. The first, predominantly backward-looking and nostalgic, deplores the disappearance of the types of control that formerly existed—or are alleged to have existed. Finding expression in sporadic attempts to use the old methods for their 'original' purposes, it has not been entirely without effect. For instance, Sir Gerald Nabarro's 'hawkishness' in the committee stage of the Finance Bill has probably forced the Government to take greater care in the presentation of its taxation proposals than it might otherwise have taken, while the revolt of Hinchingbrooke and others against passing huge sums 'on the nod' in Committee of Supply was directly responsible for the 'Butler' reforms of 1961.[8]

Progress along these lines, however, is likely to be of very limited importance because, in the long run, it cannot fundamentally change a situation in which 'the Government, through the application of its majority in Parliament, and not

6. See Basil Chubb, *The Control of Public Expenditure* (Oxford, 1952), particularly Chap. VIII; Nevil Johnson, *Parliament and Administration* (London, 1966); Gordon Reid, *The Politics of Financial Control* (London, 1966), Chap. IV.

7. See Chubb, op. cit. particularly Chap. VII; Reid, op. cit. Chap. IV and passim; E. L. Normanton, *The Accountability and Audit of Governments* (Manchester and New York, 1966).

8. See A. H. Hanson and H. V. Wiseman, *Parliament at Work* (London, 1961), pp. 271–8.

Parliament itself, carries the prime responsibility for the control (using that word in its strict sense) of both taxation and expenditure'.[9] Indeed, the whole approach is an obsolete one, in that those who adopt it are continuing to think of Parliament's main function as that of a watchdog who barks furiously when he sees an 'extravagance' or an 'anomaly' approaching, rather than that of a well-informed and constructive critic of the Government's over-all financial management.[10]

Of much greater significance is the dissatisfaction that springs from a realisation that, in matters of financial control, Parliament has 'moved with the times' far too slowly. Those who express it accept that 'the role of the Government is to govern' and that of Parliament 'to criticise the policies and acts of the government';[11] and the object of their proposals is to enable the House to exercise that critical function more effectively in an epoch when the size and complexity of the Government's financial operations have made the old machinery of 'control' look as curious as an early de Dion-Bouton driving down the M1.

Yet Parliament is not a body that readily welcomes revolutionary changes in its procedure, and one must therefore first inquire how far the adaptation or extension of existing devices could meet the requirements of the latter part of the twentieth century.

Take, first, the debates on the Finance Bill, which seem, *prima facie*, to provide the House with one of its more effective occasions for criticism. Whether they should be taken on the floor of the House or 'upstairs' is not an issue of major importance, although it has given rise to a disproportionate amount of controversy. Of far greater importance is

9. Ryle, 'Parliamentary Control of Expenditure and Taxation'. Op. cit. p. 436.

10. Mr Anthony Barker has rightly said that any anti-expenditure lobby confronts two powerful countervailing forces: 'firstly social change and, secondly, technical changes in public finance'. He adds that 'such a movement would also experience some difficulty in putting the clock back ninety years on parliamentary procedure to allow once more for the protracted consideration of financial details'. (Barker, Op. cit. p. 30.)

11. Ryle, Op. cit. p. 435.

the separation of the policy issues raised by taxation proposals from issues of a more technical kind. This was attempted for the first time in the session 1968-69 when the 'technical' aspects of the Finance Bill were sent to a standing committee. At the time of writing it is too early to assess the success of this experiment, but one may suggest that the use of a select rather than a standing committee would have been more appropriate since technical matters, as distinct from policy issues, do not lend themselves to the debating procedures that a standing committee, like the House itself, employs. Such matters need to be *inquired into*, through the taking of oral and written evidence, rather than debated. Moreover, they call for continuous rather than intermittent attention. Hence there is a strong case for the appointment of a Select Committee on Taxation to keep the whole tax *system* under review as well as to advise the House on such problems as may arise in connection with a particular Finance Bill.

It is on supply that one finds real difficulty in suggesting procedural modifications and extensions calculated to enhance Parliament's critical powers. As we have seen, the so-called Supply Days, when the House once pretended to be discussing estimates, are now quite overtly given over to general debates on subjects chosen by the Opposition. Moreover, the Estimates Committee is now *de facto* a collection of specialised sub-committees, engaged in investigations which hover somewhat uncertainly on the ill-defined borderline between policy and administration, and concerned with finance only to the extent that, within the areas it happens to be investigating, the maintenance of efficient financial control is an essential constituent of economical policy-implementation. What, if anything, can be further accomplished within this framework? Very little, one might think, apart from providing Members with better and more intelligible information, which they might or might not find the occasion to use.

If, however, a fundamentally new approach to the problems of financial control is adopted, the provision of such information becomes vital. Even under the present dispensation, Members are acutely conscious of their lack of knowledge, and have been so for many years. The main cause of their dissatisfaction is the *form* in which the Estimates are presented. This has been devised by the Treasury primarily for its own purposes—'to represent the sums required by the Departments in respect of charges likely to require payment in a financial year'—and laid out in a manner which is said to facilitate 'Departmental financial administration and Treasury control'. But however convenient it may be for the Treasury, it is of precious little use to Members of the House, who would find it even more frustrating than they already do if they ever gave the Estimates as such serious discussion. For what the House wants—or at least needs—is 'precise analyses in the Estimates of Departmental functions and costs, preferably on a comparative basis'.[12]

The revamping of the Estimates to provide such information has, over many years, been rejected as impossible or undesirable or both. Even the Plowden Committee, which both registered and stimulated the revolution in techniques of financial control which, during the late 'fifties and early 'sixties, was taking place *within* the Treasury and the other Departments of Government, decided that the existing methods of presenting the Estimates to the House were virtually sacrosanct. Although it recommended, and the Treasury subsequently implemented, a *simplification* of the Estimates 'to ensure that they would fit properly' into its 'proposed development of the system of control of public expenditure',[13] it decided against 'any change in the system of annual cash provision on which the Estimates and Exchequer Accounts and Parliamentary Supply procedures are based'. For the Departments, it considered, the existing system was 'simple, speedy and cheap'; for Parliament and the public, it provided 'a clear basis for departmental accountability in the expenditure of public funds'.[14] In other words, it could be worked by anyone possessing basic numeracy and made life difficult for those tempted to put unauthorised hands in the till. As for the Treasury itself, My Lords opined that the advantages likely to accrue from any major change would be outweighed by the

12. S. A. Walkland, 'The Form of Parliamentary Estimates'. *Yorkshire Bulletin of Economic and Social Research* Vol. 14 No. 2 Nov. 1962, p. 91.

13. *Control of Public Expenditure*, July 1961. Cmnd. 1432, p. 11, para. 27.

14. Ibid. p. 21, para. 61; p. 22, para. 63.

'great legislative and administrative operation that would be required' to effect it.[15]

It is true that Parliament is now provided with, or can easily obtain, financial information far more useful to it than that contained in the main body of the annual Estimates. For many years the Budget has provided the occasion for an annual economic survey, which is debated together with the Chancellor's taxation proposals. There have been the famous White Papers of 1963, 1966 and 1968[16] the first two of which, following the practice established in Government Departments, attempted to forecast expenditure over a five-year period. A great deal of valuable supplementary information is appended to the Estimates themselves, which now appear in the new 'Plowden' layout which relates them to the categories included in the National Income and Expenditure Accounts. The Memorandum on the Estimates by the Financial Secretary to the Treasury contains a 'General Functional Analysis' of a very broad kind. And the Select Committee on Estimates can obtain from the Treasury, if it so wishes, information about costing which is not normally published, either in the Estimates or elsewhere.

All this is to be welcomed. Nevertheless, it remains true that the Estimates, drawn up in a manner that never departs very radically from the traditional one, are still the *point d'appui* of whatever control over Supply that Parliament attempts to exert. As they are not, to say the least, very useful for that purpose, why should they not be revamped to give the House the information that it needs? In attempting to answer this question, neither the parliamentary select committees that have considered it nor the Treasury itself have succeeded in producing much more than bromides. On the one hand, it is argued that any major change would have serious consequences for the House, even to the point of undermining the foundations of the British Constitution. The Select Committee on Procedure has solemnly warned that if existing financial forms were not retained, the House would

15. Third Report from the Estimates Committee, S 1960–61: Form of Estimates (H.C. 184). Minutes of Evidence. Memorandum submitted by the Treasury, p. 2.
16. Cmnd. 2235, 2915, 3515.

be in danger of giving up 'its right to grant or refuse to grant the money required by the Executive'.[17] This is merely an act of ritual obeisance before ancient constitutional idols long since recognised by realistic students of British government as the national monuments that they really are. It would be pertinent to ask, moreover, whether this 'right', even if it were not already fictitious, would be gravely jeopardised by the presentation of the Estimates in a more rational form. Would a change in the manner of presentation make the slightest difference to what the Treasury, in its recent Green Paper, chooses to describe as the 'fact' that 'voting Supply remains an act of major constitutional importance, in which is embodied the relation of the Legislature to the Executive'.[18] Is not this rotund phrase itself a piece of arrant mystification?

On the other hand, we are told with equal persistence that although the Estimates, as at present presented, are virtually useless to the House as a means of exercising *financial* control they nevertheless enable it to exercise control over the *administration*. But just *how* they facilitate such control is by no means clear. As we have seen, most 'Supply Day' debates are quite detached from the Estimates, and would continue to be much as they are if the Estimates were presented upside down, or in Chinese. As for the Estimates Committee, this would be just as happy—and perhaps a good deal happier—with a different kind of Estimate; and one would have thought that a 'functional' classification of proposed expenditure (which, of necessity, would involve corresponding changes in the Appropriation Accounts) would actually assist the Public Accounts Committee to discharge the more 'positive' functions on which it now places increasing emphasis.

The only clear justification for the present form of Estimates is that it enables the Treasury to wield control, not over total expenditure or even over the distribution of expenditure (which it has long ceased to do through the Estimates),[19] but over the day-to-day disbursement of public funds, as the

17. Report of the Select Committee on Procedure, 1965–66. H.C. 112, para. 3.

18. *Public Expenditure, a New Presentation*, April 1969. Cmnd. 4017, p. 3.

19. See S. H. Beer *Treasury Control* (Oxford, 1958), pp. 45–56.

Plowden Committee has itself admitted.[20] Even for this purpose the present Estimates do not appear, to the layman, to be very efficacious, to judge by the frequency with which Supplementary Estimates have to be presented and by the enormous size of some of these.[21] It may be asked, therefore, whether the 'functional' classification of expenditure which the Treasury and the Departments now generally use for almost every purpose *except* day-to-day expenditure control might not be equally useful for this purpose too, particularly in view of the fact that 'the objective grouping of Estimates, introduced for the purpose of checking honesty and accuracy on the part of civil servants, is no longer very much needed for that particular purpose'.[22] There would, of course, be certain difficulties arising from the annuality of the accounting exercise; but the overcoming of these should not place an unbearable strain on human ingenuity. There would also be a fairly massive impact on the work of the Comptroller and Auditor General's Department, involving not only the adoption of new procedures but a considerable retraining of staff. Such impact, however, would hardly be comparable with that so successfully absorbed by the Department of Inland Revenue when the transition to the PAYE system of income tax was introduced.

20. 'By the autumn of each year, a large part of the expenditure for the following financial year has been committed. The defence budget, the level of departmental investment, the general grant to local authorities, and university grants make up nearly half the total Supply expenditure; and all of these are now virtually settled well in advance of Estimates-time. Many other important elements of expenditure, such as pensions and family allowances, are known within narrow limits, unless new legislation is pending. The work at Estimates-time is to an increasing extent concentrated upon financial administration—fixing the cash limits which express already decided expenditure policy.' Op. cit. p. 14, para. 37.

21. 'Supplementary Estimates,' wrote Mr Enoch Powell, 'so far from being an act of policy or a badge of shame, are now a matter of course; it is a matter of surprise and congratulation . . . if any vote manages to avoid a supplementary. An increased draft estimate is no longer always or even usually the mark of an expanding service or new developments: it commonly does no more than register the facts of life.' ('Treasury Control in the Age of Inflation'. *The Banker*, Vol. CVII, No. 387, April 1958, p. 216.)

22. Lady Hicks, op. cit. p. 155.

The case for retaining the existing form of Estimates, therefore, is by no means as strong as the Treasury's persistent defence of it would suggest. Nevertheless, the system possesses a degree of inertia that makes its radical reform, at least in the near future, most unlikely. The most we can expect is some more tinkering, accompanied by the provision of an increasing volume of supplementary information. And even if the Estimates were transformed out of all recognition Parliament's problem would by no means be solved; for it is not at present *primarily* due to the form of Estimates that 'so far as effective control of proposals for expenditure is concerned there would be no notable difference if estimates were never presented'.[23] In essence, the problem is as much procedural as informational. If effective criticism of the Government's financial policies is to be made, two things are needed, viz. (1) a decision to break with the practice of looking at expenditure year-by-year, since major expenditure commitments are nowadays made, in effect, for varying periods of years ahead; and (2) the bringing together, in *one* procedural exercise, of the two processes which are still kept more or less rigidly separated—the authorisation of expenditure and the raising of resources, whether by taxation or loan. Fortunately, both can be done without laying sacrilegious hands on the annual Estimates, which can continue—admittedly at the cost of an expenditure of trained manpower which might be better employed—as a ritual. Even more fortunately, the Government has now come forward, in the Green Paper, with proposals which will make these things possible. At last the 'Plowden' approach to financial control is to be introduced into the parliamentary arena itself, instead of being confined, in the main, to the arcana of Whitehall. If the Green Paper proposals are adopted, in fact, there will at last be a decisive change in a situation where 'the reluctance on the part of the Treasury and the government to show their hand . . . makes satisfactory parliamentary discussion of finance unrealistic'.[24]

23. H. V. Wiseman, 'Supply and Ways and Means: Procedural Changes in 1966'. *Parliamentary Affairs*, Vol. XII, No. 1, Winter 1967–68, pp. 14–15, quoting Ronald Butt, *The Power of Parliament*.
24. Alan T. Peacock: 'Economic Analysis and Government Expenditure Control' in Peacock and Robertson, op. cit. p. 10.

Admittedly, the Green Paper makes the usual ritualistic signs in the direction of the Annual Estimates. The Government, it says,

are sure that, in any revised procedures, the House of Commons will wish to continue to exercise its constitutional function of determining the provision of money for the conduct of the business of Government. The procedure for submission of annual estimates, and of Supplementary or Revised Estimates, at the appropriate time of the year is regarded by the Government as, in principle, well suited for this purpose, and they have no proposals for changing any of its essential features, or for altering the number of days devoted to the debating of Supply.[25]

There is even a proposal designed, if not actually to improve the normal 'Supply' procedure, at least to make it a little more intelligible, on the grounds that 'misunderstanding may be harmful to the national interest'.[26]

The main point of the Green Paper, however, is its proposal to present Parliament, annually, with a White Paper containing an analysis of expenditure proposals over a period of three years—and in some cases five years—ahead, and to link this with a projection of resources, in terms of existing rates of taxation. This, if accepted, will represent a real breakthrough.

For the student of parliamentary government, an interesting and encouraging feature of the evolutionary process in which the Green Paper is an important nodal point is that it was started, or at least given a very hefty push, by a Select Committee of the House of Commons. In its famous Report of 1958 on 'Treasury Control of Expenditure'. the Estimates Committee expressed 'some anxiety' about 'the natural tendency, within the present annual system of Estimates and Accounts, to concentrate too much attention on the policy

25. Public Expenditure, a New Presentation, p. 11, para. 47.
26. The present April 'Vote on Account', it considers, should be discontinued, and replaced by a clause in the Appropriation Act 'enabling the Government to spend in the period beyond the end of the financial year and before the next Appropriation Act a stated proportion of the sums voted for the current year' (ibid. p. 12, para. 51). This seems to me a sensible if minor 'rationalising' measure, comparable with the abolition of the 'Committees' of Supply and Ways and Means in its effect on the intelligibility of parliamentary procedures.

and expenditure proposals for the coming financial year with too little regard for future years'.

If both the total and the balance of expenditure are to be effectively controlled (the Committee continued) it is essential that policy decisions should be taken with full knowledge of what the policy will cost not only next year, but, if possible, the following year after that. Only in the light of such knowledge can the review of current policy be effectively pursued. Money must be voted and allocated annually, but an obsession with annual expenditure can stultify forward planning.[27]

The Treasury considered these strictures to be exaggerated, and gave evidence about its 'developing technique' of the 'forward look',[28] which at that time was largely confined to defence expenditure.

The plan to which we are working now (said the Treasury's witness) is an annual review of the programme cast forward at least three years, and each year we would cast it forward another year, so that we have continuously three clear years ahead of us. Within that programme we apply greater scrutiny and greater attention to the first year, which is the one for which we shall be doing the Estimates next.[29]

It was admitted, however, that the technique was not 'as fully developed and effectively exploited as it might be', and there is no doubt that the Estimates Committee's Report was to a very considerable extent responsible for Mr Selwyn Lloyd's announcement, in his Budget Speech of 17 April 1961,[30] that he had 'set in hand a study of the whole problem of public expenditure in relation to the prospective growth of our resources for a period of five years ahead'. This was the study undertaken by the Plowden Committee, whose report on *The Control of Expenditure* 'has formed the basis of all subsequent developments'.[31] Those who believe in the value, both to Parliament and to the public, of select committee work—now temporarily under something of a cloud as a

27. Sixth Report from the Select Committee on Estimates, 1957–58. H.C. 254–I, p. xi, para. 23.
28. Ibid. Minutes of Evidence. Qs. 2254–2334, 2772–3, 2840–3, 3107.
29. Ibíd. Q. 2256.   30. H.C. Debates, Vol. 638, Col. 793.
31. Public Expenditure, a New Presentation, p. 3. para. 3.

result of the troubles encountered by the new 'specialist' committees—can derive encouragement from this story. Even if the Sixth Report of the Select Committee on Estimates, 1957–58, had been the only report of significance that that body had ever produced—which is very far from being so—the Committee would have justified its existence.

The Plowden Committee's basic recommendation was that 'regular surveys should be made of public expenditure as a whole, over a period of years ahead, in relation to prospective resources', and that 'decisions involving substantial future expenditure should be taken in the light of these surveys'. However, as the Green Paper says, it was (and is) 'not easy' to implement this recommendation, particularly as public expenditure 'as a whole' included not only the 'current and capital expenditure of the central Government and local authorities' but also 'the capital expenditure and debt interest of the nationalised industries and other public corporations'. Hence, although the recommended surveys became, after Plowden, 'the accepted practice under successive administrations', it was not until 1969 that the Government came to the conclusion that the techniques were 'sufficiently firmly established for a new and important step forward to be made', viz. the annual publication of a White Paper presenting to Parliament 'the results of the Government's consideration for public expenditure' and thus enabling the House, 'if it so wished' to 'supplement its present financial procedures by additional discussions based on this new and more comprehensive presentation'.[32]

This 'new presentation', if it is to follow the lines envisaged by the Green Paper, will involve five major changes in previous modes of presentation. First, 'it will . . . show regularly every year figures for the year preceding publication, the year of publication (year 1) and each of the four following years (years 2 to 5)'. Year 3 will be the 'focus' year, representing the limit to which reasonably firm decisions can be taken; the figures for years 4 and 5 'will represent projections of the cost of present policies, not decisions'. Second, the capital expenditure of the nationalised industries 'will be brought into the annual public expenditure review', on the grounds that

32. Op. cit. p. 4, para. 5.

'although the bulk of this investment is determined by commercial considerations, there are generally decisions to be taken at the margin, and it is right that these should be taken in the context of public expenditure as a whole'. Third, there will be a presentation, along with expenditure, of 'all receipts from taxation, contributions and charges and of all other receipts accruing to the public sector, including the estimated gross trading surpluses of the nationalised industries and other public enterprises', the main purpose of which is 'to overcome the problem that public expenditure figures may always be misleading so long as the revenue side is not presented at the same time'. Fourthly, the presentation will 'distinguish three categories of transactions corresponding very broadly to three markedly different degrees of use of resources', viz. 'direct use of resources, tranefers, and assets' (the last being defined as 'net purchases of land, existing buildings and financial assets' on the expenditure side, and on the receipts side as 'the inflow from taxes on capital and certain similar receipts'). Fifthly, there will be included 'in the total outlays an allowance (the "relative price effect") for the likely change in the real cost of public sector purchases (particularly labour)'.[33]

Apart from a section on 'Parliament and the Proposed Presentation', to which reference has already been made, the rest of the Green Paper is occupied principally with a brief history of the developments in the control of public expenditure leading up to its own proposals (Appendix I), a discussion of 'some technical aspects of measuring public expenditure in relation to the use of resources' (Appendix II) and—most important of all—six illustrative tables.

The history of the matter we have looked at; the technical discussion and the tables will doubtless become the subject of numerous critical articles by specialists in the economics of public finance, and cannot usefully be commented on here. What can be confidently said, however, is that the new presentation will greatly enhance the power of Parliament to engage in constructive criticism of the Government's medium-term financial plans. Moreover, it will give Parliament an entirely new capacity to look at the revenue and expenditure

33. Ibid. pp. 7–10, paras. 27–36.

sides of the account simultaneously—in fact, to consider the government's financial proposals *as a whole*, instead of in two separate and, at the best, loosely-related parts. What is of major interest to us, as students of parliamentary government, is what *use* the House will make of these powers, and what *techniques* it will devise to permit their use to be of maximum effectiveness.

To envisage what can be done, if the House so wills, we need to remind ourselves of the four different 'levels' of control at which the House can effectively operate. These correspond with the levels of Treasury control as defined by the Select Committee on Estimates in its Sixth Report of 1957–58, viz.

First the Treasury must play a part in deciding the total of expenditure on all services. Secondly the Treasury must be concerned that there is a proper balance of expenditure *between* services, so that greater value could not be obtained for the total expenditure by reducing the money spent on one service and increasing expenditure on another. Thirdly, they must help to determine the total of expenditure on individual policies and services. Finally, having decided how much should be spent on each service, the Treasury must have a continuing concern in seeing that the money is being spent as wisely as possible by Departments responsible—that there is a proper balance of expenditure *within* services.[34]

The Select Committee, of course, was concerned exclusively with the Supply side; but if the proposals of the Green Paper are to be implemented, revenue must also come into the picture, principally at the first 'level', where total expenditure is being considered. This, however, does not mean that Supply procedures must be completely amalgamated with Ways and Means. A separate Finance Bill will continue to be necessary and indeed continue to provide an important occasion for parliamentary criticism of the Government's financial proposals, if only because annual or even more frequent 'changes in central Government taxation are one of the main instruments for the short-term regulation of the economy'. What, at the minimum, is needed in addition to this is an occasion when medium-term expenditure proposals can be considered in relation to the prospects of resource-raising over the same

34. Op. cit. pp. vi–vii, para. 9.

period of years, on the assumption that 'present tax rates and allowances will continue unchanged', and with due regard for 'the direct effects on revenue of expenditure decisions'. Ideally, perhaps, one would like to incorporate in the exercise medium-term, and necessarily tentative, proposals for *changes* in tax-rates and allowances, on the basis of a series of differing policy-assumptions; but it would seem that the Government is not as yet prepared to risk a forward look at 'the most desirable, or likely, pattern of taxation', and one can readily appreciate the reasons for such caution. For the time being, therefore, Parliament will have to be content with second-best.[35]

It has been suggested that the Estimates Committee's four 'levels' should correspond with four distinct stages in parliamentary scrutiny.[36] Attractive as this approach may be, however, it presents serious difficulties, since Members can hardly be expected to talk about over-all totals except in relation to broad service areas and even 'individual policies and services'. One Member, for instance, may consider that the total might well be reduced by economising on a particular service or even eliminating it; another may hold that, while no services can be cut, there are some of such importance that they must be developed faster than the Government proposes to develop them, even at the cost of raising the level of total expenditure and finding new resources to finance it; a third may present the view that the total might well be reduced, without cutting the quantity or lowering the quality of any service, by redesigning administrative organisation and procedures in such a way as to effect significant savings of cost. Whatever fresh opportunities are provided for *genuine* financial debate on the floor of the House, it will for these reasons be impossible—and in my view undesirable—to prevent Members' contributions from ranging widely over the four 'levels'.

Nevertheless, it is fully possible and highly desirable to

35. Green Paper p. 9, para. 32.
36. Originally in the evidence presented by the Study of Parliament Group to the Select Committee on Procedure (see Fourth Report, 1964–65. H.C. 303, pp. 136–7, para. 20). The suggestion is repeated in Ryle, op. cit. p. 438.

give each debate on medium-term 'expenditure-in-relation-to-resources' proposals a centre of interest. Indeed, the tables produced in the Green Paper themselves strongly suggest that, in debates on the Annual White Paper, the concentration should be on the first two levels as defined by the Select Committee's 1958 Report; since the White Paper, if it is to follow the tables in its manner of presentation, will present a grand total broken down by 'function and spending authority' —and principally by function.[37]

If separate debates on the two lower levels are thought by the House to be necessary, as a regular exercise, and if no extra time can be allocated for this purpose, one can only suggest that a certain number of Supply Days should be set aside, subject of course to the familiar convention that the subjects for discussion should be selected by the Opposition. This would, in effect, be little more than an extension of the practice of setting aside Supply Days for debating the Reports of the Estimates and Public Accounts Committees. It would require, however, that the House should be provided with information about expenditure on 'individual policies and services' and 'wise spending by individual Departments' of a kind neither provided by the present Estimates nor proposed for inclusion in the White Paper.

Exactly how all this would work out is not easy to envisage. As a start, it seems probable that the House will allocate several days—since one day would be obviously inadequate— for debating the new White Paper, while leaving the rest of its financial procedures virtually unchanged.

This would represent an important advance—perhaps the decisive one; for the overall balance of expenditure plans, seen in relation to prospective resources, could provide the

37. The relevant headings of the tables are as follows: Defence budget; Other military defence; Civil defence; Overseas aid; Other overseas services; Roads and public lighting; Transport; Technological services; Other assistance to employment and industry; Research councils etc.; Agriculture, fisheries and forestry; Housing; Local environmental services; Law and order; Arts; Education and local libraries; Health and welfare; Social security; Financial administration; Common services; Northern Ireland; Nationalised industries etc., Capital expenditure; Debt interest; Shortfall; Relative price effect; Contingency reserve.

House with a subject of the greatest political importance. Indeed, so vital is it, and so suitable for the deployment of arguments based on the rival 'philosophies' of the two main political parties, that one can only express surprise at the failure of Parliament, until very recently, seriously to consider the need to provide itself with such an opportunity. At least one would have thought that, by now, it would have become one of the main talking-points of those politicians who place such heavy emphasis on the *debating* functions of the House, as distinct from the investigatory functions with which academic critics of parliamentary government are alleged to be too exclusively concerned.

Such debates, however, would need to be properly prepared, and experience suggests that preparation could best be undertaken by a Select Committee, using the familiar investigatory techniques. The publication of the Green Paper, therefore, gives new urgency to the proposal originally made by the Study of Parliament Group, in its evidence to the Select Committee on Procedure, for the creation of a *Select Committee on Economic Affairs*,

to explore the economic, factual and policy assumptions on which forecast estimates had been prepared; to draw attention to variations in the Estimates; and to examine their economic implications in terms of availability of physical resources etc.[38]

A more up to date definition of its duties has been provided by Mr Ryle:

It would be the function of this Committee to study particular economic problems from a Parliamentary point of view, with a view to establishing the facts and clarifying the assumptions on which Government economic policy is based—and analysing the consequences as the policies are implemented. In particular, they should examine the Government's longer-term expenditure plans against the background of the current and projected economic situation. To this end they should make a specific study, as early as possible each session, of the published White Papers giving the Government's forecasts of expenditure with instructions to report on the balance of expenditure between major services over the five-year period in the light of the current economic situation. It should be the task of this Committee not to form policy conclusions

38. Op. cit. p. 136, para. 20 (a) (ii).

regarding this balance but to explore the economic and policy assumptions on which the forecasts had been prepared, to draw attention to their economic implications, with particular reference to the availability of resources, and to point out significant trends inherent in current policy, with a view to stimulating intelligent and informed parliamentary discussion of policies and expenditure priorities.[39]

Clearly, such a Committee would not be fully effective if it were appointed immediately before the publication of the proposed White Paper, held a few meetings to hear evidence and produce a necessarily brief report, and then went into hibernation for the rest of the parliamentary session. For the White Paper would represent only an annual culmination—albeit a highly important one—of a continuous process in which the Treasury was all the time engaged. Moreover, it would not be the *only* published document to engage the Committee's interest. Economic plans, for instance, would be very much its concern, and so would the reports of the Prices and Incomes Board, the Industrial Reorganisation Commission and other specialised bodies involved in making or advising on economic policy. And to do its work properly the Committee would need to acquire the experience and expertness that could come only of meeting regularly and taking a continuous interest in the matters committed to it by its terms of reference, which should be broad. It would therefore have to be set up at the beginning of each parliamentary session and remain in active existence throughout the session. Only thus, and only if a substantial number of its members were reappointed in successive sessions, could it bring to its most important annual duty, the production of a report on the White Paper, the knowledge derived from more or less continuous immersion in questions of public revenue and expenditure. Whether it would also need a permanent staff of expert advisers, or an official comparable in status to the Comptroller and Auditor General, is a question that experience would decide. My own tentative view is that a body concerned with matters as technical as those discussed in the

39. 'Parliamentary Control of Expenditure and Taxation'. Op. cit. p. 440. Although Mr Ryle wrote his article some two years before the publication of the Green Paper, his prescriptions are still difficult to improve upon.

Green Paper would greatly benefit by such assistance; but any proposal to make it available would, at least initially, meet with opposition, particularly from the front benches. There could be no even superficially valid case, however, against empowering it, like the Select Committee on Nationalised Industries, to employ ad hoc advisers whenever it considered their services necessary for the efficient pursuit of its investigations. It should also have the power, like the S.C.N.I. and the E.C., to divide into sub-committees.

The Select Committee on Economic Affairs would not, of course, be the only committee concerned with public expenditure. Its terms of reference would cover only 'levels' 1 and 2. Other committees would have to take responsibility for sifting the materials at levels 3 and 4. One would hesitate, however, to recommend the establishment of yet another collection of new committees for this purpose, as the House is already in difficulties about finding Members prepared to devote serious and sustained attention to committee work, and it must be admitted that the enthusiasm of outside commentators for the multiplication of select committees can easily get out of hand. But when all departments or areas of governmental responsibility have their corresponding specialised committees— which, one hopes, will be soon—these, together with the Nationalised Industries Committee and the Estimates Committee (which might then begin to pay more attention to finance as such than it does now), would provide the obvious instruments for investigating and making recommendations on the matters covered by the two lower levels. As Mr Ryle says, their Reports would then offer the House 'excellent opportunities for the review of individual expenditure policies'.[40]

There remains to be considered, within the limits of this very general survey, what might be described as the 'narrow' questions of efficiency and economy within the approved totals of expenditure on individual services. For looking at such matters the House is far better equipped than it used to be. The Public Accounts Committee, through a gradual interpretative extension of its unchanged terms of reference, has

40. 'Parliamentary Control of Expenditure and Taxation'. Op. cit. p. 441.

already done some excellent work in this field, while the Estimates Committee's record as an economy-promoter is by no means undistinguished. The new specialised committees, too, if they are given continuous rather than intermittent existence, should develop a comparable competence. Can one reasonably ask for more? So far as the committee structure of the House is concerned, the answer is clearly 'No'. There may even be a danger, as we have suggested, of too many committees rather than too few. But a serious gap nevertheless remains: the lack of *expert* agencies for efficiency audit. In this field, as in others, Parliament is compelled to place too great a reliance on what the 'amateur' M.P. can make of such information as the Government chooses to give him, by way of ministerial statements, White Papers, Green Papers, and oral and written evidence. *Continuous* expert help is available to him only for the familiar type of financial audit, based on the traditional criteria of legality and propriety—although often, as we have seen, going beyond them. This is not good enough, if only because, as Mr Normanton says, 'ministers and other corporate bodies which have perpetrated wasteful transactions are not likely to bring discredit on themselves by making voluntary disclosures of their failures and difficulties'. Unless, he continues, 'we have forces to conduct a search for waste we suffer harm without knowing the cause'.[41]

One must ask, however, how far information of the kind needed is already provided by the Comptroller and Auditor

41. E. Leslie Normanton, 'In Search of Value for Public Money'. *Political Quarterly*, Vol. 39, No. 2, April–June 1968, p. 158. The danger is intensified beyond the point indicated by Mr Normanton because, as Professor Peacock has pointed out, (a) waste may in some cases have a low *political* 'opportunity cost', as when, for example, 'a government may consider that it ensures more voting support by awarding a contract to a concern in an area of low employment whose costs are higher than those listed in the minimum tender', and (b) 'the costs of choosing inefficient policies' never impinge economically, and may not even impinge politically, on those responsible for their choice. ('Economic Analysis and Government Expenditure Control' in Peacock and Robertson, op. cit. pp. 5, 6.) The point here is not that 'uneconomic' choices should never be made for political reasons, but that the economic costs of making them should as far as possible be calculated and always be revealed: a counsel of perfection, perhaps, but one that makes an increasing appeal to the more intelligent politicians as well as to the more suspicious-minded economists.

General. About the central departments of government it is provided by him to an ever-increasing extent; but about local government authorities and nationalised industries, both big spenders of moneys provided by Parliament, it remains very deficient. Moreover, information even about the central Departments still tends to be dependent on the ability of the C. and A.G.'s staff, whose training is mainly in the field of *financial* audit, rather narrowly conceived, to spot unwisdom and avoidable inefficiency as well as to do the job for which they are specifically qualified, viz. ensuring that expenditures have been made in conformity with the Appropriations. But what about the 'O and M' surveys, conducted partly by the Treasury and partly by the Departments themselves? Do not these fill the gap? Unfortunately they do not—partly because their results remain confidential, partly because they are *internal* to the service, and partly because they are rather restricted in scope. What we need, according to Mr Normanton, is full, external and public accountability 'for the efficient use of manpower, equipment, buildings and other assets, provided out of the public purse for the conduct of the public services; for, in a word, the overhead expenses of Government'.[42]

Some of the things that need to be done, publicly, if 'Parliament and the executive are to be in a position to know where and how waste occurs', are pretty obvious. Mr Normanton, who has wide experience of these matters, himself offers a 'few samples' from a 'tentative list of unsolved problems which call for intensive study'. Among these are the securing of 'fair and reasonable prices when government contracts have to be placed without competition', the improvement of accuracy in the 'preliminary estimates of requirements and costs' for major capital projects, the better control of the financing of 'scientific and industrial research and development',[43] the better planning of subsidy programmes 'with a view to confounding the fraudulent as well as to the achievement of an

42. 'In Search of Value for Public Money'. Op. cit. p. 161.
43. On this, see Office of the Minister for Science: Report of the Committee on the Management and Control of Research and Development (H.M.S.O. 1961), generally known as the 'Zuckerman' Report.

economic purpose',[44] and the discovery of an answer to the question whether 'it is profitable or wasteful for public authorities to employ "direct labour" forces for services which could easily be obtained under contract'.[45]

To find the solutions to such problems—or at least to provide Parliament and the executive with a series of possible solutions—Mr Normanton considers that 'a new kind of research body' is needed—a body which, 'whilst working on behalf of the Parliamentary Committees . . . should have the same powers of access to information and documents as the state auditors'.[46] Whether a *new* body is needed, however, is arguable. The Comptroller and Auditor General's powers could conceivably be extended and the staff placed at his disposal increased and diversified. This would have the advantage of concentrating all forms of public audit in one comprehensive organisation. On the other hand, there is undoubtedly a case for separating the examination of the *regularity* of public expenditure from that of its *efficiency*. The introduction of a new and different kind of dog may be more productive than the effort to teach the old one new tricks.

On this subject more inquiry is obviously needed; but what seems certain is that an organisational response, in one form or another, to the challenge that Mr Normanton has so eloquently voiced would do more than anything else to enhance the effectiveness of Parliament's power to criticise,

44. One should add that, in the case of subsidies, the 'confounding of the fraudulent' would be one of the less important aims. The big problem here is how to achieve the purpose of an open-ended commitment with the minimum expenditure of public funds. As Mr Houston has said of the agricultural subsidies, an 'essential feature' of any effective system of control is 'the collection and publication of data, and the public assessment of the consequences of policy in all relevant sectors of the economy'. ('Control of Subsidy Expenditure' in Peacock and Robertson, op. cit. p. 72.)

45. Normanton, 'In Search of Value for Public Money'. Op. cit. pp. 162, 163–5. These are familiar examples. Some of the more esoteric but equally important problems involved in obtaining value for money, which require the use of cost/benefit calculations and the discovery, in non-commercial fields, of criteria comparable with the economist's 'opportunity cost', are discussed in Peacock and Robertson, op. cit. (See particularly the articles by Roland N. McKean, Ronald L. Meek, George Houston, J. Wiseman and Mrs U. K. (Lady) Hicks.)

46. Op. cit. p. 166.

C T.—C

in whatever detail it saw fit, the financial performance of the great variety of executive bodies which, in the last resort, are 'answerable' to it. Perhaps even more importantly, external 'efficiency audit' could lead *directly*, and not merely through parliamentary intervention, to a considerable saving of scarce national resources; but this opens up a wider field of discourse which goes well beyond the subject-matter of the present essay.

It seems probable that we are on the eve of very important developments in parliamentary supervision of the nation's finances—developments which are long overdue. The 1958 Report of the Estimates Committee, the Plowden Report and the Green Paper of 1969 have successively pointed the way to a real and positive 'control' which will supplement and perhaps eventually replace the present kind, which is largely fictitious and negative. To give effect to it, some major procedural changes will be needed; but these can be put into effect without anything in the nature of a procedural revolution. The final emphasis, however, should be on the need that Parliament now has for *help* on a scale hitherto uncontemplated, since the technical difficulties of controlling expenditure have, as Mr Normanton says, 'grown beyond recognition'.[47] On this subject the Green Paper has nothing to say. Perhaps we shall need an all-party backbench campaign on a scale considerably greater than the campaigns that produced the Statutory Instruments Committee and the Nationalised Industries Committee before the Government can be persuaded to do what is required—spend a little money in order to save a lot.

Addendum

The above essay was written before the appearance of the Report on Scrutiny of Public Expenditure and Administration by the Select Committee on Procedure.[48] This document, although its recommendations differ in detail from mine, is the product of a similar kind of thinking. Its basic criticism of present financial procedures is that they are not related to

47. Ibid. p. 157. Readers wishing to acquaint themselves with the full argument in favour of his proposals should turn to *The Accountability and Audit of Governments*.

48. Sept. 1969.

the time scale for which public expenditure plans are now made. To rectify this discrepancy, it proposes that there should be a system of expenditure scrutiny involving three distinct but related components, viz. (1) discussion of expenditure strategy and policies, based on the Government's long- and medium-term projections; (2) examination of the means of implementing this strategy and executing these policies, as reflected in the annual Estimates; and (3) retrospective scrutiny of results achieved and value for money obtained.

Strategy and policy should be the subject of an annual debate, for which material would be provided by a White Paper, along the lines suggested by the Government in its Evidence, but also containing certain additional information. This debate 'should come to occupy as important a place in parliamentary and public discussion of economic affairs as that now occupied by the annual Budget debate'. The examination of means is to be largely confided to Select Committees, making use, among other information, of Estimates presented to a greater extent than at present 'in terms of the functions or objectives of Departments'. Retrospective scrutiny is to be undertaken, as now, by the P.A.C. and the C. and A.G., who will have available to them, through the 'development of costing and other methods of measuring performance ... better yardsticks for scrutinising the results of public spending . . .'

All this I find fully acceptable. There are two specific recommendations, however, about which I have doubts. The first is that the debate on the Expenditure White Paper should take place at the beginning of the session, without any preliminary examination of it by select committee. The second is for the creation, not of an Economic Affairs Committee, but of an Expenditure Committee. This would be established 'to consider public expenditure, and to examine the form of the papers relating to public expenditure presented to the House'. A 'General Sub-Committee' of this body would, among other duties, 'scrutinise the projections of public sector expenditure as a whole *after* [my italics] the annual debate on the Expenditure White Paper', while eight 'functional' sub-committees would concern themselves with individual fields of administration.

As the Report is short, and lapidary to the point of ambiguity, it is not easy to judge how far the proposed Expenditure Committee would cover the field I have mapped out for an Economic Affairs Committee; nor can one readily assess the extent to which the investigations undertaken by its functional sub-committees would materially differ from those at present conducted by sub-committees of the Estimates Committee. The Report specifically recommends that *one* of the tasks of each sub-committee would be 'to conduct an enquiry on present Estimates Sub-Committee lines into Departmental administration, including effectiveness of management'; but priority is given to the study of 'expenditure projections for the Department or Departments in its field', to the examination 'in as much detail as possible', of 'the implications in terms of public expenditure of the policy objectives chosen by Ministers', and to the assessment of 'the success of the Departments in attaining them'. This rather suggests that the present functions of the Estimates Committee might become neglected, unless they were taken over by the new Specialist Committees, on the future of which the Report is entirely vague. There is also a tendency to assume that Members can be *made* to undertake certain types of sub-committee investigation, whereas experience strongly suggests that, having been provided with opportunities for acquiring information, they must be left free to pursue whatever lines of inquiry seem to them appropriate.

In brief, my view is that, although the Report is very much along the right lines, it is vague where it ought to be specific and rigid where it ought to be flexible. More thought will be required before one can see just how a reformed financial procedure can be properly related to the other functions of the House.

Chapter 4

Parliament and the Public Sector

A. H. Hanson

It is time that we stopped talking about parliamentary 'control' of the nationalised industries; for, in the literal sense, it obviously cannot control them, being a body quite unsuitably constituted for such a purpose. What it can and does do is to confer, by legislation, certain powers on the nationalised industries and on the Ministers within whose sphere of jurisdiction they lie and to hold these Ministers (not the industries themselves) accountable for whatever action they take or fail to take.

That Parliament finds its role vis-à-vis the nationalised industries a difficult one is obviously due to the fact that ministerial powers are simultaneously limited in theory and vague in practice. This is no new problem. It arises whenever a decision is taken to confer a measure of 'autonomy' on a ministerially-appointed agency, and becomes particularly acute when the precise scope of such autonomy cannot be neatly defined. The classical example of this dilemma is now more than 130 years old: the Poor Law Commission of 1834. During the greater part of the nineteenth century, however, there was little awareness of it, for the simple reason that most of the ad hoc bodies that were from time to time created became absorbed either by the central government or by the local authorities, while the remainder (such as the Port Trusts and the Charity Commissioners) evoked no more than sporadic parliamentary interest. The issue acquired the new importance it has never since lost from the first decade of the present century, which saw the beginning of a wave of 'ad-hockery' which has since developed into a flood. More significant, however, than the mere multiplication of ad hoc bodies has been their extension to areas far more vital, politically, administratively and economically, than those they previously occupied. Of such bodies, of course, the nationalised industries are now incomparably the most important. As the Select Committee has recently said, 'the men in charge of the nationalised industries are in big business—very big business indeed'. The total net assets of the industries 'are valued at £10,500 million, and in 1966–67 their fixed investment in the United Kingdom was some £1,500 million, over half of which is financed by the Exchequer—this is equivalent to the whole of the investment of British manufacturing industries in the private sector. In relation to the economy as a whole, they contribute about 10 per cent of the gross domestic product and their labour force of nearly 1,000,000 comprises about 7 per cent of the total labour force. Furthermore, much of this investment and effort is devoted to supplies and services— such as energy and transport—whose efficient and economic provision is essential to the well-being of the rest of industry and of the nation.'[1]

Ever since the 1920s it has been generally recognised that, to achieve success, the management of a nationalised industry needs to be endowed, either de facto or de jure, with certain immunities. It should be exempt, for instance, from the various forms of financial control and audit applicable to ordinary Government Departments; should be able to devise its own personnel structures and policies, without reference to the norms applicable to the civil service; should be free, within statutory limitations, to acquire and dispose of assets and to sue and be sued in its own name. It was to guarantee these and other immunities that the form of organisation known as the Public Corporation was devised. But the mere invention of a new structure did not, and could not, automatically solve the problems of finding the optimum point of balance between freedom and control.

The location of this point depended, and still depends, partly on Britain's traditional conceptions about the role of the state in economic life. These differ radically from those prevalent in certain other countries. For instance, France, with her traditions of étatisme dating back to Colbert, has

1. First Report of the Select Committee on Nationalised industries, 1967–68, Vol. 1, Report and Proceedings. H.C. 371–1, pp. 2–3, para. 6.

tended to regard a public enterprise as a state organisation which happens to have rather special organisational needs. Like other state organisations, it is subject to the all-pervading principle of *tutelle*. Britain, on the other hand, with her anti-étatiste traditions, has tended to equate her public enterprises with private joint-stock companies. Although, in the public interest, specific controls must be available to prevent them from abusing their powers or getting too far out of alignment with national economic policies, they remain essentially distinct from the apparatus of public administration. 'General directions' may be needed as a last resort measure, to make them do what they would not otherwise do; but general *tutelary* powers are neither necessary nor desirable. So, at least, runs the theory—to the extent that we, as a nation, have any coherent theory about these matters.

In practice, of course, there has been a clearly discernible evolution of opinion about the degree and kind of autonomy that ought to be extended—and with it a corresponding change in ideas about the supervisory role that Parliament should attempt to play.

The inter-war period, when public enterprise was still marginal to the total economy[2] and economic planning little more than a gleam in the eyes of Mr Macmillan or Mr Dalton, was the hey-day of 'autonomy'. Conservative or Conservative-dominated Governments regarded nationalisation as a device to be sparingly used. When it was forced upon them by circumstances, they saw as their main duty the appointment of the best available 'business-type' management which should then be left free to run the enterprise on accepted commercial principles, subject only to occasional directives, of a kind clearly specified in the parent statute, from the relevant Minister—largely for the purposes of ensuring probity and of preventing the abuse of monopoly powers. Parliamentary inquisitiveness was correspondingly restricted. Few Questions could be asked and little encouragement was given to the initiation of debates. There were some Members who occasionally strained at this leash, but without success in stretching

2. Despite the important part played by the Central Electricity Board in partially overcoming Britain's relative backwardness in the development of the electricity supply industry.

it very far. Even the Labour Party, under the instruction of Mr Herbert Morrison, was officially converted to the principle of maximum autonomy. Indeed, in his influential book, *Socialism and Transport*, he demanded that autonomy should not merely be granted to but thrust upon the managements. As for the managers themselves, they were only too glad to enjoy so high a degree of immunity from the attentions of those whom one of them described as 'inquisitive and irresponsible guardians of the "public interest" '.[3]

The post-war situation changed all this by bringing into office a Government which was not only committed to a massive expansion of the public sector and to the planning of the economy but far less convinced than its predecessors of the inherent wisdom of the businessman. It also had a strong predisposition to stress the 'social' as distinct from the purely commercial responsibilities of the nationalised industries. Hence the inclusion in some of the nationalisation Acts of the almost meaningless clause about 'serving the public interest in all respects' and the conferment on the relevant Minister of important powers to issue directives and give approvals. Hence, too, a very great increase in Parliament's power to discuss the affairs of the nationalised industries and to put Questions to the Minister concerned.

What we witnessed during these years was, in fact, an attempt to establish a new point of balance between autonomy and control. This was based on the now-familiar distinction between 'general policy' (for the Minister ultimately) and 'day-to-day administration' (for the Board exclusively). The distinction, of course, proved unworkable. Delimitation of responsibilities in theory was accompanied by confusion of responsibilities in practice. The development of close, informal relations between Minister and Board made the 'general directions' clause virtually a dead letter and frustrated the attempts of both Parliament and public to discover, in respect of any particular policy-decision, who was responsible for what. This was the period when the issue of parliamentary 'control' found expression in the controversy about Questions

3. The phrase is from an article by Sir Frank Pick, Vice-Chairman of the London Passenger Transport Board.

to Ministers. As it has been already adequately documented,[4] there is no need to say more about it here.

The advent to office of a series of Conservative Governments in 1951 brought with it a certain modification of 'official' theory but little change in ministerial practice. In a sense, there was an attempt to return to the pre-war 'philosophy' by making a distinction between 'commercial interest' and 'national interest' rather than between 'general policy' and 'day-to-day administration'. According to the new approach, the nationalised industries were to be regarded primarily as commercial bodies, free to pursue their own commercial interests except to the extent that they were specifically directed by the relevant Minister to have regard for wider interests. This distinction found clearest expression in the 'Herbert' Report on the Electricity Supply Industry.[5] It was given a certain superficial feasibility by the fact that all the major industries were in the process of losing some of their monopoly characteristics and hence becoming subject, to an extent greater than during the immediate post-war years, to the discipline of competition. The 'Herbert' Committee was in favour of freeing the electricity supply industry even to the extent of making it fight for its capital on the open market. This recommendation, however, was disregarded; indeed, from 1956 onwards the nationalised industries lost their right even to raise capital by public subscription and became compelled to 'go to the Exchequer'. Nor was there any less ministerial interference, by way of 'dinner-table directives', in matters supposed to fall within the commercial competence of the Boards. The record of ministerial control in respect of pricing decisions, purchasing policies, industrial relations and the provision of 'uneconomic' services—without statutory authority and full public admission of responsibility—is documented in successive reports of the Select Committee on Nationalised Industries. From parliamentary statements, it became clear that Ministers, despite their theoretical approval

4. See, for instance: A. H. Hanson, *Parliament and Public Ownership* (London, 1961), Chap. IV; David Coombes, *The Member of Parliament and the Administration, The Case of the Select Committee on Nationalised Industries* (London, 1966), Chap. II; William A. Robson, *Nationalised Industry and Public Ownership* (2nd Edn. London, 1962), Chap. VII.

5. Cmd. 9672, Jan. 1956.

of the industries' independence as commercial bodies, liked the informality of their relationships with the Boards and were not prepared to jettison it for the sake of 'correctness' à la Herbert.

This contradiction between theory and practice, which became increasingly blatant during the 1950s, naturally brought forth criticism from M.P.s. If the Minister was trying to use the Board as a screen, it was obviously the job of Parliament to prevent him. Something could be, and was, accomplished by way of using new forms of Questions, asking what General Direction the Minister had issued or whether he would issue a General Direction, etc.; and many Members made vigorous use of opportunities afforded them by Adjournment Debates, 'Reports and Accounts' debates and other occasions when, by convention or practice, there was no effective limitation on the subjects relative to the nationalised industries which might be discussed. All this, however, tended to be very ad hoc and sporadic. Increasingly, Members felt that they needed their own independent sources of information about the industries, which could be supplied only by a select committee. At last, in 1956, the Government agreed to establish such a committee with adequately broad terms of reference. After beginning its inquiries, in a very modest and tentative way, it rapidly acquired self-confidence, the respect of the House, and indeed—most surprisingly of all— the approval of the nationalised industries themselves. Its work and influence have been well described elsewhere.[6] Here we need only record that it has given considerable satisfaction, as a source of authentic information and considered proposals, both to the House and to those members of the public who are interested in the problems of public enterprise.

The continued messiness of the relationship between Minister and Board, however, gave little satisfaction to anyone; indeed the Committee itself, in its Reports, persistently nagged away at this theme, without getting much change out of the Government. The opinion of most critics, which the Committee shared, was that the relationship should assume a greater degree of formality, so that everyone should know who was responsible for what. In particular, it was held

6. Coombes, op. cit.

that if the relevant Minister wished a Board to do something incompatible with its conception of its own commercial interest, he should issue it a formal, written order, and that if the Board was thereby involved in a financial loss, it should receive compensation, by subsidy or otherwise.

Explicitly, or implicitly, the critics accepted the distinction between 'national interest' and 'commercial interest' embodied in the Herbert Report. This seemed the product of the collective wisdom of a body of highly-qualified and experienced persons, and therefore went uncriticised except by a few 'leftists' whose views could be conveniently disregarded. By the early 1960s, however, it had become evident that this distinction was as unclear, and operationally as useless, as the former distinction between 'general policy' and 'day-to-day administration'. Why? Because the application of the term 'commercial' to a nationalised industry was inherently ambiguous. As I wrote in my memorandum to subcommittee A of the Nationalised Industries Committee in July 1967:

If, by 'commercial' behaviour, one simply means enterprise, cost-consciousness and all that is associated with a 'business-like' attitude, there can be no doubt either that it is needed or that the corporation, and the corporation alone, is the body that must be entrusted with generating and sustaining it. If, however, one uses 'commercial' to mean—as the Herbert Committee apparently intended it to mean—the kind of behaviour characteristic of the private businessman, aimed at profit-maximisation, one is on much more shaky ground; for an important reason for taking our present nationalised industries into the public sector was the inappropriateness or insufficiency of profit-maximisation as an incentive for their development along lines that would bring maximum benefit to the national economy. Once the *objectives* of an industry have become detached from the 'purely commercial', interpreted in this sense, the area of commercial discretion comes to depend on a necessarily fluctuating relationship between ends and means, and ceases to be defined with a precision that offers useful criteria for distinguishing the responsibilities of the minister from those of the board. It is true, of course, that profitability can be used as *one* of the tests of performance; indeed, it has been so used, with some vigour, since the White Paper of 1961; but no one, so far, has suggested that ministerial intervention must be confined to the setting of profit-targets.[7]

7. H.C. 371–II, 1967–68, p. 527. Mr Coombes gave evidence along much the same lines: see H.C. 371–III, pp. 245–7.

Fortunately the Treasury, as the nationalised industries' 'banker', was beginning to have new thoughts. While still paying lip-service to the old Herbertian orthodoxy, it began to contemplate a Minister–Board relationship based on the setting of quantifiable objectives and the making of periodical evaluations. If Minister and Board could sit down together and, with the help of their respective experts, formulate realisable *targets*, embodying both 'commercial' and 'social' responsibilities, the industry, having been equipped with the necessary resources, could then go ahead and do its job with the minimum of outside interference but with the consciousness that, at the appointed time, it would have to give an account of its stewardship. The problem, therefore, was not one of devising a formal allocation of responsibility as between Minister and Board, but of devising techniques whereby each could make the most useful contribution towards the realisation of presumably common purposes. (It was no accident, of course, that the Treasury's new thoughts coincided with the Government's revival of interest in economic planning.)

The first formal expression of this new 'philosophy', embodied in the White Paper of 1961,[8] must now be relegated to the category of *juvenilia*. The basic criterion employed, viz. the achievement of a given rate of return on total capital, was obviously too crude. Unaccompanied by any statement of principle about pricing policies or any discussion of the various *methods* by which the rate of return might be realised, it failed to provide a serious yardstick by which the efficiency of the industries in the use of their resources might be measured. Nevertheless, the intention was good, and it is probable that experience acquired in the attempt to implement the principles of the White Paper taught a number of lessons to industries and Ministries alike.

The Treasury's more developed thoughts on the subject found expression in a second, and widely-welcomed, White Paper entitled 'Nationalised Industries, a Review of Economic and Financial Objectives' issued in November 1967.[9] This did

8. The Financial and Economic Obligations of the Nationalised Industries. Cmnd. 1337.

9. Cmnd. 3437.

not jettison the overall financial objective but laid down more sophisticated criteria for the determination of 'sound investment and pricing policy'. Proposed new investments were to be initially evaluated by the application of discounted cash flow (D.C.F) techniques, which, as the White Paper stated, were already being 'widely used by the nationalised industries'. If actual investment policy was to differ from that indicated by such calculations, it should be for well-defined 'social or wider economic reasons', some of which might be quantified by the use of social cost/benefit evaluation techniques. 'The use of correct methods of investment appraisal', however, could 'only be effective' if the industries adopted, 'within the context of national prices and incomes policy, pricing policies relevant to their economic circumstances'. Prices, it considered, should be based on 'the cost of supplying on a continuing basis those services and products whose separate costing is a practical proposition (i.e. long run marginal costs)'. Although these recommendations were hedged with many qualifications, and although it was persistently emphasised that there was 'nothing rigid or doctrinaire' about them, the general intention was clear: to enable the industries and the Government, in collaboration, to formulate economically optimum targets within a framework of broad social and economic policies. With this went the implication that to see that this exercise was regularly and efficiently performed represented the Government's main duty vis-à-vis the industries. Realistic target-setting, based upon the application of up-to-date econometric techniques, could provide the industries with that elusive charter of managerial freedom which they had been seeking ever since the early days of nationalisation, and thus help to realise the aims expressed at the conclusion of the previous White Paper, viz. the improvement of 'performance and morale' and the reduction of the 'occasion and need for outside intervention in the affairs of the industries'.

These views were enthusiastically endorsed by the Select Committee on Nationalised Industries in the largest and most controversial of its Reports, 'Ministerial Control of the Nationalised Industries'[10]—according to Professor Robson,

10. H.C. 371–I to III, 1967–68.

far too enthusiastically.[11] The Committee did indeed appear to place far greater faith than the comparatively cautious White Paper in the econometric magic of D.C.F., cost/benefit calculations and marginal cost pricing. Indeed, they went considerably beyond the White Paper in recommending that M.P.C. and D.C.F. 'should be the *standard* policies for the economic control of the nationalised industries'. Whether this enthusiasm was justified, or whether the Committee, as Professor Robson alleges, were being 'taken for an intellectual ride' by persons strong on economic theory but weak on common sense, is a matter for continuing debate which cannot detain us in the context of the present essay. What is clear is that the Committee was predisposed, by the very nature of the recommendations contained in its previous Reports, to look with favour upon anything that seemed likely to rationalise and clarify the minister–board relationship and thereby simultaneously enable the industries to discharge their duties with a minimum of day-to-day interference and provide parliament with a better idea of who should be held responsible for what.

Indeed, the Committee's previous expressions of opinion about the need for rationalisation and clarification appeared to be abundantly confirmed by the voluminous evidence it had received during the course of this latest and most wide-ranging inquiry. With a few outstanding exceptions, it seemed that Ministers had been consistently doing the things they ought not to do and not doing the things they ought to do.

Until fairly recently, wrote the Committee,

Ministers appear, on the whole, to have given the industries very little guidance in regard to either sector policies or economic obligations such as pricing policies or investment criteria; clear policies in some of these matters, including pricing, are still lacking. On the other hand they have become closely involved in many aspects of management, particularly in control of investment in some sectors and also in some aspects of pricing control and control over staff matters.[12]

11. See 'Ministerial Control of Nationalised Industries'. *Political Quarterly*, Vol. 40, No. 1, Jan.–March 1969.
12. Report, p. 190, para. 877.

This messy situation, however, cannot be cleared up by laying down rigid rules about the Minister–Board relationship, based upon unreal distinctions between 'general policy' and 'day-to-day administration' or between 'commercial considerations' and 'considerations of national interest'. As successive Governments have emphasised (although not always for the right reasons), the relationship is inevitably a conventional, informal and fluctuating one. The problem is to discover the conventions that should *normally* govern it. What both the White Paper of 1967 and the Select Committee's Report of 1968 have done is to attempt to define certain specific criteria which should be applied to these conventions, if the division of labour between Minister and Board is to be both constructive and mutually satisfactory. Whether the right criteria have yet been found may well be doubted, and it is possible that Professor Robson is quite justified in his expression of scepticism, but at least the search for them is being pursued more actively than ever before, and this is surely a sign of health.

What seems now to be fully established is that an 'arm's length' relationship between the nationalised industries and the Minister within whose field of responsibility they lie is both undesirable and impossible. This is now recognised even by some of the Board chairmen. In evidence, Sir Ronald Edwards, formerly Chairman of the Electricity Council, spoke of the evolution of his own opinions about his relations with the Minister of Power. 'The way in which experience has changed my view', he said, 'is that I then (1957) thought that relations could be kept severely at arm's length and that the informalities of the relationship were to be avoided as much as possible. Experience has taught me that they are very difficult to avoid. You have got to get a meeting of minds.'[13] The Committee itself, with a slightly nostalgic backward look at the Herbert Report, itself admits that 'the public interest responsibilities of the Boards cannot be precisely separated from their commercial interest' and that Minister and Board must collaborate 'in fulfilling both sets of obligations'. In such collaboration 'some degree of informality' is inevitable, whatever may be the 'theoretical argument in favour of

13. Ibid. p. 24, para. 97. Minutes, Q. 2407.

making all exercise of ministerial control precisely formal and authorised by statute'.[14]

For Parliament, the implications of this relationship are of the highest importance; but one may well doubt whether the Select Committee has fully appreciated them. Although attempting to develop new criteria to inform the exercise of ministerial intervention, it realises that such intervention cannot be assigned defined limits, if only because Ministers are politicians subject to political pressures. Accordingly it envisages a scope for potential ministerial intervention which is virtually limitless. The Minister is to decide 'broad policies'; to 'establish the economic guidelines for the industries' commercial decisions'; to require the industries to take whatever action he believes 'the public interest requires' and 'to be concerned with the efficiency with which industries carry out their policies and financial, economic and social obligations imposed on them'.[15] Indeed, it believes that, to discharge their duties, Ministers need greater statutory powers than they at present possess, and accordingly proposes that 'the powers of the sponsoring Ministers should be extended to enable them to give directions, particular as well as general, to Boards in regard to any matter which appears to the Minister to be in the national interest'.[16] The Committee admits that all this, 'on paper', amounts to 'a power of almost total control'. It also accepts that ministerial authority of so wide a scope 'would be sufficient to bring almost any aspect, however detailed, of the industries' affairs within the range of Parliamentary Questions'. Yet it rejects my own proposal, made in both written and oral evidence, that Questions should

14. Ibid. p. 36, para 145; p. 37, para 150.
15. Ibid. Chap. IV: 'The Guiding Principles'. It should be noted that not one but several Ministers are to be involved in the performance of these duties: the 'sponsoring' Minister, the Chancellor of the Exchequer and the Minister of Economic Affairs, as now, and also the new Minister of Nationalised Industry which the Committee wishes to be created. In this article I am not concerned with the Committee's proposed re-structuring of the apparatus of ministerial control, which I regard as the weakest, and potentially most harmful, of its suggestions. The reasons for my dislike of it are explained in 'Ministers and Boards': *Public Administration*, Vol. 48, Spring 1969. Professor Robson has expressed his (with which I agree) in the *Political Quarterly* article already cited.
16. Report p. 145, para. 664.

be 'freed' and expresses the view that the 'present rules and practices' governing them 'should remain unchanged'.[17]

That the present restrictions on parliamentary questioning achieve little more than the occasional frustration of the occasional Member is an opinion that I have defended elsewhere.[18] I have also said that the best safeguard against 'improper' Questions is the exercise of the Minister's right to refuse an answer. With the latter view the Committee appears to agree. It also holds 'that the present procedures and practice on Parliamentary Questions enable individual Members to ask reasonably detailed questions *by one means or other* and give them adequate opportunity to obtain the information they need to perform their duties as critics of both Ministers and industries'.[19] If, therefore, the original purpose of the restrictions is so easily circumvented[20] and a safeguard against harmful inquisitiveness already built into the procedure of the House of Commons, it is a little difficult to understand why the proposal to give the Minister 'a power of almost total control' should not be accompanied by a sweeping away of restrictions on questioning which are already de facto largely obsolete.

This, however, is now a comparatively small matter; the question of Questions is no longer capable of generating the heat that it generated in former years. Questions, of course, still have their place in the battery of devices for parliamentary 'control' of the nationalised industries; when used by an experienced and persistent Member, for instance, they can bring to light the occasional scandal, as in the famous case of the Yorkshire Electricity Board. But they are capricious in their incidence and rarely succeed in eliciting more than odd

17. Ibid. p. 186, para. 857; p. 187, para. 863.
18. See 'Parliamentary Questions on the Nationalised Industries'. *Public Administration*, Vol. 29, Spring 1951; *Parliament and Public Ownership* (London, 1961), Chap. IV; 'Parliament, Minister and Board'. First Report from the Select Committee on Nationalised Industries, 1967–68, Vol. II, Minutes of Evidence. H.C. 371–II, pp. 526–31.
19. Report, p. 187, paras. 861, 863.
20. The Committee itself admits, parenthetically, that 'it is not certain that removing restrictions would lead to more Questions being asked; it could be more that many of the "general direction" Questions would simply appear in a more direct, specific and less disguised form' (Ibid. p. 186, para. 857).

items of information of a kind unobtainable elsewhere. For serious 'control', other devices are much more important. The question is whether Parliament is adequately equipped with them, to exercise either its current responsibilities or the additional ones which would presumably flow from the implementation of the Select Committee's recommendations about Minister-Board relationships. There is even the possibility that, confronted with the vast 'public sector' that has resulted from nationalisation, Parliament is virtually powerless, whatever new devices it chooses to add to the old ones. Such is the opinion of Mr Kelf-Cohen, whose responsibility, as Under Secretary at the Ministry of Fuel and Power from 1942 to 1955, for implementing 'nationalisation' policies, entitles his views to be treated with respect. In his recent work on *Twenty Years of Nationalisation* he writes:

The twenty years' development of a group of large nationalised industries has shown that their addition to the public sector has resulted in an expansion in the already vast powers of the Executive. Parliament has been forced to look on, with a feeling of helpless indignation, at the fact that it has but little part to play in supervising this development. 'Parliamentary accountability' has proved a will-o'-the-wisp.[21]

What opportunities, then, does Parliament currently possess? In addition to Questions, the main ones are motions for the half-hour adjournment, the consideration of legislation, and debates on 'Reports and Accounts' from the industries and on Reports from the Select Committee. In addition, Supply Days may be used for debating the affairs of the industries, and there are many other occasions (such as the Debate on the Queen's Speech, on Confidence or No Confidence Motions, or on Private Members' Motions) when they may be brought up for discussion, should Members so wish.

On the Half Hour Adjournment, matters of the utmost detail may be freely discussed within the limited time available. However, in view of the fact that an average of 30 Members are competing every week for the right to initiate five debates, a Member may have to wait a long time before he is lucky in the

21. London, 1969, pp. 176–7.

ballot or selected by the Speaker, and meanwhile the presumably burning issue that he wished to raise may have burnt itself out. Nevertheless, in the session 1966–67 (up to 19 June 1967) there were no fewer than 14 adjournment debates on subjects relating to the nationalised industries, all except one concerned with transport.[22] The Select Committee is of the opinion that 'these debates enable useful information to be obtained and examined without making too heavy demands on the time of the House or on Ministers and their officials', and suggests that the Select Committee on Procedure might consider 'whether there should be more such opportunities and . . . whether there could be any system of earmarking some of these opportunities for nationalised industries matters . . .'[23] This suggestion, no doubt, would be attractive to Members with a special interest in the nationalised industries but less attractive to those whose interests lay elsewhere.

Legislation concerned with the nationalised industries appears quite frequently on the Order Paper. The creation of a new nationalised industry, of course, involves legislation and so does any change in an existing nationalised industry's statutory structure or powers. Private Bills promoted by the industries themselves were a feature of every parliamentary session except one (1965–66) from 1957–58 to 1966–67; all were concerned with transport. Debate on such Bills is restricted in scope unless the Bill is classified as one of 'general purposes', in which case it 'provides an opportunity for scrutiny of the detailed management of the industry or section of the industry concerned, despite the fact that the issues which a Member may wish to raise are not covered directly by the terms of the Bill'.[24] More important opportunities are afforded by Borrowing Power Bills, which authorise the Minister to advance capital to an industry over and above the previously-authorised limit. 'Since the power to advance additional capital is at issue, it is relevant to discuss any purpose for which money may be required and to inquire whether money borrowed under previous powers has been

22. First Report, 1967–68, Vol. II, Minutes of Evidence: Memorandum submitted by the Clerk of the House, Annex B, p. 483.

23. Ibid. p. 187, para. 864.

24. Memorandum submitted by the Clerk of the House. Ibid. p. 478.

properly spent.' Under the Borrowing Power Bills, the Minister from time to time issues Statutory Instruments, subject to the 'affirmative' procedure. 'The scope of debate on these orders is similar to that on bills of the same nature.'[25]

Bills relating to the nationalised industries come up frequently if irregularly; there were no fewer than 30 concerned with coal, electricity, gas, civil airways and transport during the decade 1956–57 to 1966–67. Their importance, however, varies considerably, and with it the amount of time that the Government is prepared to allow for them and that the House is prepared to give them.

Debates on Reports and Accounts and/or on Reports from the Select Committee normally occupy a parliamentary day. There have been 18 of them during the same decade. Five occupied supply days, but there were also 13 other supply days devoted to the affairs of the nationalised industries. Of the total of 31 debates (three of them occupying only half a day), no fewer than 21 were about transport—15 on the affairs of the British Transport Commission and its succeeding bodies, 6 on the air corporations. During the ten years, there were only three debates of this kind on the National Coal Board, and three on Gas and Electricity; to these must be added, however, three debates which gave general coverage to the subject of Fuel and Power. (This distribution of 'Reports and Accounts' and similar debates illustrates, as does the distribution of Adjournment Debates, the heavy concentration of parliamentary interest on Transport and serves to confirm the frequently-made point that Members tend to be actively concerned only with those industries which are not doing well or attracting persistent criticism from the public.) One should note that, of necessity irregularly, the Government gives the House opportunities to discuss policy statements embodied in White Papers for individual industries or groups of industries (e.g. Fuel and Power).

How much attention the House *should* pay to the nationalised industries is a matter of judgment. My own view is that, given the wide and increasing range of Parliament's responsibilities, it has accorded them neither an excessive nor an inadequate amount of time. The vital question is not whether

25. Ibid. p. 477.

it should spend more time or less on them, but whether it is using to best advantage the time it already has available. For one must readily admit that even if it devoted twice the amount of attention to them that it does devote, it could still be playing no more than a 'remote and fitful part' in their affairs.

Much dissatisfaction has been expressed with 'Reports and Accounts' debates, which certainly tend to be inconsequential and diffuse. On the whole, the House focuses its attention on important issues much more successfully when it has in front of it a series of definite policy proposals, as in a White Paper, or a list of criticisms and suggestions, as in a Select Committee Report. An awareness of this leads the Select Committee itself to oppose any suggestion for the 'automatic' debating of Reports and Accounts, and to suggest that 'the most valuable improvement ... that ... could be made in the methods of Parliamentary accountability would consist in the periodic publication by the Minister of a White Paper in respect of each industry'.

In fact this should be like the annual Post Office Prospects White Paper. It should set out the anticipated financial and productive performances of the industry for the forthcoming year, together with some information about pricing proposals, technical and other developments, the quality of the service aimed at, etc., all of which would add up to a picture of how they intend to achieve their financial and other objectives in the coming years. Such a White Paper, together with the Board's own Report on its past achievements, should present a balanced picture of the industry.[26]

The Committee specifically links this suggestion with its proposals for developing the techniques for the determination of investment and pricing policies (i.e. D.C.F., M.C.P. and social cost/benefit analysis). The Minister, it says, 'should use this White Paper as the medium for setting out the sector policies as they affect the industry and the policies for the industry itself ... and also the pricing and investment policies which he is requiring the industry to adopt together with specified social obligations, etc. ...'[27] Parliament would thus be enabled to play a more regular and consistent and better-informed role in the formulation of policies for the nationalised industries and, so far as proceedings on the floor of the

26. Report, p. 188, para. 867.   27. Ibid. p. 188, para. 868.

House were concerned, concentrate its attention on the big issues where general debate can be most productive.

Two difficulties in implementing this suggestion would seem to present themselves. First, even if 'White Paper' debates entirely replaced the present debates on Reports and Accounts and on Select Committee Reports, the House would have to devote more time to the discussion of the nationalised industries, at least if the presentation of White Papers was to be an annual exercise as the Committee seems to suggest. There is no reason, however, why they *should* be annual, and, in my view, the balance of advantage would lie in making them less frequent. This difficulty, therefore, could be easily overcome. Second, experience suggests that such 'White Paper' debates would be improved if each White Paper had been investigated and reported on by the Select Committee, in such a way as to elucidate its implications. Such investigation and reporting would necessarily be time-consuming and might, as a result, postpone the date of the debate for so long that it became little more than a post-mortem. Admittedly, if the White Paper was produced at less than annual frequency, and attempted to cover the proposed activities of the industry over a number of years, the delay in debating it would be much less serious. Even so, the Select Committee, which is already fully occupied, would have to take on a very significant additional burden, unless it chose to abandon or curtail its present large-scale and highly detailed investigations, each occupying the whole of a parliamentary session and sometimes more.

The Select Committee's proposal for 'White Papers on each Industry', therefore, raises rather sharply the question of its own future role. There can be no doubt, I think, that the Committee, which began its life so modestly, is now the most important instrument of parliamentary 'control'. Even when its Reports are not specifically debated, they have a direct impact, reinforced by their inter-party and near-unanimous character, on both Ministries and industries. They provide, moreover, an invaluable source of information and suggestion for both Members of Parliament and interested members of the public. Nevertheless, there is always the danger that the Committee, together with the House that has created it, will come to accept the role that it has hitherto played as the only possible one, and cease to look for improvements.

In his evidence to its Subcommittee A, which conducted the investigations leading to the Report on 'Ministerial Control of the Nationalised Industries' Mr R. H. S. Crossman tentatively suggested that the disadvantage of the series of major reports produced by the Committee was that, lacking 'topicality', they also lacked effectiveness as a means of reinforcing parliamentary control. While refraining from the suggestion that such reports should no longer be made, he said:

No doubt if you spend a year doing research the academic value of the facts you collect may be greater, but you may not be having as effective control of the executive. From my point of view the purpose of a Select Committee is not an academic investigation. The purpose of a Select Committee is to investigate as part of a continuous parliamentary control.[28]

Later in his evidence, speaking not as Leader of the House but as 'a person with 20 years Back Bench experience', he added:

I realised that there were special reasons why this Committee had to be very careful at the beginning, there was fear of political interference. You had to be extremely cautious, and even more apparently impartial and detached than one would normally have been. But I am not sure whether in the new conditions you have to be quite as careful to be remote. I would have thought that there were now shorter term aspects which a Committee of your sort could profitably study. This is not excluding the longer term when there is further work you could do, provided you had the time and the staff.[29]

Time and staff are indeed the problems that are likely to become increasingly acute. If the Committee decides to accept Mr Crossman's suggestion that it should study some of the shorter-term aspects of the nationalised industries in addition to the longer-term ones on which it has hitherto concentrated, its work-load will be significantly increased. Already it has persuaded Parliament to extend its terms of reference to embrace I.T.V., Cable and Wireless Ltd, and the

28. Minutes of Evidence, p. 498, Q. 1776.
29 Ibid. p. 500, Q. 1783.

Bank of England[30] on the grounds that these, which do not fall within the purview of any other select committee, are analogous to the institutions it already investigates.[31] Moreover, it can hardly avoid taking some interest in the affairs of the Prices and Incomes Board, now that this body has been empowered to inquire into the effectiveness of the nationalised industries' arrangements for cost control as a part of its investigations of proposed price increases; and, should the Committee's suggested Ministry of Nationalised Industries be established, it will presumably also want to keep an eye on the way in which this new organ of administrative control is operating. The proposed publication of periodical White Papers on individual industries, which might well be taken up by the Government, would involve the Committee in still further responsibilities. Although common sense, for which the Committee has consistently distinguished itself, will undoubtedly prevent it from trying to conduct an unrealistically wide and heterogeneous series of investigations, there can be no doubt that, if its service to Parliament is to increase in value, it will have to cope, somehow, with a burden of work that grows steadily heavier. How can it do so without making demands on the time and energy of its Members that they will find impossible to accept?

One way would be to secure an increase in the number of its members, which now stands at 18, and to make fuller use of its power to form subcommittees. One may well doubt, however, whether any substantial increase in its numerical strength would be practicable, particularly at a time when the House is experiencing more and more difficulty in finding enough Members prepared to devote adequate attention to a sharply increased amount of committee work. A more hopeful

30. It has not, however, been given the power to investigate *all* the activities of the Bank of England, but only those other than monetary policy, management of the money market, exchange control and banking to other banks and private customers.

31. The Committee proposed that its terms of reference should be widened to include also The British Petroleum Company, S.B. (Realisation) Ltd, Short Bros. and Harland Ltd, Beagle Aircraft Ltd, the National Seed Development Organisation Ltd, and the Horserace Totalisator Board. (See Special Report: The Committee's Order of Reference. H.C. 298, 1967–68; H.C. Debates, Vol. 777, cols 1181–1274.

approach would be the more vigorous use of the Committee's recently-acquired power 'to appoint persons with specialist knowledge for the purpose of particular enquiries, either to supply information which is not readily available or to elucidate matters of complexity within the Committee's order of reference'. The Committee has already benefited considerably from its modest use of this power; but there are arguments against the creation of a veritable corps of 'advisers', whether on a temporary or on a permanent basis, even if the Treasury were prepared to make the necessary funds available. For, although the specialist can provide knowledge otherwise unavailable to Committee members, draw their attention to problems which they might otherwise have missed and conduct investigations requiring a technical expertness which few if any of them possess, he may also persuade them that issues which require the exercise of political judgment may be safely 'left to the expert'. For specialists as well as politicians have their own built-in biases which may not be so readily recognised by Committee members as the more obvious biases displayed by ministerial and civil service witnesses. Indeed, it has already been obliquely suggested that the enthusiasm for the use of econometric techniques displayed by the Committee in its 'Ministerial Control' Report was, at least in part, an uncritical reflection of the advice it received from the specialist it employed for this enquiry. Professor Maurice Peston.

As against this, it can be argued that there is safety in numbers, and that the real danger that the Committee will have the wool pulled over its eyes mainly arises when it is limited to the services of *one* specialised adviser per enquiry. Moreover, there can be little doubt that the services of specialists, despite the possible disadvantages that may accrue from their use, is essential if the Committee is to do its work efficiently in the time available. My own view, which I have developed elsewhere, is that the bulk of such specialist services as the Committee requires should be provided by a quasi-independent agency, in some respects comparable with the *Commission de Vérification* in France—a body equipped to provide information and advice, both on its own initiative and on request, to all public bodies concerned with the control and supervision of the nationalised industries: Ministries, Parliament and consumers councils. It seems to me a great pity that, in its Report on 'Ministerial Control', the Committee has rejected Professor Robson's and Mr Thornhill's strong arguments on behalf of such an agency, and has chosen to recommend, instead, the creation of a Ministry of Nationalised Industries. Such a Ministry, in my view, would rapidly become a fifth wheel on an already clumsy chariot, and involve the imposition of new responsibilities on the Committee rather than the provision of any assistance to it in discharging its existing ones. This controversial theme, however, needs to be expounded in far greater detail than is possible in the present context.

What I would emphasise is that, properly used and intelligently developed, the Select Committee offers the most important of all devices for exercising parliamentary 'control' of the nationalised industries. Although it may not be able to satisfy all the demands that Members of Parliament may make of it, compatible with allowing the nationalised industries the degree of independence they must have, it can at least do something to make parliamentary accountability more than the mere will-o'-the-wisp of Mr Kelf-Cohen's pessimistic analysis.

So far as Parliament's relations with the existing nationalised industries are concerned, therefore, there is some ground for believing that suitable conventions can be and are being established, permitting the operational autonomy of the industries to be combined with the exercise of effective influence over them by the body that has brought them into existence and represents that amorphous entity, 'public opinion', in a way that no other body can claim to do. But new problems, so far inadequately discussed, are rapidly arising as a result of the extension of the public sector in ways almost entirely unfamiliar to those responsible for the establishment of the great public corporations.

The most familiar of these is the development of a government interest, through shareholding, in a wider variety of industrial and commercial concerns. Until recently, direct governmental participation has been comparatively limited, the best-known examples being provided by the British

Petroleum Company, the British Sugar Corporation and the engineering firm of Short Bros. and Harland. These are of occasional interest to Parliament, but apparently not as yet of sufficiently sustained interest to warrant their inclusion in the Select Committee's terms of reference. The numerous companies in which the Government indirectly participates, in so far as they are subsidiaries of the nationalised industries, already fall within the Committee's sphere of jurisdiction, although one must admit that the sheer size and importance of some of the more recent ones, which involve collaboration between public corporations and private investors, have considerably extended the Committee's coverage and hence presented it with a further challenge to its time and energy. B.O.A.C.-Cunard Ltd, for instance, is a major concern in which £19,600,000 of public money has been invested, while the Amoco Group, with which the Gas Council is associated, plays a major part in the exploitation of the extensive natural gas resources of the North Sea. More important, from the standpoint of maintaining or extending parliamentary 'control', is the establishment of the Industrial Development Corporation, which, as a result of its function of promoting industrial 'rationalisation' schemes, may well find itself the possessor of very substantial assets. Still more important are the shareholding powers conferred on the government by the Industrial Development Act, which have been condemned by the Confederation of British Industries as opening the door to 'nationalisation by stealth'. How extensively these new powers will be used depends, no doubt, on the political complexion of the government that happens to be in power; but it is clear that state shareholding results in a significant diversification of what was once a fairly neatly delineated 'public sector'. To Parliament it presents problems different from those presented by the public corporation—problems that as yet it has hardly begun seriously to consider.[32]

The likelihood is that, whatever government is in power, the

32. The Select Committee itself, however, in the Special Report already referred to, has at least opened up the subject for discussion, in a somewhat tentative way. The application of its order of reference, it says, has been 'somewhat haphazard in its effect, simply because "nationalised industries" have been defined in the Order of reference only in terms of their legal structure' (H.C. 280, 1967–68, p. vi, para. 8).

public and private sectors of British industry will increasingly interpenetrate, and in doing so raise political and constitutional issues equally important as and even more intractable than those originally raised by the creation of public corporations. How they are to be solved I would not dare attempt to predict; but I should guess that, for anyone writing an essay on 'Parliament and the Public Sector' towards the end of this century, they will loom far larger than any of the other issues here discussed.

Chapter 5

Questions in Parliament[1]

D. N. Chester

The early significance of Questions in the procedure of the House was that they developed as an exception to one of the basic principles of the rules of debate. The first edition of Erskine May's *Parliamentary Practice*, published in 1844, and the next eight editions treat Questions to Ministers not as a procedure in its own right but as an exception to the general rules of debate. In the late eighteenth and early nineteenth centuries questions were very few and were mainly concerned with the business of the House or the Government intentions in respect of legislation. By the time of the Reformed Parliament the right of Members to ask Questions of Ministers or other Members was clearly recognised. During the remainder of the century there were two important developments. On the one hand, the rules of procedure governing the form and content of Questions and their place in the proceedings of the House were worked out. On the other, the steady increase in the number of Questions asked began to raise problems for the other business of the House.

The Increasing Use of Questions
The number of Questions grew rapidly in the second half of the nineteenth century—from two or three hundred in 1850 to 4,000–5,000 a year in the 1890s. Members also started to ask supplementary or 'subsidiary' Questions. The Irish Members used the device a great deal as part of their harassing and time-consuming tactics. But the major reasons were the growth of governmental powers and the restrictions placed on other devices available to backbenchers.

Had Questions been taken at the end of each day's sitting

1. This paper, while based on *Questions in Parliament* (Oxford, 1962) by D. N. Chester and N. Bowring, takes account of changes and developments since then.

the growth in the amount of time needed for their answer would have caused less concern. But they came just before Public Business which could not commence until the last Question on the Paper had been answered. Quite apart from the legitimate use of the device, it was also used to delay the onset and reduce the time available for Government measures. Opposed Private Business and Adjournment Motions were also in the same position. Therefore though in 1900 the House usually met at 3 p.m. on four days (with a short afternoon sitting on Wednesdays) Public Business might not be reached until 5.30–6 p.m., or even later, because of those earlier items of business which had precedence. Mr Balfour therefore decided to introduce major changes. Balfour's aim was to secure pre-eminence and certainty for Public Business, much of which, by this time, was Government-arranged business. Apart from those 'of an urgent nature relating to the order of business,' he proposed that Questions were to be answered between 7.15–8 p.m. and any not then answered would be dealt with at midnight. Moreover Members were to be given the choice of an oral or a written answer. In this way Balfour hoped to reserve 'the kernel of the day' for Government Business and prevent any other business interfering with it. He also hoped to reduce the number of Questions needing answer in the House mainly by way of the new device of a written answer but also because the late evening would be a less popular time for Members, if only because their Questions would be less likely to attract newspaper publicity. The changes he proposed were part of a whole series of proposals.

However, like present-day reformers he met opposition. In particular there was strong support for Question time to continue to come at the beginning, not much later in the day's proceedings. Balfour would only agree to this providing Public Business was given a fixed and certain time for its commencement. It was agreed therefore that the House should meet at 2 p.m. and that after certain business, e.g. prayers, had been taken Question Time should start at 2.15 and continue until 2.55 p.m. when Questions of an urgent character of which private notice had been given and Questions relating to the business of the House could be asked. The Government could therefore count on Public Business beginning at 3 p.m. on the great majority of days.

Thus for the first time a limit was placed on the amount of the time of the House that would be available for oral answers. The 40 minutes of Mr Balfour was increased in 1906 by Mr Campbell-Bannerman. Instead of Questions starting at a fixed time they were to start immediately after Prayers (about 5 minutes) and certain other business, e.g. Unopposed Private Business, if any, was out of the way. It could amount to as much as 55 minutes and never be less than 45 minutes. Thus the term 'the Question Hour' came to be used. But it was a 45–55 minute not a 60 minute hour.

The change from an unlimited to a limited period came to have increasingly warping effects on the use of Questions as a parliamentary device. As a result it now works very differently than it did in say 1900 and is a much less effective weapon for the backbencher.

Mr Balfour's 40 minutes, in so far as it had a statistical justification, was based on the experience that 60 to 65 Questions could be answered in about 40 minutes and this number, plus the new device of the written answer, were sufficient, he thought, 'to bring to book even the wickedest and most flagitious Government'.

Until the First World War the time allowed was usually sufficient to enable all starred Questions to be given the oral answer to which they were entitled. This was so notwithstanding a steady increase in the average daily number of starred Questions from 38 a sitting in 1904, to 72 in 1907 and 88 in 1913. For several years after the war, however, the number rose above 100 a sitting. Perhaps more significant was the growth in the practice of asking supplementaries, a practice which Mr Balfour had, without success, tried to curb in his original reform proposals. In 1908 42 per cent of the oral answers were followed by a supplementary, rising to 51 per cent in 1918, to 62 per cent in 1928, to 70 per cent in 1938–39, until it became rare for there not to be at least one supplementary to each Question.

The House was faced, therefore, with the old problem of the quart and the pint pot. As no Government and apparently few Members were ready to increase the size of the pot the problem of how to deal with the overspill became increasingly difficult. The history of Question Time since 1902 is the history of increasing restrictions placed on the use of the starred Question.

The simplest restriction has been that imposed on the number of Questions a Member may put down to be answered orally on any one day. In 1900 it was left to the members' discretion though occasionally Mr Speaker took upon himself the responsibility of preventing a Member putting a large number of Questions on the day's Order Paper. After Question Time was limited a kind of gentleman's understanding limited the daily number of starred Questions to eight per member. In February 1919, with the big increase in total numbers, the maximum was reduced to four, and in February 1920 to three. In February 1960 it was reduced to two. The Select Committee on Procedure of 1964–65 recommended no change in the daily maximum but an overall limit of eight oral Questions a month, but this was not accepted. Thus the limit is still two starred Questions a day. There never has been any limit on the number of Questions a Member may put down for written answers.

The limitation has mainly kept the total number in check rather than substantially reducing it. The average of 100 a sitting asked in the years after the First World War was paralleled after the Second. In the 1950s the daily average of starred Questions was around 90 and more recently it has been about 70–75. The numbers fluctuate, usually being highest at the beginning of a new Parliament or at times of great party political activity. The daily average also conceals wide variations, with as many as 150 or more being put down for answer on some days.

The Rota System

Limiting the time allowed for the oral answer of Questions obviously opened up the prospect that when the time limit was reached some Questions on the Paper would remain unanswered. This fear was expressed at the time of the Balfour 'reforms'. Two possible solutions were canvassed at that time. One was that answers to any outstanding Questions should be given at the end of the day. This was not popular either with

Ministers or Members. The other was that the order of Questions should be arranged so that those which seemed to be of the greatest general interest should be reached earliest. Thus by definition any Questions left unanswered because they were at the bottom of the list would be unimportant. Mr Balfour suggested that Mr Speaker would lay down general principles which would guide the Clerks at the Table. It was not acceptable in 1902 and has never since proved acceptable because it is considered impractical to give the Clerks such discretion. The increased time made available in 1906 deferred the problem a few years though there were already occasional grumbles.

Until 1902 Questions were answered roughly in the order they had reached the Table Office. Only Questions to the Prime Minister had a special place—last on each day's list.[2] Thus the first, fifth, eighth and twenty-third Questions might be addressed to say the Home Secretary with Questions to other Ministers equally scattered throughout the list. As part of the 1902 changes Questions to the same Minister started to be grouped. At first the order in which Ministers, other than the Prime Minister, appeared was accidental but by 1906 it was arranged that Questions to the Foreign Secretary would come first on Tuesdays and Thursdays and Irish Questions should come first on some days and last on others.

Whilst the great bulk of Questions on the Paper continued to receive an oral answer the order in which Ministers appeared was largely a matter of convenience. But after 1918 as an increasing proportion of Questions failed to be reached. Ministers low down in the order were almost certain not to have to answer Questions that day. By 1929 a list headed 'Order of Questions' was printed. By then some Departments had begun to be placed in rotating order, being fourth on say Tuesday of one week, third on the same day of the following week, and so by the fourth week were at the top of the list. The parliamentary doldrums of the 1930s allowed the system to work reasonably well. But after the war the situation became more and more difficult—the number of starred Questions increased and the capacity of Question time to provide replies decreased.

2. Altered in 1902 first to No. 51 and then to No. 45.

C.T.—D

The following Table gives certain statistics for selected years 1937–1959.

Average Daily Statistics for Oral Questions in the Week before Christmas*. Selected Years 1937–59

	1937	1946	1949	1950	1952	1954	1957	1959
1. Number of Questions on Order Paper	85	128	108	124	148	109	104	131
2. Number of Questions answered orally†	61	61	42	51	42	46	46	41
3. Number of Supplementaries	70	73	86	76	70	67	64	52
4. Average number of Supplementaries allowed per Question asked††	1.15	1.20	2.04	1.49	1.66	1.52	1.39	1.27
5. Average length of Supplementaries (lines in Hansard)	5	5.1	6.5	6.4	8.3	8.5	8.9	10
6. Average length of Ministerial reply to original Question (lines in Hansard)	10	8.2	8.6	8.2	6.8	6.2	6.4	7.1
7. Average length of Ministerial reply to Supplementary (lines in Hansard)	3	3	4	5.6	5	4.7	6.1	7.8

* The week before Christmas was selected as a period normally free from stress in the House; daily averages approximated well to the weekly average.

† Figures for Questions answered orally include Questions answered together i.e. where one or more Questions have been answered together with another Question, all the Questions have been counted. In 1937 and 1946, no Supplementaries were asked on a daily average of 19 and 18 Questions respectively.

†† If Questions on which no supplementaries were asked are excluded from the calculation, the figures for 1937 and 1946 would be 1.67 and 1.70 respectively.

Source: Select Committee on Procedure, Second Report 1964–65. H.C. 188, p. 9.

The evidence is very clear. In 1937 61 out of 85 Questions were answered orally (i.e. 75 per cent); in 1946 61 out of 128 (less than 50 per cent); in 1949 42 out of 108 (less than 40 per cent); in 1952 42 out of 148 (only about 30 per cent). In absolute terms 24 Questions remained unanswered in 1937, 67 in 1946, 66 in 1949, 73 in 1950, 106 in 1952, and 90 in 1959. Had the number of Questions answered remained as high as in the pre-war days there would still have been a large carry-over, but it would have been about 20 or so a day smaller.

It will be seen that the decline in the capacity of Question Time was mainly due to the increase both in the number and the length of supplementaries. A slight increase in the length of Ministerial replies to supplementaries also did not help even though Departments clearly had been paring their replies to the original Questions.

That the House was caught in a vicious circle can be shown by comparing the position of a Member in 1901 and 1951.

In 1901 a Member could hand in a Question at the Table Office as late as 11 p.m. or 11.30 p.m. on say Monday for answer the next afternoon. His Question would be certain to be reached. If he did not like the answer he could come out of the Chamber, think out one or two further Questions, hand them in and be certain of the Minister having to reply on the Thursday.[3] If the Minister again failed to satisfy him he could put another Question which would be reached on Friday and so on, day after day if he so wished.

Contrast the position of the Member of 1951. He has to have his Question at the Table Office before 2.30 p.m. on the Monday for it to appear on the Order Paper on the Wednesday. If, however, he left it as late as that it would be almost certainly too low down the day's list to be reached, unless the Minister to whom it was addressed was at the top of the list and was not one who attracted many Questions, e.g. the Minister for Overseas Development. If the Minister to whom it was addressed was say fifth or sixth, the Member would be most unlikely to get an oral answer. He would now have two choices: to take his chance and, should his Question not be reached, go immediately to the Table Office and ask for it to

3. Question days were Monday, Tuesday, Thursday and Friday.

be transferred to a later date (unless he did this he would be automatically given an answer printed in the next day's Hansard). Or if it was clear that his Question had no chance of being reached, he could put it down for the first day it looked to have a real chance. This might be three or four weeks ahead—much longer if a recess was due in the period. Thus the elements of spontaneity and follow-up have largely ceased to be available.

However, let us suppose that by perseverance and foresight on the part of the Member his question is eventually reached and he is not satisfied with the reply. Unlike his predecessor of 1901 he knows that if he lets this chance slip he may not reach the Minister for another four or five weeks. He therefore tries to frame a supplementary on the spur of the moment. Not all Members have the quick wit and command of words to ask a single short follow-up Question immediately after hearing the Minister's reply. The 1959 figures show that on average Members took 10 lines of Hansard to make their supplementary. Even then they would be most unlikely to be allowed to ask more than one, though perhaps Mr Speaker might allow one or two other Members to put supplementaries to the Minister's reply. Thus the impossibility of a Member being able to rely on questioning a Minister on successive days or within a short period drives Members to take advantage of their rare chances, makes it difficult for Mr Speaker to curb even the most rambling of supplementaries, and so reduces the capacity of Question time which in turn means that it takes longer to answer the same number of Questions, and so extends the period during which a particular Minister is unlikely to be reached because other Ministers are above him in the rota.

The only Minister who can be reached each week with certainty is the Prime Minister whose Questions are taken at 3.15 on Tuesdays and Thursdays. All other Ministers now have their day, i.e. the day in the cycle on which they are at the top, which is normally once every five weeks but can be longer if a recess occurs during the cycle.

The Order of Questions gives the Ministerial places for a period ahead. A recent one covered the period Monday, 9 June to Thursday 31 July 1969. The Minister of Transport was at the top on the first day and did not next come at the top until 14 July. The Chancellor of the Exchequer was at the top only on 8 July, the Foreign Secretary on 23 June and 28 July, the Home Secretary on 19 June and 24 July and so on. A Member who decided on say June 15 that he would like an oral answer from the Minister of Transport could put it down for June 23 when that Minister was fourth in the answering order, or the 30th when he was third, or July 7 when he was second or he could wait until July 14 when the Minister was top. Until quite recently Members were putting Questions down four or five weeks ahead or even longer in order to make certain that their questions would appear on the day the Minister was most likely to have the time available to answer, i.e. when he was at the top of the rota. But since the Select Committee on Procedures' recommendation in 1965 the maximum notice allowed is now 21 days. A Member who wanted to be certain of receiving an oral answer from the Minister of Transport would therefore be best advised to wait until Monday 23 June before handing in his notice at the Table Office. He could try for the 7 July when the Minister was second on the list but as the Minister for the Social Services was top on that day Transport would be most unlikely to be reached, and in the event that Minister took all the time available.

The number of Questions addressed to Ministers for oral answer reflects the political significance of their departmental activities. In the first half of the 1964–65 session[4] after the Prime Minister (721 notices of Questions for oral answer) came the Minister of Transport with 632, President of the Board of Trade with 482, the Treasury with 475 whilst the Foreign Secretary received only 256 and the Minister of Labour only 183, and the Colonial Secretary 125. In 1958–59 the most questioned Departments were the Colonial Office, the Ministry of Transport, Foreign Office, Treasury, Board of Trade, Ministry of Health and Ministry of Labour in that order. As only 35 to 45 starred Questions are now reached each day and as a 'popular' Minister may attract more than that number of Questions for his day, even Members who

4. Select Committee on Procedure, 1964–65: Report on Question Time, April 1965. H.C. 188, p. 47.

put their Questions to him down for that day may not get an oral answer. Everything will depend on the order in which the Questions appear on the Notice Paper. At the moment the printer puts the day's batch of notices in the order each is pulled from the one or two bags sent over each day from the Table Office. Some Members, however, want the order to be decided strictly according to the exact time the Question was handed in, thus putting a premium on getting one's Question in early in the day. There are practical difficulties in doing this, e.g. some Members send their Questions by post. The grievance is however very revealing as showing the desperate lengths to which some Members are driven to make certain of getting an oral answer even to Questions for which three weeks' notice is given.

It may well be asked whether the increasing difficulty in obtaining replies in the Chamber has caused Members to make greater use of Questions put down for written answer. The daily average number of such Questions was no higher in the 1950s than when this device was first introduced. Between 1902 and 1913 the daily average ranged from 17 to 24; in the 1950s it ranged from 15 to 21. Since 1962–63, however, the daily average has risen very noticeably from 31 in that year to 37 in 1963–64, 46 in 1964–65, 56 in 1965–66 and to 77 in 1967–68.[5]

At one time one of the attractions of the starred Question was that an answer could be obtained more quickly than it could for an unstarred Question—for there was no obligation on Departments to answer the latter on a specified day or even to answer it quickly. In contrast, starred questions had to be answered on the day for which they were put down for even if the Minister to whom it was addressed was not reached the answer would have to be printed in the Hansard for that day. The Select Committee on Procedure of 1946 thought that if Members could be assured of a written answer within a reasonable period they would make more use of unstarred Questions and so relieve the pressure on oral Questions. The Government thereupon undertook to try and answer such Questions within seven days and this was reduced to three

5. These daily averages conceal wide variations. On 2 December 1968 there were 99 starred and 164 unstarred on the Paper.

days in 1960. Even so it is almost a matter of indifference to Members so far as speed of answer is concerned whether or not to star a question, providing of course they do not want an oral answer.

If one were to be shown a list of say 100 recent Questions and ask which would be likely to be starred and which left without the asterisk any answer would be mainly guesswork. There are no obvious criteria, no obvious differences between the two kinds. Thus on 18 June 1969, Mr Gardner asked the President of the Board of Trade 'how many prosecutions have been initiated since the Trade Descriptions Act came into force' and Mr Speed asked the Ministery of Transport 'what action he is taking to improve the accident record on the A.45 road between the Coventry and Birmingham city boundaries.' The former which demanded a numerical answer was put down for and received an oral answer and attracted two supplementaries whereas the latter was unstarred.

There are three main reasons why Members deliberately choose one form rather than the other. Questions for oral answer require the Member to be in his place on the day when his Question is called, for nobody else is allowed to ask it for him. He may have other business, or not be a regular attender at that time in the House, or he may not want to commit himself to be present on a particular day some time ahead. Second, though two Questions ask for information, e.g. about the number of civil servants employed by the Department of Economic Affairs, in one case the Member may want to use the factual answer as the basis for what he thinks will be a telling supplementary, whereas in the other case he genuinely only wants information, e.g. for a speech or an article he may be writing.

Over and above these two reasons is the glamour and publicity of Question time. It comes right at the beginning of the daily business, the Chamber is much fuller than for most of the rest of the day and it is a convenient time for the press reporters, some answers even being early enough to appear in the evening papers. There is something for everybody at Question time—a Minister may shine or be caught out and 50 or 60 Members have a chance of getting on their feet and uttering a few words, a rare event for most of them. It is a treasured British institution, loved by the public and Members and well reported by the Press. The fact that most of the information could have been obtained by way of written answer, that few Members are particularly brilliant at asking supplementaries and that few Ministers are caught napping by them still makes it a glamorous enough occasion for the Member to put an asterisk against most of his Questions.

The growth in the number of unstarred Questions in the last few years is only a partial reflection of the difficulties members have in getting an oral answer to a starred Question. There is also the limit on the numbers which can be put down for answer on any particular day—a limit which does not apply to unstarred Questions. Perhaps for this reason but also because some Members have now discovered its potential, the unstarred Question is now being extensively used mainly to obtain information but also to create an impact. It is possible, for example, for a Member to give notice of say 50, 100 or even more unstarred Questions each asking for information about an aspect of the same issue. Thus on 14 July 1969 Mr Ernest Marples put down 68 unstarred questions to eight Ministers asking for information about the procurement arrangements in their departments. The political impact of this kind of questioning is potentially quite great—on Members, who see the mass of similar Questions first on the Paper and next when they are answered, and on Ministers and civil servants who have to provide the answers.

Ministerial Responsibility

Two features of Questions and Question Time need under-lining. First, they are a very important element in the doctrine of individual ministerial responsibility and second, they are one of the last procedural devices at the complete disposal of the backbencher.

According to the 17th edition of Erskine May (1964) 'Questions addressed to Ministers should relate to the public affairs with which they are officially connected, to proceedings pending in Parliament, or to matters of administration for which they are responsible'—a definition which has hardly changed since 1893. The simplest and clearest form of ministerial answerability arises from the official actions of

Ministers and their Departments. The case of non-action is different in that the Member ought to be sure that the Minister has the power to act. Nowadays the great bulk of departmental powers are set out in Acts of Parliament in which a particular Minister, for instance the Minister of Transport, is given the power to perform certain functions—such as to build trunk roads or to appoint the members of a transport board.

One function of the Question is to enable a Minister on whom Parliament has conferred a particular power to be asked why he has exercised it in such and such a way, how he is exercising it or whether he will exercise it in a particular case or manner. It follows that if a Minister does not possess a particular power he cannot be questioned about it. He cannot, for example, be asked why the National Coal Board has dismissed a particular mine manager or closed a particular pit, for these are powers vested not in the Minister but in the Board. Similarly where powers are vested in local authorities a Minister cannot be made answerable for their performance in particular instances. On the other hand a Question to the Minister of Power about an explosion at a particular pit is perfectly in order because, quite separate from nationalisation (indeed in existence long before it) the Minister has certain responsibilities for safety in mines.

This important and obviously very desirable limitation is a barrier against Members interfering in everything that happens in the country, the appointment by a University of Dr X to its Chair of Politics, the shape of the package of a detergent or the thousands and thousands of decisions which bodies and individuals can take without the approval or interference of Whitehall. At the same time, the device enables the ordinary Member of Parliament to hold a particular Minister accountable—that is answerable—for all the functions and powers vested in him by Parliament.

In recent years the ever increasing range of departmental powers combined with an apparent desire of Members of both major parties to discuss anything that currently interests them, have perhaps made it easier to find ways round the strict interpretations of ministerial responsibility. Thus the Member who cannot ask questions about the day-to-day actions of the National Coal Board may try to link his point to the Minister's powers to issue a general direction or to approve schemes of capital development or even to collect statistics. Or he may try to bring his Question under some such broad heading as the Government's responsibility for full employment, or incomes policy, or social welfare. Nevertheless, the rule that the Minister to whom the Question is addressed must either have acted or have the power to act both limits the range of Questions and pinpoints the responsibility of a particular Minister. Questions which are misdirected, that is addressed to the wrong Minister, are transferred to the Minister responsible by the Clerks at the Table.

The fact that the Questions addressed to each Minister are grouped or bunched adds emphasis to this aspect. The whole or a major part of the Question 'hour' may be taken up by one Minister. He may answer 40 or so original Questions and even more supplementaries, 60 or so Members taking part in a fairly full Chamber.

Thus a large number of his own supporters will see how he performs, whether he appears to be on top of his job and gives an air of confidence, and what his attitude is to this or that facet of the work of his Department. It is also the part of the day's proceedings which is likely to get a greater share of press publicity than all except major speeches. Unless the Minister has a Bill to pilot through the House or is a main frontbench speaker Question Time will be the main occasion when, as the Minister responsible for a particular area of Government activity, he confronts the House.

It must also be remembered that a Minister personally handles very few of the day-to-day decisions which are taken by his civil servants in his name. These decisions are, of course, made in a way which the official thinks conforms to Ministerial policy. A Question about one of these decisions brings the case on to the Minister's desk. The decision may have been taken at quite a low level in the Department. It now is looked at by the senior members of the Department, even the Permanent Secretary as well as the Minister and one or more Parliamentary Secretaries. The P.Q. file (each Question is normally given its own file) will normally contain not only a draft answer but also any relevant facts. The Minister has no excuse for not going into the case and satisfying himself that the departmental decision was correct and conformed to his policy. When he examines it he may be surprised, even shocked, and make a different decision or clarify or redefine the policy to be followed in future. This is the internal reality of the public answerability of the Minister. Members' correspondence asking a Minister about constituency cases have a similar internal effect: they bring day-to-day decisions to the notice of the top level of a Department, and so do unstarred Questions. But the fact that the Minister has to give his answer in a full House and to be prepared for one or two supplementaries should cause him to give greater personal consideration to cases raised by starred Questions.

The growth of the public corporation or board is in large part due to the desire to avoid day-to-day matters of administration becoming subject to Questions and other forms of Parliamentary scrutiny. The process is sometimes described as taking the service or function 'out of politics'. The vesting of the function in an appointed Board precludes the Minister being asked about its day-to-day exercise.

A Backbencher's Weapon

A hundred years ago backbenchers had a wide variety of procedural opportunities open to them and at their free disposal uncontrolled by what have since come to be known as the 'usual channels', that is the whips acting mainly for their respective front benches. A Member could, for example, still move the adjournment of the House either before or during Public Business if he wished to raise an issue. Many of these opportunities disappeared or were restricted in the 1880s when the Irish used them to obstruct other business and so call attention to the wrongs of Ireland. Then, as party discipline became stronger and the Government began to dominate the business and timetable of the House, the opportunities under the complete control of the backbencher became even fewer.

Questions however have been an exception. They are not controlled by the whips nor are they a frontbench device. True the changes in 1902 limited the time available for oral answer and as we have seen this was later to impose a severe limitation on the numbers that could otherwise have been answered orally. But the time remained at the complete disposal of the ordinary Member. Suggestions that there should be some kind of control to separate important or general Questions from the rest and give them priority were always strongly opposed. It would have restricted the freedom of each Member and subordinated his wish to the wishes of the majority, which if accepted would eventually bring Question Time under the control of the usual channels. Equally significant, Questions are not normally asked by frontbenchers. The Leader and the deputy Leader of the Opposition seldom ask them except by Private Notice for matters of major current significance. Since the development of 'Shadow Ministers' it is now more usual for other leading frontbenchers to put down Questions. But the vast bulk of Questions are put down by the ordinary backbenchers on both sides of the House, many of whom will never reach even junior ministerial office nor even aspire to it. The supplementaries may however be taken up by active and ambitious Opposition Members of the junior Shadow Minister level—after the original questioner has had an opportunity to ask his supplementary.

In so far as the purpose is to seek information there is obviously no reason why Questions should be confined to Opposition backbenchers, for Government backbenchers have no special sources of information. In so far, however, as Questions are asked to embarrass a Minister or to press him to take action they are more likely to attract opposition Members. In actual practice Government supporters, particularly when Labour is in power, always ask a substantial number of Questions, many of the harassing kind. This again emphasises the backbencher character of the device.

It must be borne in mind that the opportunities to speak in the House are very limited, particularly for a backbencher. He may very occasionally 'catch the Speaker's eye' and be able to speak in a debate. He will get a greater chance in the Committee stage of a Bill if he is a member of the Standing Committee. Neither of these infrequent opportunities offer him much freedom to raise an issue of his own choosing. He may try his luck in applying or balloting for an Adjournment

Motion—but he is unlikely to get more than one of these a year. In contrast he can even now, without needing anybody's permission or approval, put down two starred Questions and an unlimited number of unstarred Questions each day which, providing they do not transgress the rules of the House, will have to appear on the Order Paper for the Minister to answer either in person or by printed answer. If the Question he asks is about an issue of importance to his constituency it and the Minister's answer are likely to get publicity in the local press. Members may correspond with Ministers about particular issues and may get satisfaction in that way. But the Question and Answer, particularly those dealt with in the House, may mean welcome publicity to the Member and may cause the Minister to ponder his reply more carefully.

The Future

If Question Time is such a good thing, and every writer and every Member seems to think that it is, why has the time allotted to it not kept pace with the growth in the number of Questions that Members desire to have answered orally? Why should Question Time in 1901 go on until all the Questions on the Paper had been answered whereas now 30 or 40 are left unanswered on most days? As late as 1965 a Select Committee on Procedure rejected a proposal that the present 55 minutes, which can be eroded by Private Business, Petitions and Motions for Writs, should be made into a full hour. A Committee mainly of experienced and interested Members were thus not willing to recommend that even another five minutes or so of Parliamentary time should be devoted to this popular element in procedure. The answer in part is that a few minutes more would make little difference. It is even argued that as Mr Speaker will allow supplementaries to be asked on the Question reached in the dying seconds of Question Time, it may on occasion be only a minute or two short of the hour.

It is generally accepted that if say another 30 minutes were made available, the number of Questions put down for oral answer would probably grow; and so some would still remain unanswered at the end of the time. This assumes that the extra time were added to the current arrangement. A proposal by Sir Edward Fellowes, then Clerk of the House, that Questions could be put down for answer in one of three Grand Committees on the mornings of Mondays and Wednesdays found no support in the Select Committee of 1959. Members want ministerial replies in the Chamber at a popular time, not in the obscurity of some committee.

Question Time could only be expanded at the expense of some other element in the daily proceedings. An extension of half an hour would mean two hours a week less for legislation or for debate. As the Government, Opposition Leaders and many Members feel there is already insufficient time for Public Business there is a reluctance to cut it further. One can understand Ministers and the Opposition frontbench not wanting to give more time to a very largely backbench activity; but why should backbenchers not give greater support to one of the last of their activities to be left uncontrolled by their party leaders?

The reason is that most starred Questions are asked by a few Members. Thus in the 1966–67 session,[6] 17 Members gave notice of 2,896 starred Questions, or 22.6 per cent of the total notices. More than half the notices in that session were given by 70 Members, a small proportion of the 500 or so Members who might be expected to ask such Questions. The great majority of Members therefore have little sympathy with any suggestion that would allow Members who already ask over 100 starred Questions a year to ask another 50 or so. Members who put down only 6 or 10 starred questions a session, and these are in the great majority, quite often feel that their Questions are not reached not because of the shortage of time, but because too much of the time available is taken by the persistent questioners. Thus each Select Committee which considers the problem is regaled with figures showing what a large part of the opportunity is taken by the few. Hence the proposal to reduce the maximum from two a day to eight a month.

There is also some feeling that the mass use of starred Questions by a group or syndicate of Members to wage a campaign is rather an abuse of the time available. In some

6. Select Committee on Procedure, Fifth Report, 1966–67. H.C. 410, p. 44.

quarters there undoubtedly prevails the view that Question Times should not be used to provide publicity for a few publicity-seeking Members or as part of the party political battle nor even to obtain factual information which can be readily obtained by a written answer. Instead it is seen as the device each Member may find necessary to use occasionally to call attention to some piece of departmental incompetence or some local or individual injustice. It is a device to be used, for example, when correspondence with the Minister has failed to secure a satisfactory answer. To ensure that only starred Questions of this type were put on the Paper would require a degree of control from which all Members shrink. Hence the uneasy situation that though all is not well with Question Time, Members are prepared to make do with it. The ordinary Member will complain of the persistent questioners and of the unnecessarily long supplementaries and ministerial replies, but any solutions proposed always appear worse than the present situation.

The only major change[7] which might affect the working of Question Time would be a much greater use of specialised committees. Excluding the persistent questioners, whose questions are likely to be concerned with a great variety of matters, most Questions reflect the current preoccupations, specialisms, and constituency interests of the Member asking them. They may all be about the aircraft industry, atomic

7. On several occasions it has been suggested that Ministerial replies should be printed on the Order Paper the day they come to the Floor. This would save the time taken by the reading out of 40 to 50 answers and enable Members to be better prepared with their supplementaries. This is said to be impracticable because the printer could not, in very many cases, get the answer from the department in sufficient time. If this is the main objection it would surely be worth while adding a day to the present period of notice and so by giving the printer the necessary extra time greatly increase the capacity of the Question Hour.

(When on 1 March 1962 Mr Frank Allaun asked the Prime Minister whether he would, for a trial period, arrange for answers to starred Questions to be circulated before the Question Hour on the day they were down to be answered, Mr Macmillan replied: 'In this contest of wits, I think it would be rather unfair if the questioner had the advantage of a full day with the reply before preparing his extempore supplementary questions.' Mr Gaitskell helpfully added 'Is the Prime Minister aware that most of us would prefer some element of surprise to remain in respect of Ministerial Answers?' (H.C. Debates, Vol. 654, col. 1530.))

energy, social security or the common market. If there were to be set up a series of Select Committees covering the whole range of governmental activity, presumably Members would serve on the committees which most interested them. This would give them the opportunity to obtain information more fully and under better follow-up arrangements than exist at Question Time. One would thus expect specialised committees to be an alternative to Questions and so relieve the pressure on that device.

It by no means follows that this would prove to be the case even if, and it is still a very big if, specialised committees existed covering the work of all or the major departments. For one thing it is most unlikely that a few questions and answers out of the many thousands during the course of the proceedings of a Select Committee would ever attract the immediate publicity received by the single question printed on the paper, answered in the House and with the printed answer also readily available to Ministers and Members. Moreover, select committees' proceedings are generally devoted to one theme at a time and the Members may want to deal urgently with quite a different theme. Finally each select committee will contain only a dozen or so members and even if these are the enthusiasts for the subject there may still remain a lot of Members of the House, including many of the persistent questioners who, not being on the appropriate committee, will still have to get their information through starred or un-starred questions.

The fact is that Question Time and specialised committees would be performing different functions. The primary purpose of the latter is to enable a small group of Members to study a governmental activity in some depth mainly so as to be better informed but also to improve the House's control over Departments. There would still be a substantial function left for Questions to perform—the raising of the individual case, the personal or group campaign to stimulate action or to change ministerial policy, the testing of the Minister's actions in a full Chamber.

At some time in the future the House will have to think afresh about the real purpose of the Question Hour. At the moment all discussion centres on getting as many questions answered as possible. Select committees recommend stricter control of supplementaries and Speakers try to restrict their number and length. But what is the point of a starred Question if supplementaries cannot be asked? How does it then differ from an unstarred Question? Surely the difference does not really lie in the Minister having to read out an answer in public. Are supplementaries being restricted merely in order to enable more of the original Questions to be answered orally or because experience shows that an average of 1.8 supplementaries a Question is sufficient to satisfy the proper curiosity of Members and that anything beyond that would be idle and wasteful? If there are many Questions which could be dealt with more satisfactorily by the asking of five to seven supplementaries, what are the relative merits, so far as the effective use of Parliamentary time is concerned, of trying to rush through 40 or so original Questions as against dealing with say 15 or 20 really effectively?

The difficulty of finding a solution satisfactory to all Members lies in the character of the device. Many Members believe that a lot of starred Questions could just as well be left without the asterisk. They know of no way of preventing what they regard as the misuse of Question Time other than by methods of control which would alter its character and limit its value to all backbenchers. Failing a satisfactory method for ensuring that only Questions warranting the use of the limited time available can find their way on the Paper, Members are likely to continue to accept each Question being treated alike.

Chapter 6

Parliament and the Ombudsman

Geoffrey Marshall

Sir Edmund Compton relates in his report, published in February 1969, that what appears to have interested visitors to his office from Europe and North America is that he is a parliamentary Ombudsman. 'The characteristics of my office which have attracted particular attention', he writes, 'are the close links with the House of Commons . . . and the provisions . . . whereby I may only consider complaints if they are referred to me by members of the House of Commons.' The visitors from Czechoslovakia, France, Japan, Laos and Tobago, who, amongst others, were particularly struck by these features, were not, one supposes, taken aback merely because the House of Lords has been so unchivalrously excluded from the benefits of the 1967 Act. What they may have been wondering was why the policing of bureaucracy in England should have been linked to the legislature at all. Might it not have been better (so the clear-sighted Laotian may have surmised) to have conceived the role as an independent one to be exercised by a judicial or quasi-judicial agency ? There is something, after all, to be said for this view. Control of the executive by Parliament is, we know, only a partially successful illusion. Some see a Parliamentary Commissioner as only a halfway house to a fully articulated system of judicial control. It may even look like a house of ill repute which respectable rule-of-law men should avoid. All theory aside, and granted our Anglican preferences for the avoidance of legalism in matters of administration, it might still be argued that the association of the Commissioner with a Parliamentary Select Committee could conceivably blur the clarity and finality of his judgments. Opportunity for further parliamentary canvassing of reports by Members who are inevitably politicians might be thought to soften the impact of

114

the Commissioner's findings, which having no more than moral force to support them, ought to have it in the sharpest possible form.

Nevertheless, it could be argued that the Parliamentary Select Committee has not demonstrably, in the first two years of its operations, had any such effect. In fact, its influence could be said to have been beneficial in several ways. It has found a role for itself which complements that of the Commissioner; it has supported and encouraged a liberal interpretation of the provisions of the 1967 Act, and it has in consequence done something to remedy the deficiencies of a limping and limiting statute. To see the manner in which this has come about we can, with some licence, divide the short history of the Ombudsman, like Dicey's nineteenth century, into three periods. In the first, there was an era of, so to speak, administrative toryism; in the second phase a piece of Benthamite initiative by the Commissioner; and in the third a period of collective interventionism by the Commissioner and Select Committee.

The First Reports

The Parliamentary Commissioner Act came into operation on 1 April 1967 and Sir Edmund Compton's first report appeared in November of that year. It explained the organisation of his office and the procedure followed in dealing with Members' complaints. It was suggested that Members should decide for themselves to what extent they would scrutinise a complaint for eligibility before referring it to the Commissioner, but that the Commissioner would be ready to receive any case on which a Member felt doubt or wished the jurisdictional tests to be applied on his behalf. The question of eligibility obviously presents difficulty for Ministers, since whether a complaint falls within the provisions of the Act is often not·a simple matter. In general, complaints must refer to the action of one of the central government departments scheduled in the Act. Local government, the police and public corporations are excluded. But since Members have a number of powers in these fields (appellate, financial and inquiry powers in planning, education and police, for example) it may often be that a complaint which appears to be excluded may be framed in relation to the action or inaction[1] of a Minister or Department. Sometimes the issue cannot be settled without some preliminary investigation by the Commissioner's staff and there is a further class of cases which under the Act may be excluded (e.g. which are out of time or where recourse to a tribunal or to a court of law is possible) but which may be admitted at the Commissioner's discretion. Moreover, the Act does not contain any definition of 'maladministration' and both investigation and reflection may be needed before an allegation of injustice can be characterised as proper for further inquiry.

This point was underlined by Sir Edmund at some length. His concern, he noted, was not with injustice as such, but only with that specific variety of injustice brought about by maladministration. What complainants usually wanted, he said, was a review of an unwelcome decision on the ground that it was biased or perverse. But the area of investigation which was properly within the Commissioner's ambit was the administrative process attendant on a discretionary decision, where there might be 'defects or failings on the part of the departmental operator' or mistakes detrimental to a complainant in the collection of evidence or in the presentation of a case to a Minister. The quality of a decision itself (whether actually made by a Minister or in effect by a civil servant) was thus excluded from questioning. The distinction between the decision and its antecedents was recognised as unsatisfactory and difficult to draw. But the difficulty is written into the 1967 Act. Section 12(3) forbids the Commissioner 'to question the merits of a decision taken without maladministration by a government department or other authority in the exercise of a discretion vested in that department or authority'. When Parliament said that, it presumably intended to say something, and Sir Edmund was doing his valiant best to find and apply the intention of the Legislature.

In December 1967 the Commissioner's second report (on noise at London airport) showed precisely how 'grievances' and 'maladministration' might fail to coincide. The complainants alleged that the Board of Trade, as the responsible department, was failing to control the noise caused by air

1. Section 12(1) of the Act provides that 'action' includes failure to act.

traffic at Heathrow. The Commissioner examined the procedure for regulating aircraft noise, and the manner in which complaints were handled. He did not ask whether the complainants were suffering from an unjust or unreasonable burden but whether the decisions involved had been taken 'after proper consideration of all the relevant factors'. Since they had, the Board of Trade had not been guilty of maladministration. The first annual report, containing summaries of the facts and decisions in about 70 cases, showed even more clearly what maladministration might or might not be. Elements of maladministration were found in 19 cases (10 per cent of the total). There had been some lost files, delays in correspondence, wrong information and minor discourtesy—all of them remedied to the Commissioner's satisfaction. In a number of cases complainants had argued that a departmental decision in their case had been unjust or unreasonable. But the Commissioner, after investigating the handling of the cases, had concluded that the decisions had been consistent with the Department's normal arrangements or general policy. In one such case (refusal to allow a householder to construct a pedestrian access to a trunk road at the back of his house) the report concluded that 'the rigid application of the Ministry's policy to this case bore hardly on the complainant'. But this in itself was not maladministration and the merits of the general policy were outside the scope of investigation.

Some cases suggested a further ground of potential consumer frustration. Many complaints were against actions taken in accordance with the provisions of legislation or of regulations made under statutory powers. Complainants thought the actions, and often the regulations and legislation themselves unfair. But these did not constitute 'administrative' action (being 'legislative' in character) and could not therefore terminate in 'maladministration'. Political science, unfortunately, has failed to supply a serviceable label to describe the malfunctioning of the legislative role.

The Sachsenhausen Case
At the end of 1967 some lamentation was in order. Administrative justice seemed to be spluttering amongst the filing cabinets

and the odd inconsiderate 'departmental operator'. But Sir Edmund rescued it by a decision which might be conceived as important on a minor scale to the development of British ombudsmanship as was *Marbury* v. *Madison* in the history of constitutional adjudication in the United States. The complaint related to the treatment during the Second World War of twelve prisoners of war in a special camp and cell block at Sachsenhausen. An Anglo-German agreement in 1964 had made available £1,000,000 for United Kingdom nationals who were victims of Nazi persecution, but the Foreign Office had refused to pay compensation to the twelve applicants, who alleged that they had suffered injustice by reason of the Foreign Office's maladministration. The issues were a mixture of fact and judgment. A lawyer might have said that they related solely to questions of fact, meaning that they involved matters of opinion about where to draw the line. The Foreign Office had laid down for itself certain criteria which were roughly that a victim of persecution, to qualify for compensation, should have been interned in a concentration camp or in conditions which were equally severe. Amongst the questions in issue were the camp boundaries and whether the applicants had been interned inside them. In his report the Commissioner found in favour of the complainants' version of the facts about their internment. He held that there had been defects in the procedure by which the unfavourable decisions had been reached. 'The original decision was based', Sir Edmund stated, 'on partial and largely irrelevant information and the decision was maintained in disregard of additional information and evidence.'[2]

This characterisation was disputed by the then Foreign Secretary, Mr George Brown. In February 1967 Mr Brown had seen three of the complainants at the Foreign Office. Mr Airey Neave's account of the meeting at which he had been present was as follows: 'After they had given an account of their sufferings, he told them "to forget it and get it out of their systems". He said that "all the money was gone".'[3] In March the Foreign Office dispatched a letter to Mr David

2. H.C 54, 1967–68, p. 18.

3. Evidence to the Select Committee on the Parliamentary Commissioner for Administration. H.C. 258, 1967–68, p. 57.

Ginsburg M.P. declining to set up an inquiry into the complaints. 'No proper function,' they said, could be served by an inquiry of this kind. 'Our legal advice is that the Notes for guidance, upon which the distribution of compensation were based, were administrative instructions authorised by the Foreign Secretary at the time. As such they were not creative of rights and only the authority issuing them is competent to say what they mean.' The issuing authority, the Foreign Secretary at the time, Mr R. A. Butler, was by then busily occupied in Cambridge and the Foreign Office did not suggest that he should be consulted. Mr Brown's view on the other hand does not seem to have been quite the same as that of the legal advisers, for he strongly implied that he too knew what the administrative instructions meant. As he later said in the Commons 'I read every piece of paper in the file. I came to my own conclusions by my own processes of judgment.'

Mr Brown's judgment was three-fold: first, that the Parliamentary Commissioner was wrong; secondly, that it was none of his business; thirdly, that he would pay compensation as if the Commissioner had been right. In the Commons debate to take note of the Commissioner's report on 5 February 1968 he insisted that none of his officials had misled him. Nobody had blundered or bungled. The matter was one of judgment and he personally had judged it.

Having said this, the Foreign Secretary went on to suggest that a serious constitutional question had been placed in issue, namely the maintenance of the convention of ministerial responsibility. The House, he said, should not start holding officials responsible for things that had gone wrong. If things were wrongly done, they were wrongly done by Ministers. It was Ministers who must be attacked, not officials. If the office of Parliamentary Commissioner were to lead to changing this constitutional position the whole function of ministerial accountability to Parliament would be undermined.

These reflections and the apparent conflict between the Minister's and the Parliamentary Commissioner's conclusions provided the material for the first report of the Commons Select Committee which had been set up in November 1967 to examine the Commissioner's reports.

The Select Committee and Parliamentary Accountability

Three obvious questions were raised at this point about the function of the Parliamentary Commissioner and the Select Committee. First: in what sense may a ministerial decision (as distinct from the activity of 'departmental operators') constitute an example of maladministration? Secondly: to what extent is it proper for the Commissioner in his reports to indicate where actual blame or responsibility lies in a department, and should he name the officials concerned? Thirdly: what is the role of the Select Committee when there is a conflict between the Commissioner and a Minister? Are they themselves to resolve it?

The Committee in effect answered all these questions in their Sachsenhausen report. They began by regretting that the issue had been the subject of a statement by the Foreign Secretary and a debate in the House before their report had been heard. They concluded by saying that they regarded as a serious lapse in administrative standards the Foreign Office's persistent refusal over a period of nearly two years to attend to the significance of the fresh evidence available to them. There were, they thought, shortcomings on the part of both Ministers and officials. There were defects in the information and advice provided to Ministers and this was 'the collective responsibility of Foreign Office Officials'.[4]

Thus the Committee, though denying any intention of acting as a court of appeal or substituting their judgment either for the Commissioner's or the Minister's, firmly took the part of the Commissioner against the Minister. They accepted his characterisation of the case rather than the Foreign Secretary's; and they felt it their duty to discover what the Department had done to put right what the Commissioner said was wrong. With the Foreign Office's subsequent evidence on this point the Committee were dissatisfied. The Permanent Under Secretary, Sir Paul Gore Booth, they said, 'was unable to give your Committee any specific indication either of the defects of the system that the Sachsenhausen case had brought to light or of the action that was being taken to mend the system'.[5] This was not altogether surprising, since the Foreign Secretary had not conceded that any defects

4. H.C. 258, 1967–68, pp. ix–xi. 5. Ibid. p. xii.

in the system had occurred. Sir Paul was placed in further difficulties by the Committee. They wished to know whether the Foreign Office now accepted the conclusions of the Parliamentary Commissioner on the basis of which they were paying compensation. Sir Paul found it difficult to say, because his Minister had given no clear guidance. He had said that compensation should be paid but he had completely rejected the Commissioner's conclusions, if not his facts. Did the Foreign Office (Mr Fletcher-Cooke, wanted to know) now say, having reviewed the cases, that the complainants were or were not in the concentration camp. 'The answer', Sir Paul said, 'is that the Foreign Office takes its instructions from the Foreign Secretary.'[6] Sir Paul also declined to say which civil servants had dealt with the question—'I am not authorised certainly by the Foreign Secretary to name individuals.'[7]

The Committee returned to the implications of this topic in their second report issued in July 1968. In the interim they had met with some opposition from Mr Brown's successor, Mr Michael Stewart, who had sent the Attorney-General to tell the Committee that it must not for the Constitution's sake start taking evidence from junior civil servants. Mr Airey Neave in his evidence to the Committee had named the official whom he thought had had the greatest responsibility for the day-to-day administration of the Sachsenhausen case (though the name does not appear in the minutes of evidence). Sir Elwyn Jones suggested that ministerial responsibility would be undermined if the Committee were to examine anyone other than the Permanent Under Secretary.

To this the Committee replied that if the doctrine of ministerial responsibility meant that all decisions were assumed to have been made by Ministers, the whole point of the Parliamentary Commissioner Act was to undermine it, since Parliament had authorised the Commissioner to find out exactly how decisions had been made and to interview civil servants. The Legislature had decided 'to let this independent official go through the files behind the Minister's back and talk to Tom, Dick, and Harry in his department.'[8]

The dialogue between Sir Elwyn and Committee members

6. H.C. 258, 1967–68, p. 33.   7. Ibid. p. 30.
8. H.C. 350, 1967–68, p. 82.

remained spirited. The Civil Service, it was suggested, might be terrified if the Commissioner's cases were to be reopened by the Select Committee and they would lose the right of privacy guaranteed to them by the Act when questioned by the Commissioner. To this Committee replied that they were not reopening investigations, but it was their duty to see how a Department had remedied defects discovered in its procedures and this they could only properly find out from those actually working the system. But, said the Attorney-General, a junior civil servant might, in defending himself, implicate others and even contradict his Minister. So indeed, said the Committee, he might; and the conversation (as Lord Haldane once said) then fell off.

The report laid before the House clearly states the Committee's conclusion, that the complete anonymity of civil servants forms no part of the doctrine of ministerial accountability as it stands today. It can, with Parliament's authority in the 1967 Act, be infringed by the Commissioner's findings, since a complaint may be directed against specific individuals or branches of government. The Committee do not agree that they should confine themselves to taking such evidence from the Principal Officer of a Department when they are considering what a Department should do to remedy administrative defects, since they may sometimes need the evidence of officials concerned at first hand with the working of the system and they are 'satisfied that they will be able to take evidence from subordinate officials for this purpose without exposing them to unfair publicity or criticism'.[9] Departments, they think, can be relied upon to indicate the appropriate witnesses; and the Fulton Report, in commenting on the relations between the Civil Service and Parliament, has, they add, envisaged a greater involvement of civil servants below the level of Permanent Secretary.

'Bad Decisions' and 'Bad Rules'

The Report of July 1968 took up another central issue. The Commissioner had asked for guidance upon the extent to which the quality of a decision could properly come within his field of inquiry, as distinct from the propriety of the pro-

9. H.C. 350, 1967–68, p. xii.

cedures leading up to it. Another area of difficulty was that in which hardship to individuals might be caused by the correct application by a Department of an administrative rule or policy. Individual hardship would not necessarily indicate that the rule was defective, but it might indicate that the Department should review its operation. Should it not be open to the Commissioner, if necessary, to find maladministration where a Department had failed to review its rules and procedures?

The Committee's conclusion was that both the 'bad rule' and the 'bad decision' could in suitable cases constitute maladministration. That term was not defined in the Act, but in the parliamentary debates on the Bill in October 1966 Ministers had conceded that it might cover 'bias', 'prejudice' and 'perversity'—and could not decisions themselves be biased, prejudiced or perverse? The Committee were not encouraging the Commissioner (they said) 'to substitute his decision for that of the Government' but if he found a decision which, judged by its effect upon an aggrieved person, appeared to him to be thoroughly bad in quality 'he might infer from the quality of the decision itself that there had been an element of maladministration in the taking of it'.[10] All conclusions and decisions, the argument implies, are taken on evidence or by weighing one thing against another. Though the Parliamentary Commissioner Act says that the merits of a decision may not be questioned if it is reached without maladministration, it is, it seems, now permissible to infer that if a decision has no merits at all, there *must* have been maladministration in the way it was reached. Thus the stuffing is knocked out of s.12 of the 1967 Act, as it always deserved to be.

Expansion of the Commissioner's Role

The Second Annual Report by the Commissioner allows some judgment to be made of the potentially wider role which the Select Committee has encouraged him to undertake and it suggests some further questions.

By the end of 1968, 542 Members of the House of Commons had referred complaints to the Commissioner's Office. During the year 374 cases had been completed and the results reported to the relevant Member. 727 cases (or 54 per cent) had,

10. H.C. 350, 1967–68, p. vii.

however, been rejected as being outside the Commissioner's jurisdiction, as had 808 written complaints received direct from members of the public. Nearly one-fifth of the complaints received related to bodies not within the scope of the Act (such as local authorities, other public bodies, legal bodies, the police and tribunals). A number of the case reports suggest, however, that complaints relating at least in part to bodies outside the Act may be brought in via ministerial powers. A complainant allegedly ill-treated by the police complains, for example, that the Home Office has failed to exercise its power under the Police Act to set up an inquiry (case C–442/68). The three Departments against which most complaints were received in 1968 were Health and Social Security, Housing and Local Government and Inland Revenue. In 38 (10 per cent) of the 374 cases completed in 1968 there had been 'elements of maladministration which had led to some measure of injustice'. In the main these were minor matters involving confusion between departments, correspondence going astray, or loss caused to a complainant by delay. In two cases of the last kind the Inland Revenue were found by the Commissioner to have caused damage (to a Canadian company and to a scientist holding a Swiss research fellowship) by delaying a tax refund and a PAYE code readjustment until after the devaluation of sterling. In each case the Department agreed to make an ex gratia compensation payment on the Commissioner's suggestion. There is one feature of these proceedings which must strike anyone who reads the summarised facts of a number of 'hardship' cases (and it is suggested equally by a reading of the New Zealand Parliamentary Commissioner's reports). A department will often declare that it is powerless to remedy a hardship ('Although the Revenue conceded their responsibility . . . they considered that there was nothing that they could do to meet the loss incurred').[11] After the Commissioner's intervention they concede that something is, after all, possible. It seems not unlikely that if the Commissioner did not exist the departmental refusal, if contested only by the complainant, would often have been maintained. But stimulated by the Commissioner,

11. Second Report of the Parliamentary Commissioner, 1968–69. H.C. 129, pp. 85, 86.

a Department will sometimes make a positive suggestion for surmounting a difficulty produced by its earlier decision. In one case the Home Office refused an application for an Australian opera singer to remain in the country. After the Commissioner began his inquiries they 'thought they should consider whether her employment with the Opera company could be regarded as training for a profession under a scheme for Commonwealth Citizens administered by the Department of Employment and Productivity. This would enable her to remain in the UK.'[12] Ministerial changes of mind are also underlined. In a case involving alleged injustice arising out of the betterment levy 'The Minister stated that he could do nothing ... since the Land Commission was bound to act in accordance with the Statute'. Yet within a few weeks the Government acknowledged that there was a genuine case and that it could be met by an extra statutory concession.'[13]

In the 1968 annual report the Commissioner also commented on the effect of his decision to accept the Select Committee's suggestion that he should consider departmental rules and the quality of departmental decisions as within the scope of his investigations. In relation to rules and policies Sir Edmund indicated that his practice would be to inquire whether a department had reviewed a rule which, though correctly applied, had caused hardship. But he went on to say that he would not question a decision to maintain a rule if the review of the rule had been conducted without maladministration. Three points were made in support of this conclusion: first, that a decision as to whether a rule should be changed must rest with the department; secondly, that there might be grounds of public hardship which overrode the hardship to the individual; and thirdly, that s.12 (3) of the Act prevented any questioning of a decision to maintain a departmental rule. None of these seems adequate support for this restricted form of review of departmental rules and policies. No one suggests that a decision to change a rule does not rest with a department (as indeed does a decision to modify a particular decision). The point is not relevant to the question of the form of the Commissioner's inquiries or his recommendations for action. As to hardship to individuals

12. Ibid. p. 53.   13. Ibid. p. 72.

125

being overridden by other grounds for maintaining a rule—it may well be so overridden. But in some cases, perhaps it ought not to be. A departmental decision on that question may conceivably be bad or perverse as it may on any other. The citation of s.12 (3) here is puzzling. If the section does not prevent the questioning of 'bad' decisions—and the Committee has persuaded the Commissioner that it does not—the Committee's reasoning is equally applicable to bad decisions which happen to be about maintaining rules. One case, in fact, is mentioned by the Commissioner in which he did consider whether the maintenance of a rule causing hardship might involve maladministration. In this case the Ministry of Transport, Sir Edmund says, 'satisfied me that it did not'.[14] But did he consider the merits of the Ministry's decision or not? The case report concludes by noting that 'the ministry have exercised discretion according to their normal policy and procedures' and adds 'I do not question the merits of their decision'.[15] This final sentence is of course ambiguous. It might suggest that the Commissioner did not direct his mind at all to the merits of the Ministry's decision not to depart from their policy but merely assured himself that it was in fact their policy,[16] and that they had considered it in the light of the particular case of hardship. On the other hand it could mean that having considered the merits, the Commissioner did not feel that there was anything questionable in them or in the Ministry's decision.

Oddly enough the same ambiguity is still present in the phraseology of the reports on allegedly bad decisions where a general administrative rule is not in issue but only an individual decision. Here the Commissioner has clearly undertaken to consider the quality of the decision itself. In the introduction to his report the Commissioner states that the effect of the new practice 'has so far been slight' and 'I have not yet come across any decision which *after full investigation* has seemed to me so bad as to indicate bias or perversity on the

14. Ibid. p. 7   15. Ibid. p. 140.

16. An element of maladministration was found where a Ministry *had* departed from its policy. A decision to uphold an enforcement notice served by the Ministry of Housing and Local Government 'was not in my view in accordance with the Ministry's usual practice as they have described it to me'. Ibid. p. 62.

part of the person who took it'.[17] Yet in a number of cases the difference between the old and the new approach is hard to see and the Commissioner seems on the face of it still to be fighting shy of the quality and merits of the decision—Case C 56/68 for example involves the decision of the Ministry of Transport to close a railway station. The Report concludes: 'In reaching the decision to consent to the closure of the station the Minister took into account and fully considered all the relevant facts and . . . the decision was taken without maladministration. Consequently the *merits of the decision are not for me to question*'.[18] What surely ought to be said is that the merits are open to question but in this case after 'full investigation' the decision is not bad or perverse or unreasonable. The distinction still being drawn here between 'merits' and 'maladministration' is question-begging if the new willingness to consider the 'bad decision' is to have any bite at all. The only alternative conclusion is that there is some distinction between the 'badness or goodness' of a decision and its 'merits' which awaits exegesis.

Further Problems

In the Second Report of the Select Committee for 1967–68 and in the Commissioner's first report for 1968–69 the question of treating statutory instruments as within the Commissioner's field of investigation was left open for further review. The argument that they should not be considered within his compass is that they constitute legislative rather than administrative activity. Consequently the Commissioner has classed complaints against statutory rules and orders as being complaints whose thrust is against legislation. The first and second annual reports list many cases. A complaint about assessment of income in connection with student grants, for example, was held to be a complaint about the relevant Awards regulations of the Department of Education and Science and thus excluded. But the case for reviewing departmental rule making when it emerges as delegated legislation seems as strong as that which the Committee has already conceded in relation to informal administrative rules and policies. In his evidence to the Select Committee in

17. Ibid. p. 6. 18. Ibid. p. 131.

May 1968 Sir Edmund Compton conceded that it might be argued that though formally a legislative act, 'the making of statutory orders is one way in which Departments administer Acts of Parliament and is, in that sense, part of the administrative process'.[19] That being so Sir Edmund wondered whether a Department might be questioned by him as to whether they had considered administrative action to amend the orders which they have made. Why not?

Indeed the argument can be taken further. Much legislation, and not just delegated legislation, is in reality the work of Departments and the greater part of the legislative output is the handiwork of Ministers generally. Since the preparation and revision of legislation is in practice in large part a function of the Executive there is much to be said for including statute law within the province of a Parliamentary Commissioner, as is done in New Zealand. It perhaps sounds odd and even reckless to invest a non-elected person with power to declare an Act of Parliament to be unjust. But, no one would expect a British or New Zealand Ombudsman to make such declarations. The power would simply be a useful enlargement of the Commissioner's freedom to point out marginal and often unforeseen consequences of Statutes. A number of examples could be drawn from the Commissioner's reported cases particularly where Income Tax, compensation or welfare legislation is concerned. It is pointed out in one case (C–867/68) that the Housing Subsidies Act 1967 makes no provision for a mortgage option notice to be withdrawn during the continuation of the mortgage. Is there any very great derogation from the sovereignty of Parliament in the Parliamentary Commissioner's making a recommendation on such a matter? No one else will do it so effectively. Very often (as the Revenue cases show) a Department may be able to make an extra-statutory concession even if a complaint of hardship is prima facie caused by the provisions of a statute, and the Minister is the best possible person to procure an amendment to the law. Not to do so when amendment is necessary could without absurdity be called an administrative failing and possibly maladministration.

In the Commissioner and the Select Committee, Parliament

19. H.C. 350, 1967–68, p. 91.

has given itself a potentially flexible dual instrument whose freedom to manoeuvre within the boundaries of administrative law and justice ought not to be hindered by unnecessary fetters. The notion of 'maladministration' has proved to be such a fetter and the Select Committee by a bold piece of private statutory interpretation have tried to prise it loose. Parliament itself ought really to review the 1967 Act and set the Commissioner free. Several other matters are ripe for consideration. There are difficulties about the notion of an 'aggrieved person' in s. 6 (2) of the 1967 Act.[20] There is the question of allowing the Commissioner to act without a complaint and make inquiries, if he feels it necessary, on his own initiative. There is also a difficulty about the publishing of decisions. The Commissioner's practice has been to send to the Press reports of his investigations in selected cases which might otherwise be partially or misleadingly reported. But both decisions of and references to the Commissioner are almost always partially and often misleadingly reported. There is a legitimate public interest in an accurate and reasonably contemporaneous statement of what issues have been referred to the Parliamentary Commissioner and how they have been resolved. Selective press handouts and a belated annual narrative are not a substitute for a proper system of reporting.

20. See the Commissioner's comments in the Annual Report for 1968. G.C. 129, 1968–69, p. 6.

Chapter 7

The Role of the Library with a note on official publications

G. F. Lock

Staffing the House: Numbers and costs

The staff of the House of Commons are little mentioned in the standard textbooks on Parliament, and even well-informed people may not realise that they exist, imagining for example that Members look up all their facts for themselves. The nature of their work makes them back-room figures, but collectively they fulfil an essential role in the legislative and deliberative process. This chapter is largely concerned with the Library, but it attempts to set the staff and work of the Library within the context of the staff of the House of Commons as a whole.

The Estimates for the current year (1969–70) provide for 335 directly-employed staff in the House of Commons, and their salaries etc. cost £727,000. As public organisations go, this is obviously quite small, ranking below, for example, the Natural History Museum but above the Charity Commission; the Science Museum would be of the same order of magnitude, with 389 staff costing £585,000. However, the numbers of directly-employed staff do not tell the whole story, as some functions are carried out by staff employed by Government Departments. The maintenance, heating and so on of the building are carried out by the Ministry of Public Building and Works. (The upkeep and improvement of the Houses of Parliament were estimated to cost £673,000 in 1967–68, the last year for which there was a separate Estimate. Of this, £539,500 was current expenditure and £135,000 capital expenditure. In 1969–70, expenditure connected with the House of Commons included in the Votes of other departments is put at £1,647,000; well over half this is for stationery and printing.) The G.P.O. provides postal and telephone services and a contingent of the Metropolitan Police is

130

stationed in the building. The custodians of the building (who also carry out policing functions) are a charge upon the House of Lords Vote; amplification and communications services are provided by private companies, and the travel office, which arranges Members' official journeys etc., is a branch of a nationalised industry (Thomas Cook's). In addition, the Refreshment Department of the Commons employs its own staff direct. These services between them account for some 500–600 additional staff, the number varying according to whether the House is in recess or in session, and some of the services are shared with the House of Lords. The remainder of this chapter covers only the directly-employed staff of the Commons.

Control and Conditions of Service

The staff of the Commons are not civil servants, but they have some things in common with the Civil Service. The senior staff of both the Clerk's Department and the Department of the Library[1] are recruited through the Civil Service Commission, the basic qualifications for permanent posts in both Departments being a first or second class degree. (The Clerks take the examination for the Administrative Class of the Civil Service; Library Clerks are selected by interview.) Pay scales are linked with civil service grades and pension arrangements are similar. The ban on political activities applies even more strongly to Commons staff than to civil servants. The staff of the Commons are servants of the House, not of Ministers, and there are no rights of transfer between the Civil Service and the Commons.[2] Though this means that the loyalty of staff is undivided, a factor to which Committees and Members have ascribed much importance,[3] it does mean

1. But not the equivalent staff of the House of Lords.

2. Transfer even within the service of the House is very rare, though the former Librarian was for much of his career in the Clerk's Department and Erskine May himself was at one time Assistant Librarian.

3. See for example the Select Committee on Agriculture: the Committee 'consider it of vital importance that their staff should be independent of the Executive—and be seen to be independent'. A system of secondment of a civil servant to the service of the Committee 'would be scarcely fair to the civil servant attached to the Committee, whose future would lie with the Department under scrutiny and whose loyalties would inevitably be divided'. Report, 1966–67. H.C. 378–XVII, para. 7

that the expansion of services is dependent on the recruitment of additional staff—a lengthy process, whereas in Government departments new services can often be more rapidly developed by the switching of staff. The respects in which Commons staff differ from civil servants range from such minor things as having no control over their canteen facilities, not signing a declaration under the Official Secrets Acts on taking up their appointments, and being exempt from jury service, to more important things like non-participation in Civil Service training arrangements, for example courses at the Centre for Administrative Studies. There are no formal arrangements for staff associations, of the Whitley Council type that exist in the Civil Service. (There is a body called the Staff Board, consisting of senior officials, which is the rough equivalent of the official side of a Whitley Council.) In 1954, the Staff side of the Civil Service National Whitley Council made representations about this to a Select Committee then sitting on accommodation and other matters,[4] who included a recommendation on such arrangements in their Report. In July 1960, a ballot on trade union representation was held among the staff, and the voting was 67 to 181 against the institution of trade union arrangements, with 17 abstentions.[5] However, the staff voted in nine groups and there was a majority in favour of trade union arrangements within two groups. Arrangements were set up for these two groups and they have been extended since, but many of the staff are still not covered by them. On 24 March 1955, the then Prime Minister stated: 'Her Majesty's Government . . . favour the compilation of a code to govern the conditions of service of the staff of the House.'[6] As far as I know, no such code has been compiled.

The pay, pensions and terms of service of the staff are theoretically settled by a body called the House of Commons Offices Commission, set up under an Act of 1812 and con-

4. Report from the Select Committee on Accommodation . . . (The 'Stokes' Committee). H.C. 184, 1953–54, pp. xvi, 165–7.
5. H.C. Debates, 3 Nov. 1960, cols. 366–7. Earlier in the year, Mrs Castle, Mr Gaitskell and others had questioned the Prime Minister about the lack of trade union arrangements for the staff of the House; Ibid. 24 May 1960, cols. 213–14.
6. Ibid. 24 March 1955, col. 2266.

sisting of the Speaker, Chancellor of the Exchequer, Secretaries of State and the Law Officers (if they are Members of the House). Each year the Estimates for the House of Commons solemnly bear the note: 'Treasury control over this Estimate is confined to items which do not relate to the personal remuneration and retired allowances of officers of the House of Commons. General control is vested in the House of Commons Offices Commission.' Thus one might think that this lucky group of public servants is free from the oversight of the Treasury. In practice, as was recently pointed out by the Clerk of the House,[7] Treasury control is exercised by the presence of the Chancellor of the Exchequer on the Commission. Until 1955, the Commission made no Annual Report, but it now presents one to the House[8] which records, inter alia, staff appointments, resignations and promotions. Since 1965, a Select Committee on House of Commons Services has been set up each session 'to advise Mr Speaker on the control of the accommodation and services in that part of the Palace of Westminster and its precincts, occupied by or on behalf of the House of Commons'. This Committee, which appoints sub-committees for different services and groups of services, tenders advice on staff matters,[9] but strictly the statutory body responsible is still the Commission. Until the setting up of the House of Commons Services Committee, the Library came under an unofficial Committee advisory to the Speaker; there is now a sub-committee of the Services Committee specially concerned with the Library, and the Services Committee publishes Reports on the Library when necessary.

7. Evidence taken before the Select Committee on Science and Technology: Sub-Committee on Coastal Pollution, 21 May 1968. H.C. 421–I, 1967–68, p. 236.

8. In typescript, it is not published. The undertaking to present an Annual Report is to be found in H.C. Debates, 24 March 1955, col. 2266.

9. It is not always accepted by the Treasury—see Evidence to the Sub-Committee on Coastal Pollution, op. cit. p. 231.

The setting up of the Services Committee was recommended in the Report of the Select Committee on the Palace of Westminster, H.C. 285, 1964–65.

Staffing the Library

The 1969–70 Estimates provide for a total staff of 53, and of these 20 are in the 'graduate grade'.[10] The latter come from nine different universities (including two post-war foundations), though products of Oxford and Cambridge (8 and 4 respectively) outnumber those of other universities. As might be expected, the social sciences predominate among the subjects studied, but there are five historians, two modern linguists and graduates in English and Science; there is a respectable proportion of staff with first-class and higher degrees. The Library has for a long time had a small executive grade, and there have been instances of staff promotions from it to the graduate grade as there have been from the clerical to the executive grade.

One distinguishing feature of the staff structure is the high proportion of women in the graduate grade. This has been as high as 9 in 20, but is currently 8. The employment of women on this scale is a comparatively recent development; although one woman Library Clerk served between 1946 and 1951 and another between 1951 and 1953, women started to arrive in force only in 1963.[11] Of the 16 appointments made since then, 12 have been of women. While there can be no doubt that the policy of selecting the best candidates who apply, irrespective of sex, is the correct one, this imbalance is likely to result in a rather peculiar structure of the senior staff of the Library, with the top ranks filled predominantly by long-serving men and the lower and middle ranks filled mostly by women, many of whom may resign after a few years' service. There is thus some loss in continuity and expertise, but this is largely offset by the high calibre of the new staff. Such an arrangement may not be ideal, but it has permitted the Library to keep its staff usually up to strength over a period of some difficulty in recruitment. In fact, so far the turnover among

10. This phrase is used as convenient shorthand for staff of the rank of Library Clerk up to Librarian. It does not imply that members of the staff in other grades cannot be graduates and they sometimes are.

11. In 1955, the advertising of a post as being open to men only was raised at Question Time (H.C. Debates 30 June 1955 col. 503). Similarly in 1967 a question was also put about an advertisement for a post which stated that preference might be given to male applicants. (Ibid. 23 Jan. 1967, col. 965.)

the female recruits of the 1960s has been lower than the turn-over among the male recruits of the 1950s.[12] Of the twelve women appointed since 1963 only two have left for reasons connected with marriage; two others left for reasons for which a man might have left—to improve their career prospects, one in the Administrative Class and one in the Foreign Service. Ambitious and able women are of course just as likely to move on as men if they feel that their jobs do not measure up to their capabilities. Recruitment to some specialist posts has always been difficult—for example, for economists or statisticians, as the Civil Service offers higher salaries. Luckily the idea of working at the House of Commons has had an attraction for some people who would perhaps not be attracted to the Civil Service, but there can be no certainty that this idea will retain its appeal.

The General Services of the Library

This is not the place to describe at length characteristics that the Library has in common with other libraries, and the reader will probably prefer me to concentrate on its distinctive features.[13] It can of course be taken for granted that it is rich in official publications, with an enormous run of Parliamentary Papers lining a long and lofty corridor from floor to ceiling. It has a strong law section which is found very useful by the numerous lawyer-Members, and can call if necessary on the even greater resources of the Library of the House of Lords, which naturally specialises in this field, because of the

12. The 'Stokes' Committee commented upon the 'considerable number of resignations amongst the senior Library staff', at a period when the staff, apart from secretaries, was almost entirely male. Op. cit. p. xiii.

13. The services offered to Members are outlined in a Handbook published by the Library and sent to new M.P.s. The work and organisation of the Library have been described in R. Irwin and R. Staveley (eds.) 'The Libraries of London', 1961, pp. 94–8—chapter by S. Gordon; D. Menhennet 'The Library of the House of Commons'. *Political Quarterly*, July–Oct. 1965, pp. 323–32; D. Menhennet, 'The House of Commons Library: research and information services'. *Information Scientist*, Sept. 1967, pp. 75–83; D. Menhennet and J. B. Poole, 'Information services of the Commons Library'. *New Scientist*, 7 Sept. 1967, pp. 499–502; D. Menhennet, 'Parliamentary Libraries IV—Information and Research Services'. *The Parliamentarian*, April 1969, pp. 111–16.

Lords' legal functions. Broadly, it receives all publications of the United Nations and international organisations—these are very numerous, and considerable skill is needed for their arrangement and indexing. The Reference Room has a wide range of periodicals, all the national newspapers and a selection of provincial and foreign ones, reference books, year books and annual reports. There are special sections of the Library for statistical and scientific publications, built up by the research staff in those fields. Last, in this very brief summary of the Library's holdings, comes the collection of general books in which the emphasis is placed on history, biography and the social sciences, but which also includes books on many other subjects, including some of a lighter character suitable for providing distraction during an all-night sitting. Most of this description agrees with what the outsider would expect to find in the Library, but many of the resources have been built up only since 1946. Until then, by all accounts, the Library had the atmosphere of a rather old-fashioned West-End club. The staff was small, money for buying books was scarce and a wide coverage was not attempted. As a result of an enquiry into the Library by a Select Committee,[14] its development was then started along the lines which have guided it until now, so that it ceased to be just a repository of books and official publications where Members could work in peaceful and bookish surroundings. Its aim became the provision of information for Members on a much wider scale than had previously been possible—both quick answers provided from readily available sources by staff working on the floor of the Library, and longer answers, usually in writing, by back-room staff manning the new Research service, founded in 1946. The two Divisions of the Library are interdependent and complementary. The non-research staff (called the 'Parliamentary Division') organise the holdings of the Library, answer the enquiries that can be readily dealt with (including many telephone calls from outside the House), and maintain various specialised indexes that have been developed to fulfil specific needs. (The indexes are compiled in 'strip' form on panels and among them are: a 'Parliamentary Index' to all papers presented to the House

14. Report. H.C. 99–I, 1945–46.

and to debates; a 'Home Affairs Index' to selected newspaper and periodical articles, pamphlets, government press notices and other material; an 'International Affairs Index' to the documents of international organisations and material on foreign countries; and a 'Committee Index' to Royal Commissions and Committees of Enquiry, giving their composition, terms of reference and so on.) The research staff draws heavily on the work of their colleagues in the Parliamentary Division, and indeed would find it impossible to function without it; in return they assist the Parliamentary Division by helping with the maintenance of services available to the Library as a whole (for instance, by contributing to collections of press cuttings) and taking over all the more time-consuming enquiries. I discuss the Research Division in more detail in the next section.

The Research Division

As mentioned above, the research service was instituted in 1946, with two graduates to do statistical and two to do non-statistical work, plus a small supporting staff. It remained at this modest strength for over 15 years, though increasingly overloaded towards the end of the period. It now consists of 12 members of the 'graduate grade', one of the executive grade and supporting clerical and secretarial staff. This expansion has enabled it to attempt limited specialisation, and with this aim scientific and economic sections have been set up in addition to the general and statistical sections already in being. (However, because of various difficulties, it has not been possible to staff the economic section wholly with people with economic training.) Library clerks at the International Affairs desk deal with research on international questions and with most enquiries on foreign countries; they do not, however, form part of the Research Division.

The word 'research' is something of a stumbling block in the understanding of what the Division does. Part of the meaning will have emerged from the previous section; the Library uses the term to mean most of the work done in writing for individual Members and also the preparation of duplicated background material made available to Members as a whole. It is not 'research' in the academic sense at all;

nobody writes lengthy dissertations on any subject—the staff would not have time to write them, nor Members to read them. Nor should we claim that any of the work was original or 'pushed forward the frontiers of knowledge', though we should claim that our answers were very useful in bringing together and boiling down material from a wide range of different sources. Enquiries vary enormously in subject and answers in length—from half a page to several pages. The scope of the service covers replies to specific enquiries put by Members and arising out of their parliamentary activities; it does not extend to general briefing, and replies are of course strictly factual and impartial. A general characteristic is the urgency of the work; about two-thirds of the answers are required within 48 hours, and for many only two or three hours' notice is given.

In addition to answering specific enquiries for individual Members, the Research Division makes available to Members as a whole several series of compilations. These are: digests of selected scientific articles and of comment on British affairs in overseas newspapers; a new series of 'Background Papers' on such subjects as 'The situation in Czechoslovakia' and 'Government Economic Measures since October 1964'; and finally a series of 'Reference Sheets', of which some 30–40 are produced per year. These are fully annotated lists of legislation, debates, pamphlets, periodical articles and press comment on a given subject. Most major Bills and debates are covered, and a set of copies of the items listed is put in boxes in the Library for Members to consult. Examples of recent subjects are: trade union reform, redistribution of parliamentary seats and national health service charges. At one time statistical memoranda were also prepared giving figures on a major topic in a fair amount of depth—for example the nationalisation of iron and steel. These have however been discontinued because of the pressure of work on enquiries.

Why should Members have a research service at all, when they are free to bombard Ministers with parliamentary questions? It might be thought unnecessary to ask and answer this question in the 1960s, but it was only eight years ago that an Estimates Sub-Committee wrote: 'The House should decide whether it requires a research service'; and later: 'Wherever possible information . . . should be sought from other libraries'.[15] In its reply, the Library Committee wrote: 'To question the need for . . . [research] services would be to advocate a complete reversal of policy. They are of proven value and we believe that their abolition would be strongly resented by the large numbers of Members who use them.'[16]

The research service fulfils a different need from the parliamentary Question, though there may be some overlap between the short research answers and those Questions (especially written ones) which are genuinely prompted by a thirst for information. Research answers can cover subjects for which there is no ministerial responsibility, and on which parliamentary Questions would therefore be rejected, e.g. requests for information on other countries (though some slip through in the form 'what information is available to the Minister from international organisations?'). The research service can answer theoretical questions, e.g. the difference between the historic and replacement cost basis for depreciation in company accounts; it can provide detail on individual companies, local authorities and nationalised industries; and it can deal with historical enquiries—and in none of these fields would parliamentary Questions be admissible. The researcher can deal with a subject at more length than can a civil servant drafting a Hansard answer, and can meet an enquirer to discuss points of difficulty with him. Just as there are some subjects for which Members seek publicity—and for which a parliamentary Question is appropriate—so there are others on which they wish to seek information privately. Sometimes a Member may need a good deal of background information to enable him to draft a telling parliamentary Question, and this the Library can provide. The research service can be quicker, as there are no rules about minimum periods of notice; it is open for all the hours that the House sits, whereas Ministries close during the evening and at night.

There is also the question of cost. Parliamentary Questions

15. Second Report from the Estimates Committee. H.C. 168, 1960–61, pp. vii, xv.
16. Tenth Special Report from the Estimates Committee. H.C. 246 1960–61, p. 4.

are not cheap: the average cost of an oral answer in June–July 1965 worked out at £10 10s. 11d. and a written answer at £7 11s 4d. Total costs for parliamentary questions incurred in Government Departments in Session 1964–65 were of the order of £110,000 and must have risen considerably since, because of the rise in both numbers of Questions and in civil servants' salaries.[17] Without the Library's services, in both Divisions, the volume of parliamentary Questions, already large, would probably be considerably larger.

Two classes of research enquiry owe their origin to parliamentary Questions. The first consists of Questions rejected by the Table Office on various grounds, among which is that the information is already available in print. The Library staff is able on request to help discover what information is published and what is not; thus it sometimes finds itself answering a draft Question after finding a published source containing the data required, whereupon it has to extract and 'work it up' into the form required by the Member. The second class consists of parliamentary Questions, the answers to which are inadequate for Members' needs. As the volume of Questions grows, a greater proportion of the answers is coming to consist of references to publications. Sometimes these are specific (though unfortunately not always accurate) with titles and page numbers given; sometimes they are very general, e.g.: 'All the information requested can be obtained from published documents.' A fair proportion of Questions receiving this sort of answer ends up with the Library, and the actual work of preparing proper answers to the original Question falls upon the research staff. Thus the curious system has grown up whereby an official employed by a Ministry has one shot at dealing with some parliamentary Questions and another employed by the House of Commons has a second and, one hopes, final shot at them.[18]

17. On the cost of parliamentary questions, see H.C. Debates, Vol. 718, Col. 96–7W; Vol. 758, Col. 383–4W; and Vol. 759, Cols. 77–8W and 250–1W. The highest cost found in the 1965 survey was over £475. A 1968 figure for the average cost of civil service time alone for replying to an oral question was over £10.

18. On this system, see H.C. Debates, 22 July 1968, written answers Col. 18. The question asked the Chancellor if he were aware that the practice was 'overburdening the Library Research Unit, which was less

The Library staff like to think that they can on occasion provide a better service than a government department, even though it is a much smaller organisation than most of them. It is a matter of remark that some Ministers continue to use the Library's research service after their appointment, even at times on matters connected with their own departments. The Lawrence Committee of 1964, while saying that facilities for Members were really outside their terms of reference, nevertheless observed 'that Members referred with gratitude to the assistance which they receive from the staff of the Library of the House, while suggesting that a further strengthening of this staff would be of great assistance to them'.[19]

The Library and Select Committees
A field that has widened considerably in the last two years or so has been the Library's activities in connection with select committees. For some time there had been a small flow of work from committees, e.g. the drawing up of a bibliography or a list of statistical sources at the beginning of an enquiry, supplying information on specific points during the enquiry both to individual members and to the committee as a whole,[20] and checking the odd fact for inclusion in the final Report. It took a long time for the principle to be accepted that committees should use specialist assistance; the traditional view was that the place of the expert was in the witness-chair and that committees would obtain all the help from experts that they needed from the examination of witnesses. (An exception was made for the help given to the Public Accounts Committee by the Comptroller and Auditor General.) In 1959, the Select Committee on the Nationalised Industries considered the question of specialist assistance, and one of the courses they reviewed was the use of the Library's research staff, enlarged

---

well equipped to give the information than his own Department'. The reply spoke of the practice as being on many occasions 'reasonable convenient and well-established'.

19. Report of the Committee on the Remuneration of Ministers and Members of Parliament, Cmnd. 2516 p. 18.

20. For an example, see Report by the Select Committee on the Nationalised Industries on the Post Office, Vol. II. H.C. 340–I, 1966–67, p. 559.

for the Committee's needs. Mr Gaitskell favoured this course in his evidence to the Committee.[21] However at the end of its Report, in the words of the *Economist*, the Committee gave 'little positive guidance to the House to help it decide whether to employ any extra assistance and, if so, from what source'.[22] No specialist assistance was in fact provided at this period, but the Committee obtained the services of an extra Clerk.

In 1965, the Estimates Committee recommended the provision of specialist assistance,[23] but on an ad hoc basis for particular enquiries. The first sub-committee to be assisted in this way was that on Government Statistical Services,[24] which had as their adviser Professor G. Pyatt, of the University of Warwick. The Library statisticians had had to decline the opportunity of giving extensive assistance to this Sub-Committee because of the pressure of their normal work, but submitted two memoranda to it which were used both in the drafting of the Report and as the basis of questions. Specialist consultants have been used by other Committees, e.g. the Select Committee on Nationalised Industries (Professor Maurice Peston[25]) and the Committee on Science and Technology for their enquiries into marine pollution and on defence research. The Library has also assisted the Science and Technology Committee with their various enquiries; the Scientific Section of the Research Division has a special role in connection with this Committee.[26] The Committees on Education and Science and on Race Relations have also been

21. Special Report from the Select Committee. H.C. 276 1958–59, pp. ix, 47. Five years earlier, the 'Stokes' Committee had recommended that the Estimates Committee should be empowered 'to secure the assistance of an accountant, actuary or other qualified person'. Op. cit. p. xii.

22. *Economist*, 21 March 1960, p. 972—'The House's Servants'.

23. Fifth Special Report. H.C. 161, 1964–65; subsequently considered and approved by the Services Committee (First Report. H.C. 70, 1965–66), and first included in the Order of Reference of the Estimates Committee in 1966–67 (First Special Report. H.C. 52, 1966–67). See also *Economist*, 28 Aug. 1965, p. 799—'Not Enough Teeth'.

24. Fourth Report. H.C. 246, 1966–67.

25. *The Times*, 25 Sept. 1967, p. 23.

26. The Marine Pollution Sub-Committee acknowledged having derived 'much benefit from our scientific assessor, Professor Ely and from Dr Poole of the Scientific Staff of the Library of the House'. (H.C. 421–I, 1967–68, p. xlix.)

assisted by Library Staff, and the other committee that received significant assistance was the Select Committee on Agriculture. A section of that Committee's First Report, on British Agriculture and the E.E.C., was drafted by a member of the Library staff, and the Committee expressed their thanks in the Report. They went on: 'Unfortunately staffing difficulties there [in the Library] have precluded assistance on a large scale. In the future, your Committee hope to make more use of the Library's research facilities which they were informed towards the end of the inquiry are being expanded with the aim of assisting specialist Committees very much in mind.'[27] Early in 1968, a graduate in agricultural economics joined the Library staff; her services were made available to the Committee about one day a week, and in its final Report, the Committee paid tribute 'to the able and willing assistance given to us by the Departments of the Clerk of the House and the Library during the period of our existence'.[28] During the year in which she assisted them, the main Committee made an extensive enquiry into agricultural import-saving and the mechanism of the price review, and two sub-committees examined fisheries and horticulture.

The degree of involvement with committee work varies with the requirements of the committee and with the amount of time that the Library researcher is able to devote to it (and committee work does tend to be time-consuming). At its maximum it may involve, in addition to research, assisting the Clerk to the committee with the following tasks: suggesting organisations and individuals who should be invited to submit memoranda or give evidence and possible lines of investigation for the committee to follow; reading the memoranda submitted by witnesses, commenting on them and suggesting topics for questions; reading the printed oral evidence to see if there are points that the committee might pursue at subsequent meetings; attending some meetings or parts of meetings of the committee; and assistance with the final report.

27. Report from the Select Committee on Agriculture, Vol. I. H.C. 378–XVII, 1966–67, p. vii.
28. Special Report from the Select Committee on Agriculture. H.C. 138, 1968–69, pp. 8, 9.

It is too early to say what eventual form the system of specialist select committees will take, so that one cannot define precisely the role that the Library might play in connection with it. The principal advisers and servants of committees must of course always be their Clerks, but it is clear that there is also a place for both expert consultants and research assistance. Whether this research assistance is provided by the permanent staff of the House or by people temporarily employed for the purpose depends on several factors. Some subjects of enquiry are so narrow that only an academic specialist could provide the service that a Committee would want. (With some enquiries it may be difficult or impossible to find an expert who is not involved in the body or service under investigation.) Other enquiries might ideally require a succession of consultants to deal with separate aspects of the subject-matter. On others there is no reason why a member of the Library staff should not provide a service at least equal to that which would be given by an outside specialist. It may sometimes happen that the Library has on its strength a person with exactly the right qualifications for a committee, for instance the agricultural economist for the Select Committee on Agriculture. The need for committee researchers can often not be predicted very far ahead; before a committee can start its work each session, it has to be set up by resolution of the House (which may be some time after the start of the session if there are any disagreements about the composition or terms of reference), choose its subject, and decide whether or not it requires research assistance. It will then wish to pursue its enquiry fairly promptly and intensively, and whereas academics may find it difficult to make time available at short notice well on in the academic year, Library staff are 'on tap' and can perhaps contrive some flexibility in their programmes. A knowledge of the ways of the House and of Members contributes to the effectiveness of assistance to Committees, and so does experience of previous enquiries. Library staff are able to provide an element of continuity in research assistance to committees, but they are not numerous enough, or wide-ranging enough in their subject specialities, to enable committees always to dispense with outside assistance hired on a temporary basis for specific enquiries.

Conclusions

This chapter has surveyed only a few of the factors that have affected the development of the Library over the post-war period. In 1966 a Report was published on short-term needs,[29] which stated that the views of Members would be welcome on the future scope of Library services over the longer term. No Report on the long-term development of the Library has yet appeared, but one can predict that Members will continue to want extensions and improvements to the services available to them (and after each General Election there is a group of newly-elected and usually fairly demanding Members). The last major expansion saw the setting-up of the Scientific Section of the Research Division and of a limited press cuttings service. A service mentioned by some Members, and not officially provided by the Library, is a translation service, and many have favoured the setting-up, on a permanent basis, of a computerised information system which ran experimentally for three months last year.[30] Such a system could provide a 'current awareness' service for Members tailored to their individual interests as well as indexes of permanent value. An unsuccessful amendment to the 1959 Report of the Select Committee on Procedure mentioned the desire of its sponsors for assistance in the drafting of Bills and amendments and for an 'information service for speedily answering the smaller technical problems of constituents'.[31] At present the Library has no lawyer on its staff, although the need for one can arise with some enquiries, and all staff have perforce to develop a familiarity with the language and documentation of the law. Thus the Library is of course some way from providing a comprehensive legislative reference service on the American model, as the number of subject specialities it can offer is limited by the size of its staff. Within these

29. First Report from the Select Committee on House of Commons (Services). H.C. 76, 1966–67.

30. See J. B. Poole, 'Information Services for the Commons: a computer experiment'. *Parliamentary Affairs*, Spring 1969, pp. 161–69.

31. H.C. 92, 1958–59, p. liii. A service for drafting assistance would possibly not be best located in the Library.

limits, the work of the Research Division is analagous with some of the legislative reference work carried out in the larger parliamentary libraries in other countries.

The Library has links with the Civil Service on both pay and recruitment, and as the profound changes in grading structure resulting from the Fulton Report are worked out in the Civil Service, they are bound to have repercussions on the staff structure of the Library. These may form one influence on the Library's development in the coming decade. Another that has been mooted—though its likelihood has probably now receded—is the possibility of amalgamation with the House of Lords Library.[32] The proposal was made mainly with the aim of saving space, and the implications for service to the Members of both Houses would need very careful working out. One can say with certainty that the economic climate will be unfavourable to the growth of the public service, as much in the House of Commons as elsewhere, so that if Members desire improved Library services, they will have to press their case in the context of other competing claims on scarce resources. At the same time, at an overall annual cost of around £6m., the legislature is a small item in the total of central government costs. A growing number of 'professional' M.P.s feel that the House of Commons has far too long denied its Members facilities adequate to their role.

A Note on Official Publications

The Library naturally has large holdings of official publications, and arranges and indexes parliamentary papers, preparing for publication an index for each session and cumulations of these indexes covering 10-year and 50-year periods. It is also a most intensive user of the contents of publications, which it consults to answer the varied questions continually put to it. It is worth considering how adequate official publications are for the use that Members, or staff acting on their behalf, make of them.

In Trollope's political novels, his ideal British statesman, Plantagenet Palliser, is depicted as frequently retiring to the

32. Fifteenth Report from the Services Committee, New Parliamentary Buildings. H.C. 652, 1966–67, p. x.

libraries of his various country houses to immerse himself in
Blue Books and evolve from them his political programme.
Any contemporary politician who depended today largely on
parliamentary papers would find large gaps in their coverage.
By 'parliamentary papers', one means in this context Bills,
House of Commons Papers and Command Papers; these are
the publications which are available immediately on demand
to Members and which therefore secure the widest distribution. At one time non-parliamentary official papers were
supplied to Members only on payment; now they are supplied
free on a restricted basis, but have to be ordered specially, and
therefore secure a much lower circulation. One might have
thought that the distinction between the two classes of paper
would depend on the importance of their contents and this is
indeed the theory: a Treasury Circular of 1921 stated that
Command Papers should be 'documents relating to matters
likely to be the subject of early legislation, or which may be
regarded as otherwise essential to Members of Parliament as a
whole to enable them to discharge their responsibilities'.[33]
In practice, one of the criteria is the size of the paper, as by
another rule made in 1921,[34] no paper can be a parliamentary
paper if it is larger than royal octavo.[35] This rule not only
excludes such papers as most of the Regional Economic Studies
and the Buchanan Report on Traffic in Towns but almost all
the statistical papers of any importance. Before the Second
World War, most major statistical publications were parliamentary papers and therefore obtainable on demand by
Members. Over the post-war period a larger size has been
adopted for these publications, and this has taken them into
the non-parliamentary class. However, even when papers are
of the right size, and would appear to be of considerable

33. Treasury letter 38/21; the most recent Treasury guidance on
categories of papers is of very little help. See 'Official Publications'
(H.M. Treasury, 1958), p. 9.

34. Treasury letter, 19A/21.

35. This rule is broken from time to time, e.g. for part of the evidence
of the Monckton Commission on the Constitution of the Federation of
Rhodesia and Nyasaland and for certain of the Reports of the Boundary
Commissioners. The Parliament of Northern Ireland allows two sizes
for its Parliamentary Papers and thus avoids the absurdities that stem
from this rule.

importance, their appearance as parliamentary papers is not assured. The following are examples of reports that have appeared as non-parliamentary papers in recent years: the Beeching Report on the Future of the Railways, '15 to 18' (the Crowther Report), the Plowden Report on Children and their Primary Schools, the N.E.D.C. Green Books on the Growth of U.K. Economy, the Newsom Report on the Public Schools and the Wootton Report on Cannabis. Some departmental variation in practice is apparent; evidently the Home Office wishes to keep Parliament informed of developments in its field (and even continues to present its statistics as parliamentary papers), whereas the Department of Education and Science, for example, excludes some important reports from the papers it presents to Parliament.

It can cause difficulty to users when some in a series are parliamentary and some not: for example, three large papers were published between 1963 and 1966 on plans for local authorities' welfare services. The first and third were Command Papers, the second was non-parliamentary. The same was true of the 'Hospital Plans' for England and Wales and Scotland. These papers at least continue to appear, in one form or another, whereas some series are simply discontinued, leaving a gap in the information available to Parliament and the public. A major casualty was the Public Investment White Paper, which during its short run (to October 1963) provided a great deal of information that is not now available. Other examples of discontinued series are the Annual Reports on Colonial Territories, on Industry and Employment in Scotland and of the Ministry of Labour, the White Papers on numbers of civil servants, and the Government Actuary's Annual Report on the National Insurance Scheme. (Also, no Quinquennial Review of the National Insurance scheme is to be published for the period 1964–69.) Some series are not wholly discontinued, but are reduced in size or appear less frequently.[36] The Report of the Ministry of Housing and Local Govern-

36. The outstanding recent example of the reduction of size of papers is the Civil and Defence Estimates, drastically cut in 1962 and 1963, with the loss of much valuable detail. But Parliament, in the shape of the Estimates and Public Accounts Committees, was at least consulted on the proposal for this reduction before it was implemented.

ment is an example of both tendencies; in the 1950s this was among the fullest Annual Reports, having the valuable feature that each issue took a special subject (in addition to the regular topics) and treated it in some length, e.g. new towns, water supply and the planning of Greater London. The 1961 Report was reduced to 60 pages compared with the 205 pages of the previous issue, and the special features disappeared. The Report no longer appears annually, but one hopes that it will not suffer the fate of other Annual Reports—discontinuance 'as an economy measure'.[37]

Except where it is laid down by statute, it appears to be quite arbitrary which Departments make annual reports and which do not; or, in the case of Departments not making comprehensive reports, which activities are reported on and which are not. Not all the nationalised industries are under an obligation to report to Parliament; thus, there is no statutory requirement for a report from the Bank of England, but until 1959 the Bank's Report did appear as a Command Paper.[38] The reports of some nationalised industries have become rather slight compared with early issues, and there is a surprising lack of uniformity among them. To take a simple example, some area electricity and gas boards show their retail tariffs in their reports and some do not.[39]

There have, however, been some improvements in recent years, off-setting the deterioration in other directions. When refusing to grant Members' requests for economic forecasts in March 1967, the then Chancellor of the Exchequer said he was 'considering whether the House could be given fuller and more regular information'.[40] As a result, the House is now given at Budget time (in the Financial Statement) fore-

37. E.g. those of the Ministries of Labour and Works. Reports can also dry up because of the transfer of functions among ministries: e.g. the annual report on Civil Aviation which appeared throughout the inter-war years and the late 1940s, but ceased with the merger of the Ministries of Transport and Civil Aviation.

38. The Radcliffe Committee said that its 'meagreness . . . has become a by-word' (Cmnd. 827, p. 124). It has since been somewhat improved.

39. Similarly in the field of departmental reports, one finds that some information is published for Scotland, but not for England and Wales, and vice versa.

40. H.C. Debates, 14 March 1967: written answers col. 46.

casts of the national income and balance of payments. A monthly official article on the economic situation has appeared since January 1967,[41] but this, like the annual 'Economic Report' (now deceased) tends to be somewhat non-committal, and for more definite economic comment Members must turn to such publications as the 'Economic Review' of the National Institute of Economic and Social Research and the annual 'Economic Survey' of the U.K. published by O.E.C.D. In 1969 the Economic Report ceased altogether as a separate publication, though a few pages of economic comment were included in the 'Financial Statement and Budget Report'.[42] Its predecessor—the Economic Survey—was in the late 1950s and early 1960s a document of 60 pages or more. There have been two White Papers, in 1963 and 1966, giving 3-year 'forward looks' of public expenditure and two covering shorter periods,[43] and a recent memorandum presented to the Select Committee on Procedure by the Treasury proposes to make this a regular practice.[44] This may be very useful, as long as sufficient information is published to make the forecasts verifiable (which has not usually been the case in the past).

The Fulton Committee stated that: 'We welcome the increasing provision of the detailed information on which decisions are made',[45] and certainly several valuable new series of statistical publications have appeared over recent years, usually as non-parliamentary papers.[46] Policy on publishing varies from Department to Department, and such

41. In 'Economic Trends'.
42. See H.C. Debates, 25 March 1969: written answers cols. 257–58.
43. Cmnd. 2235, 2915, 3515 and 3936 respectively.
44. Public Expenditure: A New Presentation. Cmnd. 4017.
45. Cmnd. 3638, p. 91.
46. Some are surveyed briefly in 'Information and the Public Interest.' Cmnd. 4089. They are also mentioned in 'Statistical News' published quarterly since May 1968 by the Central Statistical Office. But a cardinal need of research workers is for the resumption of the 'Guide to Official Statistics of the U.K.', which appeared annually between the Wars and has since sunk without trace. It is hoped that something similar, though limited to social science, will emerge from a project at present being carried out under the auspices of the Social Science Research Council for a guide to published and unpublished data in government departments of interest to people researching in the social sciences. (See Annual Report of the S.S.R.C. 1967–68, p. 16; H.C. 5, 1968–69.)

co-ordination as exists is applied by the Treasury in the interests of economy in government printing. The result is that, though official publications appear in great numbers and on a large variety of subjects, there must be some doubts on whether either the range or form of some of them are ideally suited to the needs of Members of Parliament.

Chapter 8

Parliament and Science since 1945[1]

S. A. Walkland

The debate about science and Parliament, fairly intense in the early 1930s amongst a small group of left-wing Parliamentarians, publicists and scientists, was on the whole quiescent in the post-war period until the early 1960s. The normal characteristics of those occasions when Parliament contemplated science policy were unease, a sense of being taken out of its accustomed depth, and an appreciation of its general impotence in this rapidly growing and important field. In opposition to the popular scientism which was current in Labour Party circles in the early 'thirties, in the post-war period there developed in any case a quite powerful intellectual tradition militating against political pressures being brought to bear on science policy. On the premise that science has an intellectual structure which in itself determines research priorities, an elaborate theory of non-intervention in science matters was built up, until recently reflected in the administrative structure of publicly-sponsored science, and in the hesitant, bi-partisan approach of Parliament to the subject. Michael Polyani has long been identified with this theory, which has been opposed to the pressures towards guiding the process of scientific enquiry in the direction of politically-determined goals,[2] and for a short period a version of this theory of non-intervention was the avowed personal philosophy of the first Conservative Minister for Science, Lord Hailsham.[3] It may be argued that such a position was more

1. The writer is grateful to the Editor of *Parliamentary Affairs* for permission to use material which originally appeared in articles in that Journal.
2. Michael Polyani, 'The Republic of Science: its Political and Economic Theory'. *Minerva* I, Autumn 1962.
3. See N. J. Vig, *Science and Technology in British Politics*, 1968, Chap. IV.

appropriate a generation ago, when the integrity of science appeared to need safeguarding from centralising political theories which overstressed social utility in the development of science policy. Few theorists would now defend such an uncompromising position, which in any case was always more relevant to pure rather than applied science. Recent attempts to develop theories of scientific choice have extended the debate about research priorities into the technological sphere, and have admitted the importance of social and economic criteria, as well as scientific factors, in developing a policy for science.[4] The new Council on Scientific Policy similarly in its first Report accepted responsibility for developing criteria for scientific growth based, inter alia, on social, educational and economic effects.[5] In more direct fashion, the Labour Party's conscious linking of scientific policy with economic growth and technological stimulus for British industry, the reorganisations in the government of civil science which were put in hand after 1963, the development of the Ministry of Technology as Britain's foremost scientific agency have also played a part in changing the focus of attention of Parliament, which, in common with European assemblies generally, is now seeking a larger role and an improved competence in science and technological affairs.

In the recent debate about Parliamentary competence in this field two preoccupations can be discerned. One stresses the helplessness of Parliament in the face of growing executive expertise and secrecy, particularly in those fields of 'closed' politics in which government decisions are taken as a result of expert advice, to which Parliament has no access. This is a bi-partisan concern, and provided a strong strand in the parliamentary reformist agitation of the first half of the 1960s. In the field of science policy its most fluent exponent has been Austen Albu, who, before his elevation to ministerial rank, had served for a number of years on the Parliamentary and Scientific Committee and on the Estimates and Nationalised

4. See the numerous articles on this subject in the first two volumes of *Minerva*. For an attempted synthesis, see Stephen Toulmin, 'The Complexity of Scientific Choice'. *Minerva* II, Summer, 1964.

5. First Report of the Council for Scientific Policy. Cmnd. 3007 May 1966. 'Report on Science Policy'.

Industries Committees, and who was inclined, both by his training as an engineer and his parliamentary experience, to a technocratic view of governmental processes. In a paper published whilst chairman of the Parliamentary and Scientific Committee[6] Albu set out his fears regarding parliamentary authority in the making of science policy. His concern was with the comparatively narrow issue of the lack of opportunities of Parliament to participate in the process of decision-making in cases where decisions are concerned with or rest on scientific or technical considerations, and with the consequent ousting of parliamentary and public criticism from these areas. He illustrates his argument by reference to the post-1945 development of advisory agencies which have been set up by the Government in a variety of technical and scientific fields, and sets out a number of important R & D decisions which were made by Ministers on advice furnished by such agencies but withheld from Parliament. From his varied backbench experience Albu was able to demonstrate the paucity of opportunities for M.P.s to gain background information on these decisions, with the result that 'the equality of opinion of Parliament and the executive has been destroyed'. His conclusions, which were largely embodied in a memorandum on parliamentary reform which the Parliamentary and Scientific Committee submitted to the Select Committee on Procedure of 1964–65, reiterated the need for a more inquisitorial procedure in the Commons, and the creation of Select Committees 'charged with the duty of informing Parliament on the scientific components in Government decisions'—a point of view to which, if anything, the new Select Committee on Science and Technology, staffed as it is with Albu's erstwhile parliamentary colleagues from the Parliamentary and Scientific Committee, seems to be inclining.

In sharp contrast with the technocratic attitude of Albu, concerned to establish machinery which would enable the House of Commons to share responsibility with the executive for the 'correctness' of technical decisions, can be set the broader view held by Nigel Calder, editor of the *New Scientist*. In a contribution to the 1964 Vienna Conference on Science

6. Austen Albu, 'The Member of Parliament, the Executive and Scientific Policy'. *Minerva* II, Winter 1964.

and Parliament, sponsored by O.E.C.D. and the Council of Europe,[7] Calder attempted to divert the Parliamentarians present from their somewhat narrow preoccupation with administrative machinery and with particular decisions in the R & D field. Whilst supporting most of the usual suggestions for improving the capacity of Parliament in this field, Calder argues for more politics of the old-fashioned kind in Parliament's involvement with science. 'Politicians have laid too much emphasis on the machinery of government support for science, which is relatively easy to deal with, involving only a superficial knowledge of scientific organisations and of the psychology of scientists; they have shirked, until it is unavoidable, study of the applications of science in relation to general policy, which means understanding the substance, the potentialities and the complex implications of actual scientific advances.' Calder rejects both the traditional bi-partisan approach of politicians to science and the administrative theory which has accompanied it. 'To suppose that Parliament should deal with science on a non-partisan basis is to kill from the outset the hope that the consequences of science will receive the whole-hearted attention from politicians that they deserve . . . in fact, I do not think that Parliaments should be looking wistfully for some little technical influence to mend their self-respect. They should instead be seizing on the greatly neglected business of mapping out a course for our scientific civilisation.'

Neither of these opposing views of parliamentary involvement has gained full currency with politicians. The signs are that those few M.P.s who have shown a marked interest in science matters over the last few years are more inclined towards the parliamentary appraisal of actual decisions than to the broader concerns which Calder would direct them to. But although Calder's insistence on the importance of broad social and political criteria in developing Parliament's awareness of science furthered the debate beyond the special concerns of Austen Albu and other members of the Parliamentary and Scientific Committee, his attempt to derive broad ideologically-determined science policies for the opposing parties

7. See Nigel Calder, 'Parliament and Science'. *New Scientist*, No. 393, 28 May 1964, pp. 533–5.

seems very unrealistic. Moreover he failed to recognise that in the period prior to the 1964 election the disputes over science policy were to some extent intra-party rather than inter-party.

Nor can his conclusion that the process of educating the parties in the social potential of different science programmes should begin in the backbench party science committees, which both Parliamentary parties set up in 1959 in response to the establishment of a Minister for Science, survive an examination of the work of these committees over the last few years. The Conservative Science and Technology group in the 1959–64 Parliament, under the successive chairmanships of Mr Robert Carr and Sir Harry Legge-Bourke, reflected to some extent the deep division of opinion between Lord Hailsham, the Minister for Science, and those committed Conservative Members who were pressing for more action on applied industrial research. But a recent study has shown how comparatively easy it was for the Minister to carry the group with him on all important issues, and Conservative policy on civil science proved to be not essentially different in 1964 from what it had been in 1959.[8] In the same Parliament the Labour backbench Science Group was even less influential. It was by-passed in the policy thinking on science and technology which the Shadow Science Minister, Richard Crossman, initiated in 1963. Some individual members of the group were influential with Crossman, but the main impetus in developing Labour's plans came from the Labour leadership and its immediate scientific associates rather than from the Labour backbenches. On the other hand, the political parties' general activities in science policy, although intermittent and undertaken largely in response to electoral exigencies and pressures, have been much more coherent than that of Parliament as such. It is only necessary to cite, for example, as well as the work of the Labour Science Group, the 1962 Conservative 'Carr Report' on scientific policy relating to industry, initiated by the party's Advisory Committee on Policy. But neither of these party initiatives was 'ideological' in Calder's sense of attempting to relate science policy to basic party objectives. Both were an

8. See N. J. Vig, op. cit. p. 116.

aspect of that competitive technocratic appeal, based on claims to be able to manage successfully the processes of modernisation and economic growth, which both parties made to the electorate in the 1964 campaign.

If at times party politicians, especially in the period from the late 1950s onwards, when science became politicised, have played a considerable part in the development of basic policy, what of Parliament's formal role? Parliamentary involvement with science matters has, until recently, been intermittent and fairly superficial. Until the establishment in 1966 of the Select Committee on Science and Technology the only official machinery available to the Commons to probe administration and occasionally to touch on policy were the older Select Committees, in particular the S.C.E. and P.A.C. This was bi-partisan involvement, motivated not as a result of parliamentary interest in science policy and administration as such, but by concern with public expenditure. Much of the parliamentary concern with research and development in the late 1940s and 1950s was the result of the impression which it gained, especially in defence research, of heavy and wasteful spending and the seeming inability of the normal political and parliamentary processes to contain it. The two financial Select Committees found it necessary to spend a growing proportion of their time on this category of expenditure. The Public Accounts Committee, with its severely formal philosophy of financial accountability, has on a number of occasions clashed head-on with highly speculative and expensive research activities. Although the Committee has often skilfully clarified the financial implications of R & D programmes, the impression remains that it is fundamentally disturbed by this type of activity, and little that is positive or helpful has emerged from some of its investigations. The Select Committee on Estimates, so far as its hard-pressed time has permitted, has investigated the broad administrative structure and occasionally the policies of a number of research agencies, with varying degrees of success.[9] After the stimulus

9. See S. A. Walkland, 'Science and Parliament: the role of the Select Committees of the House of Commons'. *Parliamentary Affairs*, Summer 1965. See also N. Johnson, *Parliament and Administration* (London, 1966), Chap. 2, Section 8, 'Scientific Research'.

to its development which the Select Committee on Procedure
of 1964–65 gave to the Estimates Committee its sub-committees
were given latitude for the first time to specialise in particular
fields, and in 1965 a sub-committee was appointed on Technological Affairs, covering labour, education, science and
technology. Overt specialisation between the sub-committees has, however, recently been discontinued, and in the
sphere of science it seems that the S.C.E. assumes that the
new Select Committee on Science and Technology will super-
sede it.

In the field of science policy, and in questions concerning
the government of civil science, Parliament's main agent in
the post-war period has been the unofficial Parliamentary
and Scientific Committee. This all-party body derived from
a smaller and more militant Parliamentary Science Committee
of the early 1930s, set up to draw the attention of M.P.s and
Ministers to scientific opinion and to the results of research
and development which might bear on public policy. The
Committee has a constitution which relates individual
members of the Commons and the Lords to all the main
scientific research and professional institutions in the country.
The result is a slow-moving, rather cumbersome, but so far
as civil science is concerned, a comprehensive body whose
opinion, once formed, carries weight. Its length of continuous
experience and its network of contacts has at times proved
highly useful and influential. Much of its work has been low-
keyed, admittedly, and it has often failed to provide an
aggressive parliamentary lead when this has been needed.
For example, apart from the efforts of one or two of its
constituent organisations, collectively the Committee did not
take sides in the brain-drain issue of the early 1960s, nor play
any role in the controversy over the proposals of the Trend
Committee on the Organisation of Civil Science in 1963.
The first omission is inexplicable; the second probably a
product of conflicting views in the Committee's member
organisations.

The Committee's officers, both from Parliament and from
its affiliated organisations, have been of high calibre, and the
Committee has done much to bring together as a working
team the parliamentary 'scientific elite', which has seldom

numbered more than 20–30 M.P.s and Peers, and whose names recur with singular regularity in any parliamentary organisation on science. As an all-party committee, straddling also both the Commons and the Lords, it has never been able to operate much in advance of dominant government opinion, and its interests have usually been concentrated, with one or two exceptions, in fields where there has been basic unanimity between the political parties. As such it was well suited to act as the main channel of parliamentary influence in this field in the decade after 1945. There was very little party disagreement on the initial post-war reforms which set the pattern of civil science administration and policy until 1964–65, and the Parliamentary and Scientific Committee was able to lend its support to the consolidations and changes in the machinery of government for civil science which Labour made after 1945, and established something approaching regular consultative status with the Government on administrative detail.

In 1964 the writer concluded a review of the development and achievements of this unofficial Committee with some rather depressing observations concerning it.[10] It seemed then, at a time when pressure for parliamentary reform had not yet borne fruit, that the Committee had belied its early promise, and had been overtaken by events. To some extent this was true—it was proving incapable of bearing the weight of political controversy which was then centring around science policy, and its initial role as a forceful defence and pressure organisation for science had receded. As Vig has remarked, Parliament's need had become 'less one of representing scientific interests than make them accountable; less that of spreading the "scientific point of view" than understanding its application in government agencies'.[11] On the other hand, as a centre for those Parliamentarians who think science and technology important, and who are willing to make efforts to extend their interest and to play a role, however sporadic, in keeping some broad issues in front of the Government, the

10. See S. A. Walkland, 'Science and Parliament: the origins and influence of the Parliamentary and Scientific Committee'. *Parliamentary Affairs*, Summer and Autumn 1964.

11. Vig, op. cit. pp. 121–2.

Parliamentary and Scientific Committee has been both useful and competent. It has undoubtedly played a part in changing the focus of attention in Parliament.

Its main contribution to post-war policy was in the field of higher technological education, reform of which was probably the most significant achievement in the sphere of science of the Conservative Governments of the 1950s. The Committee was well in advance of official thinking on future British scientific man-power needs, and in its conviction that basic reform in the structure of higher technological education was needed. It was sensitive to comparisons with the U.S.A. and U.S.S.R. in this field, and to the need for greater British technological effort in face of industrial competition from the revivified economies of Western Europe. In the event, the long and arduous pressure campaign which the Parliamentary and Scientific Committee mounted contributed decisively to the policy reversal embodied in the White Paper on Technical Education of 1956.

The controversy over technological education catalysed the general disquiet about British efforts in the field of applied science, and after 1956 concern over the pace and extent of applied technological research and the weakness of the machinery of civil science spread from the Parliamentary and Scientific Committee to the political parties, and the post-war political consensus which had been established in this field broke down. A full and detailed account of this process of the politicisation of science is the main content of a recent book by Norman J. Vig, *Science and Technology in British Politics*. As Vig shows, in many ways this period is a confused one, with the political parties, both national and Parliamentary, grappling for the first time with the unaccustomed issue of 'big science' and its proper government, and with the main divisions of opinion to some extent cutting across party lines. As the debate continued, party differences over science became more structured, and science policy was consciously linked by the Labour Party and some Conservative elements to economic growth and technological stimulus for British industry. Parliamentary reaction was confused, but considerable. Statistically, the 1959–64 Parliament demonstrated more concern with science administration and policy than any previous post-war Parliament[12] and interest shifted rapidly from the Parliamentary and Scientific Committee to the backbench subject groups on science and technology.

There were more general debates on science and technology in the 1959–64 Parliament than in the previous four Parliaments combined, with a similar increase in the volume of Questions on science topics. Debate served as a vehicle for the expression of competing party policies, and Questions produced a superficial but broad front of pressure on the Government on the details of science policy. In fields such as manpower, industrial research and government organisation Parliament covered matters of considerable political significance, but, as Vig concludes, 'neither Questions nor debates contributed much detailed and concrete intelligence on Executive decisions and policy'.[13] More interesting in this Parliament was the work of the Conservative Science and Technology backbench group, which, apart from its general opposition to Hailsham, was active in debating the machinery of government for science, submitting evidence to the Trend Committee on the Organisation of Civil Science, whilst maintaining a detailed interest in atomic energy and space research.

In contrast with the immediate post-war reorganisation in the structure of government science, the reorganisations of 1964–66 owed little, however, to parliamentary opinions or pressures. The Parliamentary and Scientific Committee itself played no formal role, as opposed to its deep involvement in the late 1940s, and parliamentary reaction to this increasingly pertinent and important subject was on the whole confused and ineffective. The most significant parliamentary development in this period was its growing appreciation that in science matters it was more deficient in basic knowledge and expertise than in any other subject. Science and technology had become one of Parliament's main challenges; it was ill-equipped to meet it, and M.P.s were increasingly aware of this. All analyses appeared to confirm the deficiencies of the existing institutional and party arrangements either for educating M.P.s in the inter-relationships of science and policy, or for bringing educated opinion to bear on govern-

12. Vig, op. cit. Chap. VI. 13. Vig, op. cit. p. 112.

ment arrangements, and the strong reformist thinking of the early 1960s produced a separate and powerful strand of concern over science and technology, reflected in numerous references in Commons' debates to the need for improved facilities. In 1963 Sir Lionel Heald called attention to the fact that 'this House is not sufficiently equipped to deal with technical and scientific matters', and suggested the need for more scientists as M.P.s and the co-option of outside experts as advisers to specialist committees. John Osborn and Airey Neave supported specialist committees, and also for the Conservatives Sir Ian Orr-Ewing proposed that a sub-committee of the Estimates Committee might investigate science policy. For Labour, Austen Albu, Jeremy Bray and Tam Dalyell were strong supporters of the select committee idea. All of these M.P.s were members of the steering committee of the Parliamentary and Scientific Committee, and the main contribution of this body to the general debate was frankly to admit its own deficiencies as a vehicle for informed criticism of science policy and administration, and to formally endorse Parliamentary reform. Late in the 1964 Session it established a sub-committee, with Austen Albu as chairman, which produced for the Commons' Select Committee on Procedure a memorandum proposing a Select Committee on Science. Other memoranda proposing extensions to the Commons' committee system were also submitted to the Procedure Committee, one of them, from the Study of Parliament Group, also singling out science and technology as an appropriate subject.[14]

After such well-publicised concern, it was inevitable that the first of the new-style Select Committees should be on Science and Technology, although there is little evidence that the Government, in acquiescing in its establishment, had clear ideas concerning its functions. This is obvious from its very broad remit—'to consider science and technology and to report'. The Committee itself interpreted its terms of reference rather more precisely[15] after a fashion which makes it seem

14. For details of this period, see N. J. Vig and S. A. Walkland, 'Science Policy, Science Administration and Parliamentary Reform'. *Parliamentary Affairs*, Summer 1966.

15. 'To examine national scientific and technological expenditure

as if it is committed to both particular Estimates, Committee-style enquiries into administrative efficiency, and investigations of the factors which determine policy in this field. The new Committee published its first Report, on the United Kingdom Nuclear Reactor Programme, in November 1967. The success of the innovation which the Committee represents, and the general direction its enquiries will take, cannot be fully judged after only two years and one main Report. It was obviously anxious in its first investigation to establish a role for itself, and to secure its status both with the Government and with the House of Commons, and this, partly as a result of the scale and importance of its first enquiry, it can fairly be said to have done. An investigation into the nuclear industry was by any standards overdue—the older Select Committees of the Commons had made specialised and partial investigations into aspects of the nuclear programme, but there had never been a full-scale parliamentary evaluation of an enterprise which has attracted a huge government investment. The enquiry was well timed, and served to focus a debate which was already proceeding on the future of the industry. The Report's conclusions were many and technical, the main recommendations going to the heart of the organisation of the nuclear industry. It might have been expected that there could be no unanimous or 'correct' view of what such organisation should be—the Committee itself disagreed with the published views of one expert witness, and the Government subsequently disagreed to some extent with the recommendations of the Committee. But where political, economic and technical themes are closely interwoven, there can be no set of arguments which is not open to challenge from some quarter, and it is the educative and informative function of the Parliamentary Committee which is more valuable, rather than its conclusions. The quality of the evidence which the Science Committee elicits from its witnesses is of much greater significance than its own pronouncements on that evidence.

together with the skills and use of manpower and resources involved, in both the public and the private sectors, in order to discover whether full value for money is being obtained; to examine the relative merits of priorities, and to make recommendations.' Second Special Report. H.C. 351, 16 Feb. 1967.

On the basis of this first enquiry it is obvious that the committee sees itself as competent to evaluate technical policy, and the Government, judging from its reference to the Committee of the problems of coastal pollution following the Torrey Canyon affair, also regards the Committee as a primarily technical agency. This interpretation is also corroborated by the Committee's enthusiasm for the U.S. Joint Congressional Committee on Atomic Energy, a version of which the Committee would have liked to have seen established in Britain. It may be asked whether the Committee should develop into a body whose sole concern is technical policy, to the exclusion of wider considerations more appropriate to a parliamentary body. It was, for example, obvious that in places the Committee in its first investigation was at an informational disadvantage on technical matters, despite its use of the Scientific Section of the Commons' Library. During this investigation several members of the Committee drew on personal contacts within the industry, but the Committee did not appoint experts for this first enquiry. The sub-committee on coastal pollution, however, took expert advice, and the full Committee appointed two experts for its second investigation, into defence research establishments. It is not likely that even so the Committee will ever have informational parity with the executive.

Detailed technical information, from reputable and independent sources, has always been lacking, in the degree required, for M.P.s. The Parliamentary and Scientific Committee had always assumed that one of its more important functions was to act as a main channel of scientific intelligence for M.P.s, until in 1964 it directed an enquiry to its affiliated associations which revealed that direct contacts between M.P.s and outside scientific organisations were rare, and that there was little flow of information to the parliamentary members of the Committee. As a result the Committee recommended the strengthening of parliamentary library services on science. In 1966, in view of the increasing demands of M.P.s for this sort of information, a small Scientific Section was added to the establishment of the House of Commons' Library. In 1967 it comprised a Senior Library Clerk, a Second Clerk (both with science qualifications) and an executive library assistant, with secretarial and clerical support. In large measure the Section aims to replicate in the field of science and technology the services produced by the Research Division generally—the answering of research enquiries of a scientific or technological nature and the provision of Reference Sheets—bibliographies and similar surveys. The Library's scientific holdings are being built up, and an indexed collection of cuttings from the scientific press and journals has been started. The Section also produces a fortnightly *Science Digest*—a short collection of summaries of articles on topics judged to be of interest and significance for Members. The Section has established connections with both the Parliamentary and Scientific Committee and the new Select Committee, preparing background papers for both the investigation of the nuclear industry and that of coastal pollution; it has assembled relevant press and journal cuttings and has given technical assistance and advice to the Clerk to the committee.[16]

Some questions of demarcation still remain to be solved—between the Committee on Science and Technology and the latest 'Departmental' Committee on Education and Science, and between these and the S.C.E., P.A.C. and S.C.N.I. There is also the question of the future of the Parliamentary and Scientific Committee. It would be a loss if this body were to be superseded entirely by the new official Committees. At the moment the balance of interest and enthusiasm has been tilted in the new Committee's direction, and the Parliamentary and Scientific Committee has receded into the background.[17] But its educational work for M.P.s, its function as an informed lobby for science interests, still give it an important general role. The new Select Committee seems set to develop into a high-powered and specialised investigatory body, with contacts at a higher level of policy-making than those usually tapped by the Parliamentary and Scientific Committee. The latter is essentially a grass roots of science organisation, and

16. For a survey of the work of the Science Section see 'Information Services of the Commons' Library' (*New Scientist*, 7 Sept. 1967) by Dr David Menhennet and Dr John Poole.

17. In 1964, moving the adoption of the Committee's annual Report, the Chairman, Austen Albu, opined that most of the original objects of the Committee had been achieved.

as such can be valuable in registering for Parliament the reflexes amongst the scientific world of official policy. Some changes are likely, as the new institutions bed down with the old, but in this area, at least, Parliament can now be said to have overcome its latent fear of professionalism and specialisation. Where science affairs once demonstrated parliamentary weakness at its most pathological, Parliament now disposes of more powerful and varied machinery than in any other field.

Chapter 9

Standing Committees

H. Victor Wiseman

The House of Commons spends almost half its time dealing with Public Bill legislation. The Select Committee on Procedure, 1966–67, stated that the average number of days spent in the House itself on legislation, including Private Members' Bills and the Finance Bill, was 73 out of 160; the hours spent in standing committees amounted to a further 80 days of average length. They regarded this proportion of time as 'about right'.

The argument that the House no longer 'legislates' in any effective sense is now well known. The vast majority of Public Bills are Government Bills and few Private Members' Bills proceed far without Government support or acquiescence. Governments can rely upon their majority to pass any Bill in principle on Second Reading and in subsequent stages amendments are generally made only with Government approval. Adverse votes in committee can be reversed on Report. A great deal of law is contained in delegated legislation which is not effectively controlled or supervised by the House.

Nevertheless, the imprimatur of Parliament, of which the Commons is the effective part, is necessary for all legislation. Time must therefore be found for its consideration by the House and, at least in theory, sufficient time for adequate discussion of details. There is little likelihood that the volume of legislation can be reduced or that the time spent on it can be shortened; indeed, as Mr Crossman has said, effective scrutiny may require more time. The basic problem, therefore, is how to make more effective use of the time available and, if possible, to improve procedures for this purpose. The point at which this can be achieved, if at all, is predominantly at the Committee stage.

This stage is now for the most part taken in standing committees 'upstairs'. These committees are predominantly concerned with the committee stage of Public Bills generally and this is the main concern of this chapter, though the use of a standing committee for the Finance Bill is also discussed.[1] We need, for our purposes, go no further back historically than 1947.[2] As part of its procedural reforms aimed to speed up the process of legislation, the Labour Government decided that all Bills, with the exception of Finance Bills, Provisional Order Bills, Bills of great constitutional importance and urgent or minor non-controversial Bills, should be automatically referred to a standing committee. As many committees were authorised as might be necessary (the maximum number at any one time has been nine); the size of the '*nucleus*' (those Members appointed first to the committee) was reduced to 20, chosen only with regard to the composition of the House; 'added' members up to 30 were chosen with regard to their qualifications; the maximum membership was 50, 15 being the quorum. The Government also applied the Allocation of Time Order, the 'guillotine', to standing committees, while the allocation of time for sections of Bills was the responsibility of a sub-committee of the standing committee.

These standing committees are not specialised as are their counterparts in the U.S. and France. In 1907 standing committees were lettered A, B, C etc., whereas before that there were (following Gladstone's reforms) three committees concerned with law, trade, and Scottish Bills. Specialisation, however, was declining even before 1907, as Sir Henry Campbell-Bannerman told the House. In 1947 the lettered system was retained, though the limit on the number of committees was removed and their size reduced. Bills are allocated to them by Mr Speaker—one committee taking Private Members' Bills. However, writing in 1955, Sir Kenneth

1. In 1919 Estimates were sent to standing committees but the experiment was never repeated except in relation to the Scottish Estimates. This is referred to below. In addition we later consider the use of standing committees for Second Reading and for the Report stage.
2. For an excellent account of standing committees from their inception in 1882 until 1958 see David Pring, 'Standing Committees in the House of Commons'. *Parliamentary Affairs*, Vol. XI, No. 3, Summer 1958.

Wheare suggested that 'the committees by adjusting their membership to members' interests give much more scope to special knowledge and interest than might seem possible at first sight. In fact, one might say that the essential contrast between the British system of committees and the American and French systems in the matter of bringing specialised knowledge and interest to bear on bills is that whereas in the French and American systems the Bills go to the members with special knowledge and interest, in the British system the members with special knowledge and interest go to the Bills, pursuing them to the committees to which Mr Speaker has referred them.'[3]

The validity of this judgment depends in part on the role played by nucleus ('unspecialised') members and added ('specialised') members. For the former, the 1907 requirement that regard should be had to the class of Bills the committee considers *and* to the members' qualifications (as well as to the composition of the House) was repealed in 1933; it had in practice been ignored all along and no standing committee had ever stuck throughout a session to a particular class of Bill. Since 1933 the nucleus has been chosen only with regard to the composition of the House, while the added members have been chosen for their qualifications. In 1958 Mr David Pring queried whether the 'two part' system added anything to the usefulness of the work of the Committees. The ease with which nucleus members could join or leave committees made it possible to include specialists in the nuclear just as readily as in the added group. Doubt was expressed as to whether the nucleus was really significant; there was some evidence that most of the speeches were made by added members. The majority of the nucleus added little except their votes; the quality of debate and care of examination were not enhanced by their presence. One suggestion was that there should be no compulsion to add members, thus reducing the minimum size of a committee to 20. Specialists would then be nominated to the nucleus. To ensure a further degree of specialisation, either all bills on a particular subject-matter might be sent to the same committee or—if this might lead to congestion in some

3. K. C. Wheare, *Government by Committee* (Oxford, 1955), p. 135.

committees and idleness in others—the nucleus could be re-nominated for each bill.

The Select Committee on Procedure, 1959, was not pre-pared to accept much smaller committees as a general rule, though they did accept the necessity for some reduction in numbers. Their recommendations, implemented in 1960, were: to appoint committees in respect of each Bill; to abolish the distinction between the nucleus and the added members; to choose the experts first and then consider party balance; to establish a maximum size of 50 and a minimum of 20, the quorum being fixed at one-third of the membership. The Committee clearly envisaged a greater use of standing com-mittees. They pointed out that in 1956–57, while major constitutional bills and bills of which the committee stage was a formality occupied 27 hours, and the Finance Bills 70 hours in Committee of the Whole House, bills thus taken 'for urgent reasons or for reasons of expediency' occupied 62 hours. If this practice continued, the Committee stated, it would not be possible to reach the objective of relieving the House of the pressure of detailed work. It should be exceptional to keep a Bill on the floor of the House, even for urgent or expedient reasons.

The abolition of the distinction between the nucleus and the added members was only marginally, if at all, a move towards specialisation. The changes in 1960 simply recognised that it was individual Members who specialised and that all that was needed was to get them on to the committee. Since, on the whole, the specialist Members are the only people, together with the Minister, who do any talking, the object of informed comment on the Bill is achieved. The question then arises whether procedure could be changed to avoid the need for automatic Government majorities and even formal amendment in committee, so as to avoid wasting the time of the conscien-tious added members.

Professor Crick has argued that the basic problem is that of manning. Do even the specialist Members attend regularly? For committees to sit for two-and-a-half hours in the morning twice a week required about 250 M.P.s before 1960. The Select Committee on Procedure stated that about 200 attended 'regularly'. This, however, was misleading. There were many committees and M.P.s came and went. In 1961–62 one M.P. made 78 attendances but 65 who were appointed did not attend at all. About 100 (excluding Ministers) were not even summoned. Only 112 attended more than 20 times; just under 200 attended more than 10 times. If 'fairly regularly' means, say, once a week in 30 weeks, only about 70 M.P.s qualify.[4] Clearly no high degree of specialisation is possible unless the problem of manning can be solved. Yet to attempt as part of the solution a drastic reduction in the size of committees, especially when the Government has only a small majority in the House, might result in fewer Bills being sent upstairs. With small majorities, larger committees might be required; otherwise most Bills would be retained on the floor of the House.

The precise use of standing committees is an aspect of procedure about which no one ever seems to be satisfied. Such committees, according to Lord Campion, have 'never quite fulfilled the hopes entertained of them, or given that relief which was expected of them'. Debates are frequently protracted despite the fact that government backbenchers are often enjoined to silence. The time taken is often considerably longer 'at a guess' (according to Mr David Pring) than would have been needed on the Floor of the House. For example, in 1957–58, 31 sittings were required for a Bill on Local Government, equivalent to 12 full sittings in the House—even longer than the 11 days required for the Finance Bill. Various reasons have been suggested for these long-drawn-out proceedings. Committees get comparatively little publicity; M.P.s perhaps feel constrained to examine proposals with more care than if newspapers and letters had drawn their attention to points of special note. There is no sense of urgency during short sittings in the morning in the quiet of a committee room. Committees lack the natural time-limit which governs the procedure of the House.

Nor is there general agreement as to the precise functions of standing committees. Mr S. A. Walkland considers that the

4. Bernard Crick, *The Reform of Parliament* (London, 1964), p. 84. For an account of specialisation in parliamentary standing committees cf. article by Richard Kimber and J. J. Richardson, *Political Studies*, Vol. XVI, No. 1, Feb. 1968.

main purpose of the committee stage is fairly well understood but lacks a degree of precision. It is never fully clear in theory whether the function is technical, i.e. shaping the details of Bills in the light of the collective wisdom of the committee, or whether it is to extend political advocacy and opposition beyond the Second Reading. He appears to accept that the first is at least as important as the second. The committee stage, he argues, is (1) to enable Ministers to 'tidy up' the Bill—'refinements are added and administrative oversight corrected'—and (2) to enable amendments to be presented on behalf of affected pressure groups—'the continuation on a different level of the processes of consultation which began earlier is the explanation of most group-sponsored amendments moved by well-disposed M.P.s at the Committee stage'. On this point, Sir Ivor Jennings suggested that many M.P.s who have asked to be put on for a particular Bill pay less attention to the broader view adopted by the Government than to the axes they have to grind. Sir Kenneth Wheare was 'impressed by the close and careful discussion on each clause, by the critical attitude of the Opposition and by the trouble taken on the Government side to give a reasoned defence'. The personal temperament and characteristics of the Minister and the Opposition Leader affect the atmosphere; some M.P.s make mere debating points, but this is 'not usual in standing committee'.

Nevertheless, others with considerable experience of standing committee work have suggested that it is in large part a continuation in another guise of the policy-confrontation of the Second Reading—an approach which may be encouraged by the physical arrangement of the committee, which follows the pattern of the House. The prolonged discussion on Clause I, which embodies the principles of a Bill, is often a repetition of the broad arguments of Second Reading. It is sometimes, also, an ill-disguised attempt to prove that inadequate time is being allowed for full discussion, particularly if an allocation of time order has been made from the start. If the latter is not the case, it is often too late. after some eight sittings occupying three or four weeks, to introduce a satisfactory time-table.

The Select Committee on Procedure, 1959, devoted some

attention to this particular problem. The drawing-out of proceedings for longer than is necessary, they suggested, is due to protracted discussion on the earlier clauses of the Bill, leading to inadequate treatment of later clauses. They wanted a business committee to consider all bills committed to a standing committee after Second Reading. It should recommend to the House the date by which each Bill should be reported back and, if thought appropriate, the number of sittings required, subject to the right of later amendment. The Government, or Private Member in charge of his Bill, might then move a motion instructing the standing committee in the sense of the report. Such motion would be debatable, though not necessarily so if the business committee were unanimous. There should, however, be no obligation on the part of the Government 'to move' if they thought the most expeditious handling of the Bill could best be achieved by other methods. The actual details of clauses and amendments to be considered at each sitting should be settled by the chairman of the standing committee in consultation with the Minister in charge and Opposition representatives. Mr Butler had suggested in evidence that a date for the return of a Bill should be fixed by Order of the House; the Select Committee had demurred because this took no account of the number of sittings required. By July 1959, Mr Butler had come round to the view that the business committee should name the date. But since the Select Committee had recommended that the Government should not be compelled to move the business motion if it were debatable, he expressed 'doubt whether we could do better than our present system—namely, that we have a voluntary time-table imposed with a debate on the floor of the House'.

No changes were introduced and the Select Committee on Procedure, 1966–67, considered the matter again. Attention was once more drawn to the excessive time spent on the first three or four clauses. There was no question of reducing the time available for the committee stage; indeed, for full consideration it might have to be longer, as Mr Crossman admitted. What was needed was predictability. The approach to change was cautious: the chance of the Opposition 'to delay and attenuate the Government programme' must not be destroyed. If no agreement about time-tabling could be reached, then a guillotine motion would be necessary. But the Committee did recommend a Steering Committee for both committee and Report stages of bills; its report must be unanimous and must be agreed to by both sides. Finally, if its recommendations were subsequently not observed, then a Government motion would be needed. On this point, however, it should be noted that experienced observers of standing committees have been impressed by the extent to which informal agreements as to the length of committee proceedings are honoured. Only when the Opposition suspects that during the progress of a Bill the Minister is not co-operating do they put on pressure or depart from the agreed time-table—which, of course, under present procedure is private and subject to revision. We shall return to these proposals in our consideration of the Finance Bill.

Before discussing possible changes in the procedures of standing committees, it is convenient to deal briefly with matters other than that of the committee stage. The Select Committee on Procedure, 1964–65, considered the possible use of standing committees for *Second Reading* debates. They recognised the danger of preventing M.P.s from making a contribution at this stage, and of insufficient publicity. But they did recommend that 'bills on any subject which are not measures involving large questions of policy nor likely to give rise to differences on party lines' might, if agreement were reached through the usual channels, be sent for Second Reading to a committee consisting of not less than 30 nor more than 80 M.P.s. M.P.s not members of the committee might table reasoned amendments to the motion that the bill be given a second reading. Ten days' notice of intention to send a bill to a Second Reading Committee must be given and not less than 20 M.P.s might prevent such action. The Leader of the House must give a definite recommendation and the Question for Second Reading in the House would be decided without amendment or debate. These recommendations were accepted experimentally. The Select Committee on Procedure, 1966–67, however, noted that only seven Bills had gone through this procedure in 'the present exceptionally long session'. They considered that the experiment had succeeded and should be embodied in Standing Orders, and that more Bills should go through in this way. This same Committee, noting that in the Autumn there was a long queue of bills awaiting Second Reading and that therefore the work of standing committees had to be compressed into the first months of the calendar year, recommended that a limited number of Bills which were read a second time at the end of one session might proceed to the committee stage in the *next* session. This carry-over procedure would apply to Bills considered by a Second Reading Committee; ten days' notice should be given and the objection of not less than 20 M.P.s would prevent such action.

Since 1945 proposals have been consistently made and equally consistently rejected that in certain cases the *Report* stage of Bills might also go to a standing committee. To go no further back than 1959, the Select Committee on Procedure rejected such a proposal. If the same standing committee were used, there would be repetition; if it were enlarged, it might be difficult to man it; if it were a new committee the value of expert knowledge would be lost. They would not entertain the idea that a non-member of the committee might have the right to move an amendment on Report but be without the right to vote. In its evidence to the 1966–67 Select Committee on Procedure, the Study of Parliament Group proposed that, after publication of a Bill as amended in committee, the report stage should be taken by the committee to which the Bill was originally committed. If at this time some members of the original committee should no longer be available because of the claims of other business of the House, they could be replaced by substitutes. They also suggested once more that Members of the House not being members of the committee could be then allowed to move amendments as at the committee stage; Ministers would have the same facilities. None of this was accepted. There was, however, a slight breakthrough. The Select Committee recommended that Bills of secondary importance might go to a standing committee for the Report stage if such a committee were large enough and if there were adequate safeguards to prevent 'unsuitable' Bills from being so treated. They suggested this procedure for Bills which had gone for Second Reading to a standing committee (including the Scottish Grand Committee), with the possibility of some adjustment in membership. Notice must be given and, again, 20 M.P.s might prevent such action. It was a relatively small concession—though perhaps important in principle, and the Committee pointed out that not much time would be saved on the floor of the House.

Although according to one view[5] 'the history of the Scottish Committees since 1948 is not a very favourable augury for some of the bolder extensions of the committee system that have been recently discussed', at least a brief reference to them cannot be omitted. Mr Burns himself has, in fact, pointed out that the precedent has been followed by the setting up of a Welsh Grand Committee[6] and further 'regional committees' have been suggested.[7] The Scottish Standing Committee had appeared briefly in 1894–95, was permanently established in 1907 and was retained in 1947; it consisted of all Members sitting for Scottish constituencies together with between 10 and 15 other Members. Its function was to take the committee stage of all public bills certified by Mr Speaker as relating exclusively to Scotland. In 1948 new Standing Orders provided that such Bills might also be referred to the Committee for Second Reading, though not less than 10 M.P.s might prevent this by objecting. It was also provided that the estimates, or any part of them, for which the Secretary of State for Scotland was responsible might be referred to the Committee for consideration on not more than six days in any session. In 1957 a distinction was drawn between the Scottish *Grand* Committee, constituted as above, and the Scottish *Standing* Committee which was to be composed of 30 Scottish Members nominated for each Bill and not more than 20 other Members nominated with regard to their qualifications and the balance of parties. In fact the Standing Committee has normally not exceeded 35 members, excluding the Chairman. Indeed, in practice there are never any non-Scottish added members on the Standing Committee and in the Grand

5. J. H. Burns, 'The Scottish Committees of the House of Commons 1948–59).' *Political Studies*, Vol. VIII, No. 3, Oct. 1960.

6. cf. R. L. Borthwick, 'The Welsh Grand Committee'. *Parliamentary Affairs*, Vol. XXI, No. 3, Summer 1968.

7. G. W. Jones, B. C. Smith, H. V. Wiseman, 'Regionalism and Parliament'. *Political Quarterly*, Vol. 38, No. 4, Oct.–Dec. 1967.

Committee the added members rarely appear and still more rarely speak.

The Grand Committee now deals with estimates, second readings, and motions dealing with matters exclusively Scottish (on two days in each session). The Standing Committee takes the committee stage of Scottish Bills. A second Scottish Standing Committee was first set up in the 1962–63 Session; it was put on a permanent basis by inclusion in Standing Orders in December, 1968. Mr Burns shows that some time has certainly been saved on the floor of the House by these measures; on the other hand the lack of time available to the Committees themselves has limited the scope of the procedure. Perhaps the most pertinent comment is that of Professor Crick: 'This peculiar dispensation to the Scots is not without its wider interest since it shows the quite elaborate exceptions the Government and the House will allow when they have the mind.'[8] On the other hand, it must be borne in mind that standing committees exist to process law and the Scots have a legal system of their own, in form at least. The report stage debates on Scottish Bills are generally limited to Scottish Members; usually no one else is interested and English Members are only too pleased to get Scottish matters off the Floor of the House. There is no clear analogy with intra-English regional devolution.

We now turn to possible changes in the procedure and methods of working of standing committees which lie outside the fairly orthodox proposals and changes considered so far. None of them has been considered by a Select Committee on Procedure.

Two possible changes not involving radical modification of the general procedures in standing committees have been suggested. Amendments to meet opposition arguments are generally made at the Report stage in response to assurances given during the Committee stage. This, it may be argued, involves an unnecessary waste of time. Failure to complete the amending process as far as possible during the committee stage may to some extent be due to the rigidity of committee procedure and to inadequate consultation between back-benchers and Departments to ensure that amendments are

8. Crick, op. cit. p. 85.

drawn in a form acceptable to the Government. Even if amendments are merely 'a peg on which to hang a debate or to probe the intentions of the Government', proceedings might be improved. It is difficult to scrutinise a Bill without knowing something of the departmental minutes relating to it and of the data on which the decision to legislate is based. (For some Bills the problem might be solved, at least in part, by the suggestion of the Select Committee on Procedure, 1966–67, that the subjects and details of potential legislation might be discussed either by specialist committees or by ad hoc committees on future legislation *before* the Government finally prepares its Bill.) An alternative—or perhaps supplementary—approach, might be to accept the fact that chance defeats of the Government in standing committee are generally reversed on Report and, therefore, to abolish the procedure of formal amendment in committee altogether. This would obviate the need to maintain a permanent government majority and make possible the expression of the wide range of opinions which in any case exists. Amendments could still be *discussed* in committee, on the basis of the increased information and consultation referred to above, but they would actually be *made* at the Report stage.

In considering even more fundamental changes in standing committee procedure, we may begin with the evidence presented by the Study of Parliament Group to the Select Committee on Procedure, 1966–67. The Group proposed that every Bill (with rare exceptions) should be sent after Second Reading to a committee. There should be some flexibility regarding the type and size of the committee to which any particular bill should be sent. Most Bills would go to committees which would proceed in the same way as the existing standing committees, but in most cases membership would be as low as 15. The decision on the type and size of committee appropriate for each particular Bill could be taken by a business committee on which Government and Opposition front benches would be represented.

As membership of standing committees would be small, it should be provided that any Member not being a member of a committee should be allowed to attend a meeting of the committee with the right to speak to any amendment of which he had given notice and which was in order and had been selected by the Chair. Such a Member would not be allowed to vote in any division in the committee. In setting up a committee the Committee of Selection should name a number of substitutes who could, when so requested, take the place of any member of the committee who had satisfied the Chairman of his inability to attend, either through illness or through being engaged in some other business of the House.

Alternative proposals were made about the position of Ministers. The first would make the Minister in charge of a Bill a member of the committee; like other members he could be replaced by a substitute, which in his case would be one of his Junior Ministers (unless a Junior Minister were in charge of the Bill, which is invariably the case in the Scottish Committee) or a Junior Minister of another Department concerned with part of the Bill. The Committee of Selection, in naming substitutes, would thus normally include among them all office-holders who might expect to take part. The provision that such substitution should be possible only when the committee member to be replaced was engaged on other business of the *House* would have to be interpreted very liberally in the case of a Minister. The alternative would be that normally no Minister should be a member of the committee but should be allowed to attend any of its meetings, move amendments and take part in its deliberations but not vote. The effect of this provision would be to allow several different Ministers to take part. This would be convenient for the Government without damaging the interests of the House. On a substantial and complex Bill it might be desirable for two or more Ministers to be in charge of different sections, but not for every one of these Ministers to be present throughout the whole proceedings on the Bill. Such provision would allow the Government freedom in the choice of its spokesmen on the different sections of the Bill, unfettered by any need to have Ministers attend merely so as to maintain a Government majority.

The Select Committee on Procedure accepted neither of these proposals and made only brief reference to a matter which might be significant in the light of our further comments below. The evidence of our Group clearly implied that some Bills might go to a select rather than to a standing committee. The House of Commons Disqualification Bill, 1955–56, the Army and Air Force Bill, 1960–61, and the Armed Forces Bill, 1966–67, were all considered by select committees before being recommitted to a Committee of the Whole House. The Obscene Publications Bill, 1956–57, went first to a select committee and then to a standing committee. The Procedure Committee did not consider the use of a select committee *instead* of a standing committee. But it did suggest that Select Committees might be used for the discussion of details, especially in complicated and technical matters; evidence might then be taken from experts and more informal discussions would be possible. However, this would be an *additional* stage for such Bills.

Is there not a case, however, for the greater use of select committees as *substitutes* for standing committees? When standing committees were first established it was stated that their procedures should be those of a select committee. In practice, however, their problems soon appeared as more akin to those of a Committee of the Whole House and their adoption of procedures similar to those of the latter was inferred long before 1947 when reference to select committee procedure was excluded from Standing Orders. Those who advocate the use of select committee procedure at the Committee stage of Bills aim to make discussion more informed and effective. If the committee stage is to be more than part of Mr Butler's 'struggle for power', these proposals are at least worthy of consideration.

In this context we may discuss the views of a Legislation Study Group set up in 1967 by the Study of Parliament Group. Starting with the proposition that the main constraints on legislative time are the length of the session and the sessional 'cut-off', the size of the Government's programme both as envisaged and realised, and the congestion of business in standing committees, the Group considered that only in the organisation of standing committees was 'there any real scope for adaptation'. There was a need to reduce the size of standing committees and to increase their number so as to reduce the queue of Bills waiting to be considered and also the haste with which each is examined.

The Group, however, heard more fundamental criticism, both from within the civil service and from Members, relating to the lack of information and to the lack of contact between Government and Members. From the civil service side, it was said that, because there is little direct contact between administrators in charge of steering a Bill through committee and the members of that committee, a civil servant sometimes found it difficult to decide what a particular amendment meant before advising his Minister. The converse case, of the Member in committee who wishes to elucidate a question of fact from the administrator and has to ask, and receive an answer to, his question through the Minister, equally demonstrated the rigidity of existing procedure. The more extensive use of select committees, where civil servants can address the committee directly and answer questions without the mediation of a Minister, would do much to ease this situation.

Members too are concerned at the paucity of 'hard' information from Government sources. Information as such is not lacking; outside bodies interested in Bills frequently make valuable data available. The Government, by comparison, tends to be secretive about the information on which it bases its decisions, especially when its views of the facts differ from those of outsiders. White Papers, in particular, are too brief, and memoranda do not go beyond the bare bones of the Bill and its financial and public service manpower implications. The idea that a secretive Government faces groping backbenchers is widely held. If true, it must vitiate attempts to improve the scrutiny of legislation by Parliament.

Much more investigation and research are required before any attempt to formulate detailed proposals is made. Case studies are needed of the committee stage of actual Bills, how adequately they are considered and how procedures might be improved. If some of the procedures of a select committee were adopted, would this lead to a further demand for publicised investigatory proceedings like those of Congressional Committees? Canada has, in fact, recently adopted this procedure. Would anything be gained by making specialist committees the nucleus of standing committees, or by handing over to them the committee stages of those Bills falling within their spheres of interest? How far is the House prepared to go in delegating its legislative work to small committees, even with the safeguard that non-members might speak but not vote? How much time on the Floor of the House would be saved? Does the Opposition really want greater opportunity for constructive criticism—which may lead to the emergence of a 'cross-bench' attitude similar to that which normally prevails in Select Committees—or does it regard the Committee stage primarily as a continuation in another guise of the policy-confrontation of Second Reading? Do all government backbenchers want greater use of standing committees if the critics among them are unlikely to be nominated to such committees—witness the qualms about sending the Industrial Relations Bill upstairs in April 1969? Some light may be thrown on these questions by our consideration of the Finance Bill, though this may be so much sui generis that public legislation in general may be more apt for reform than financial legislation.

The Finance Bill

The Select Committee on Procedure in 1959 believed that 'the greatest single economy that could be produced in the time spent on the floor of the House would be to commit the Finance Bill at least in part to a standing committee'. The evidence showed that there had been a steady increase in the time thus spent since World War II and that the number of days taken even on a relatively short and uncomplicated Finance Bill exceeded the time taken on longer and more complicated bills in the past. They referred to the tradition that matters of taxation ought always to be taken on the floor of the House, but considered that 'tradition ought not to stand in the way of reform'.

One suggestion was that the fiscal proposals might be divided into two Finance Bills, one implementing major budget decisions, the other dealing with technicalities. The former would be taken on the floor, the latter upstairs. Beyond commenting that the Government could put such proposal into effect whenever it wished, the Committee made no further observations. An alternative proposal was to divide the Bill into those clauses containing the more important changes in taxation and those involving complicated details or requiring close legal argument. Again, the former would remain on the floor, the latter go upstairs. The Treasury, however, had shown that such division would be extremely difficult and that, in a normal year, it would result in five-sixths of the Bill remaining on the Floor of the House. These arguments, however, would not apply if the Bill were divided according to the 'parts' in which it is normally drafted. From a purely procedural point of view the Bill could be divided on the basis of these 'parts' between the floor and a standing committee, or between two or more standing committees. If the Bill was sent upstairs in its entirety, one committee would be unable to complete consideration of it in time to comply with the Parliament Act 1911, and the Provisional Collection of Taxes Act 1913. In an average year 70 hours were spent in Committee of the Whole House on the Bill. (Presumably this argument applied only in the absence of an Allocation of Time Order?) The Committee left the choice of alternatives to the House, to be determined in the light of circumstances obtaining at the time and the nature and content of the Finance Bill. But if the entire Bill were not sent upstairs the Committee recommended the experiment of committing a part or parts to a standing committee.

This proposal was welcomed guardedly by Mr Butler in July 1959. He thought that 'an experimental approach to the Finance Bill would be the best'. Mr Morrison would have the whole Bill sent upstairs. Mr Philips Price wanted to send parts of the Bill upstairs; certain clauses might be selected and dealt with by the 'experts', while those 'likely to arouse emotions and dealing with first principles' would be kept on the floor. Mr Mitchison, who in the Select Committee on Procedure had voted against sending the Bill upstairs, had now come round to the view that parts might be so treated. In the same debate, Mr Blackburn tabled an amendment to Standing Order No. 38 in order automatically to commit the Finance Bill to a standing committee unless the House otherwise determined. Mr Douglas Houghton, however, thought that, 'bearing in mind the number of hon. Members who take part in the debates on the Finance Bill . . . a proposal to send it to a standing committee . . . would lead to many inconveniences and disappointments.' He suggested a Taxes Management Act to separate administrative questions from the Finance Bill. When Mr Butler declared that he would rather deal with the question of taking part of the Bill upstairs *ab initio* and not by amending standing orders, Mr Blackburn 'felt that Mr Butler was in full agreement with the object he had in mind' and withdrew his amendment.

Despite Mr Butler's cautious approval of some experiment in dealing with the Finance Bill, nothing was done in the next few sessions, and the Select Committee on Procedure, 1962–63, once again, in its Second Report, considered the question of 'Expediting the Finance Bill'. They firmly rejected any proposal to send the Bill either as a whole or in part to a standing committee. If only part were sent upstairs, the maximum saving of time would be two or three days; against this there would have to be a guillotine motion, which would be debatable, and probably a longer Report Stage would be necessary in order to enable Members not appointed to the standing committee to move amendments. Although it would be possible to send certain parts or clauses of a Finance Bill upstairs, it did not appear to the Committee 'that the main object of saving the time of the House would be achieved by such a step'.

Even to send parts upstairs—still more, to send the whole Bill upstairs—would offend a 'strong body of opinion which believes that [this] would be a breach of a constitutional principle, namely that the House as a whole must keep control over the executive in the matter of taxation'. On average, the House spent about 10 per cent of its time on the Budget and the subsequent Finance Bill. 'This does not seem to Your Committee to be an undue proportion of time to spend on the most important legislation of the Parliamentary year, one by which every person in the country is affected and in which a large number of Members is interested.' The Committee was firmly against even an experiment.

The reformers, however, remained unconvinced and the problem continued to be presented to subsequent Procedure Committees.

The matter was again considered by the Select Committee on Procedure, 1964–65. In its evidence to this Committee the Study of Parliament Group recommended that both the Committee and Report stages of the Finance Bill should continue to be taken on the Floor of the House. They did suggest, however, that those clauses which were agreed to raise technical problems should be referred for study to a select committee, with sub-committees if necessary. This 'taxation' committee should report on as many clauses as possible in time for their recommendations to be incorporated, if thought fit, in amendments to the Bill at the Report stage. Clauses requiring more time should be examined by the select committee during the course of the year, but these would only be 'referred to the select committee for examination, not committed'. It was hoped that time spent on debate in committee and on report on technical matters of interest only to a very limited number of Members would thus be considerably reduced; more relevant information, together with the views of outside experts, could be obtained and published, better drafting of technical proposals might be ensured, and a corpus of Members knowledgeable on taxation administration could be built up.

The Group may have been somewhat unwilling to recommend more radical proposals in view of its reluctance to express a view on matters of profound constitutional import and of its desire to keep its recommendations within what seemed to be the bounds of practical possibility. Many M.P.s, however, wished to pursue the matter of reducing the burden of detailed consideration on the Floor of the House and they were to some extent encouraged by further recommendations from the Select Committee on Procedure, 1964–65. In their Third Report, the Committee expressed the firm belief that further efforts should be made to relieve the pressure on the time of the whole House and to avoid unduly late sittings, although they reiterated the need to have particular regard for the rights of Members and to preserve the reasonable opportunities of an Opposition to subject the Government of the day to responsible parliamentary pressures. They considered that 'one way by which these conflicting objectives can be reconciled is by continuing the search for a method of identifying those parts of a Finance Bill which could with propriety be examined by a standing committee'. This, of course, harked back to the recommendation of the Select Committee in 1959.

If it were known that it was the desire of the House to consider as much as possible of the Finance Bill upstairs, Governments might well be able to draft the Bill in such a way as to assist the House to make a division. One approach to this, already considered earlier, would be to separate, as far as possible, 'administrative' from 'budgetary' provisions. A select committee, whose nucleus would be members of the Speaker's panel of chairmen, should make recommendations on proceedings on the Finance Bill, after hearing proposals from Ministers concerned and other interested Members. Recommendations should be made only after a reasonable time had elapsed after Second Reading, so that regard might be had to the number and character of amendments tabled. The select committee should also be authorised when it thought it appropriate to draw up a time-table for the consideration of the Bill. Recommendations on a lengthy or highly controversial Bill might be made in instalments in the light of experience gained in the earlier stages of the time-table. Such proposals would be debatable in the House but 'Your Committee believe that it might well be found that these recommendations, coming from a body of senior Members, represented an acceptable *modus vivendi*'. The Committee felt that its proposals would result both in a saving of time on the Floor of the House and in a more appropriate consideration of the technical features of the Bill.

No action was taken on these proposals and the Select Committee on Procedure returned once more to the matter in its Fourth Report, 1966–67. Four possible methods of dealing with the Finance Bill were considered. First, the whole Bill might be committed to a standing committee. Arguments were heard that Bills of comparable importance and complexity were already sent upstairs. Large parts of the Finance Bill were of minor interest or of main interest only to specialists. If the standing committee were made sufficiently large and there was an extended Report stage, Members who wished to take part in debate would be able to do so. Six sometimes very long days might be saved in the House. Against this, the Finance Bill affected the interests of all the constituents of every Member. Since about 175 Members took part in committee proceedings, to reduce the number able to speak and vote to about 50 would constitute an attack on the rights of Private Members. Mr Speaker might have to be so generous in his selection of amendments and new clauses on the Report stage that little time might be saved. The reputation and work of the House might suffer if all Treasury Ministers, leading members of the Opposition front bench and a considerable number of other Members were continuously occupied for three or four weeks in May and June upstairs and were thus prevented from taking part in other important business in the House.

It would be necessary to complete the Committee stage in a definite and relatively short time and the House would need to instruct the Committee to report the Bill by a fixed date. Assuming the same amount of time were required upstairs as on the floor of the House, a standing committee sitting six hours a day for three days a week could be expected to complete the Bill in four weeks. But to meet the problem of continuous attendance, the Committee of Selection might appoint up to ten Members (Ministers or frontbench spokesmen) who would be able to attend as Law Officers do now. It might also be possible to allow *any* Member to address the Committee and move amendments but not vote, though there were obvious objections to this. Finally, and as an alternative to the last suggestion, there might be a 'recommittal' stage at which priority would be given to Members not on the standing committee. The Select Committee on Procedure preferred the latter alternative.

The second suggestion was that the Bill should be divided between the House and the standing committee, as discussed both in 1959 and 1964–65. Finance Bills often contained provisions of considerable complexity not involving much party controversy but requiring careful scrutiny by Members such as lawyers or accountants with special knowledge. In some cases the principle behind the proposed change might be simple though controversial, but its implementation might involve separating out lengthy and complicated clauses and schedules; the latter might go upstairs. Certain Private Members' new clauses, which cannot involve increases in taxation, might also go to standing committee. The division of a Bill would have to be agreed between the Chancellor of the Exchequer and his opposite number on the Opposition Front Bench. But would it be possible to divide the Bill in a satisfactory manner? Further, the time spent in committee on recent Finance Bills on 'administrative' or 'machinery' matters amounted to only one-sixth of the total—little over one day. There would also be difficulties if the Standing Committee were to meet while other parts of the Bill were being taken on the floor of the House. The evidence of the Treasury Ministers was against this second suggestion.

The third suggestion was the adoption of a voluntary time-table. The Opposition Chief Whip thought that the Committee stage on the Floor of the House ought normally to be completed in eight or nine days, without sitting later than 11.30 p.m. If a voluntary agreement were reached, a business committee nominated by Mr Speaker would (under Standing Order No. 43b) plan the time-table within the days allotted. If there was failure to reach a voluntary agreement then a Minister should be able to move a Resolution, debatable for a short time, setting up a business committee to determine the number of days to be allotted to the Bill and the allocation of time within the overall total. The whole House would thus still participate in the Committee stage, the strong opposition which might be provoked by sending upstairs a Bill of this constitutional significance and annual importance would be avoided, and the allocation of time involved would be largely voluntary if the House accepted the principle of the system proposed. On the other hand, while late sittings might be avoided, the number of days spent on the Bill at an over-crowded period of the year might not be reduced. The scheme also failed to meet the arguments of those who believed that the House should not be kept for discussion and votes on many amendments and clauses which affect and interest only a small minority of Members.

The fourth suggestion was simply to retain existing procedures.

The Committee was clearly impressed by the arguments against committal of all or part of the Finance Bill to a standing committee, which had, indeed, been considered conclusive by its predecessor in 1963. The latter, however, had been satisfied that restraint on the length of committee proceedings would be inappropriate for the Finance Bill, and in this they were *not* followed by their successor. The Committee, having recorded its differences of opinion, stated that 'both those Members who favour sending all or part of the Bill to a standing committee and those who believe that no change should be made are, therefore, prepared to support an experiment in voluntary time-tabling for proceedings in the House'.

In a procedure debate on 19 April 1967, Mr Crossman indicated that the Government had decided to adopt the proposal for a voluntary arrangement. He made it clear, however, that if an agreed time-table could not be reached, or if, having been arrived at, it was not working properly, the Government would propose that the Business Committee should consider and recommend a time-table. Two hours would be allowed for debate on this motion. He added that although a very large number of Members had come to the conclusion that the whole Bill should go upstairs, this 'radical suggestion' should be considered as part of the overall reform of Public Bill procedure. The House should await the major report promised by the Select Committee on Procedure. (In fact, this report contained no specific proposals about the Finance Bill.) Meanwhile, the Finance Bill should not be the first but one of the last measures to be submitted to any experiment in 'upstairs time-tabling' which the House might adopt. Later, however, he expressed the opinion that 'in due course the House will come to the conviction that the right thing to do with the Finance Bill is to send it to a Special Committee upstairs'.

The Opposition was not altogether happy with the proposed arrangements. In particular, Mr Boyd-Carpenter feared that if the Minister were to be the judge of whether the voluntary time-table were working properly, he would not be unbiased. Moreover, if a motion were introduced for a time-table it should be debatable for six not for two hours. Many Members were unwilling to accept the use of a guillotine, however modified or disguised, on the Finance Bill. One oft-voiced fear was that once a time-table had been imposed, Government backbenchers might filibuster and thus reduce the opportunities open to the Opposition for criticism. Alternatively, the Government might suddenly put down a great number of amendments after a time-table had been agreed or imposed. The House had to be content with Mr Crossman's 'assurances' on all these matters. The new Sessional Order was duly accepted.

The procedure, however, was not, in fact, applied to the Finance Bill 1967, and the Government decided to send the whole Bill upstairs to a standing committee in 1968. The background to this decision is to be found in the debates on 6 December 1967, when Mr Crossman moved (1) to amend Standing Order No. 40 so as to make it possible to take the Finance Bill upstairs, (2) to make a new Standing Order based on the Sessional Order described above, and (3) to enable Ministers, like Law Officers, to attend any standing committee as required.

Mr Crossman had, it will be recalled, ventured the opinion that the House would eventually decide to send the whole of the Finance Bill upstairs. None of the arguments for or against this had changed between April, when the Government accepted the 'compromise' of a voluntary time-table with a 'sanction' if this were not observed, and December, when the decision to send the Bill upstairs was taken. Mr Crossman simply stated that the Sessional Order was a dead letter because the Shadow Chancellor, Mr Macleod, disliked it and preferred to rely on the traditional informal discussions. Mr Macleod had stated that he would have nothing to do with 'dark, nefarious schemes for having what he called a so-called voluntary time-table'. Mr Michael Stewart asserted bluntly that the compromise had been 'rejected'.

Mr Macleod described the proposal to take the Bill upstairs as 'a breach of faith' in view of the way in which the 1967 Finance Bill had gone through. He argued that the 'gentleman's agreement' had worked; the eight days spent in committee ended at 10.12 p.m., 11.59 p.m., 11.45 p.m., 10.51 p.m., 9.53 p.m., 11.40 p.m., 9.38 p.m., and 7.45 p.m.—not once after midnight. He, like Mr Boyd-Carpenter, alleged that the reason for the present proposal was the prospect of a tough, controversial Budget and he stated categorically that the 1968 Finance Bill would take place under a guillotine. More generally, he deplored the increasing tendency of the House of Commons to try to make formal matters out of matters best left imprecise: 'I would not sign on the dotted line. No one must make an agreement unless it is certain he can carry it out. Governments may so infuriate Oppositions that more time is essential; many amendments might be tabled at a late stage; Government backbenchers might talk at length once a time limit is imposed.'

We shall not deal at length with the arguments about the merits of the proposals; nothing new emerged. Both Mr Crossman and Mr Stewart argued that there was little 'constitutional' difference between the Finance Bill and other major Bills; Mr Macleod and others insisted on the unique importance of the Finance Bill. They also doubted whether very much time would be saved on the Floor of the House and, suggested that much of what might be so saved would be taken for Government business rather than for the 'topical debates' so dear to the hearts of some backbenchers. Many speakers referred to the more effective discussion possible in a small committee; some, even, to the possibility of crossbench consensus and to the smaller likelihood of automatic Government majorities—which they appeared to regard as advantages. Against this, others argued for the right of the Opposition to delay Government business; if a long and controversial Finance Bill were introduced the Government might have to sacrifice some of its other business. It was again pointed out that if a large committee sat frequently in the afternoons this would lead to a disruption of business on the Floor of the House. There was the usual reference to the rights of backbenchers, particularly since the Government opposed a Liberal amendment that ordinary Members, like Ministers, should be allowed to attend meetings even if not members of the Committee. Only Mr Boyd-Carpenter and Mr Selwyn Lloyd referred briefly to the possibility of taking 'technical' clauses upstairs, though Mr Grimond reminded them of the difficulty of dividing the Finance Bill. The Government proposals were, nevertheless, carried and the 1968 Finance Bill as a whole was taken upstairs.

Before attempting to assess the significance of this experiment we record briefly that Mr Macleod's prophecy—or threat

—of a guillotine was borne out when on 21 May 1968 an Allocation of Time Order was introduced by Mr Peart. There was little attempt in the two hours available to canvass the broad arguments about sending the Bill upstairs. Mr Donald Chapman, Chairman of the Select Committee on Procedure, thought that the Government had made a mistake in not having fixed from the beginning a date for the return of the Bill to the House. He, like Mr Edward du Cann, also referred briefly to the possibility in future of sending the 'technical' clauses of the Bill upstairs. For the rest, Mr Peart pointed out that in nine sittings, totalling 62 hours, only 14 of 56 clauses had been considered, not taking into account 58 new clauses. If this manner of proceeding had continued until 13 June (the proposed date for the return of the Bill) the Committee would have spent 90 hours with 'no indication that it would have finished its work'. Even so, as Mr Roy Jenkins pointed out, the Government was offering another 50 hours, making about 110 in all—the longest period but one in 45 years. Many Members were unconvinced by Mr Peart's argument that between 1951 and 1964 the average time spent in committee was 64 hours. It was pointed out that in 1965, 163 and in 1966, 99 hours had been required. But the Government inevitably obtained its guillotine order.

Any balanced judgment on the 1968 experiment must first take into account a number of factors not directly related to the merits of the exercise. Mr Ian Trethowan ascribed some of the difficulties to 'sheer bad management', especially the attempt to push through four major Bills, with the consequent proliferation of standing committees which were not easy to man. The Finance Bill experiment, in his view, was of doubtful utility, though worth trying. The *Economist* expressed the hope that the Opposition would give the experiment 'a fair trial' but, like David Wood, had doubts about the wisdom of trying it with a controversial Bill which proposed an additional £923,000,000 in taxation.

Opposition to the principle of the experiment also took the form of prolonged criticism of the physical conditions in which the Bill was discussed. The acoustics of the Committee Room were appalling; one side of the room was too hot, the other too cold; improvements eventually made were at the expense of the press and public, robbing the Committee, it was said, of desirable publicity. Much time was consumed in arguments as to whether the break for dinner should be one hour, one-and-a-quarter or one-and-a-half hours; whether the time allowed for divisions should be two or six minutes; whether Members should be allowed to appear in shirt-sleeves. David Wood commented on 'how shoddily the most important bill of the session is being put through'. No objective observer can do other than suspect at least that some of this was due to a desire on the part of some Members to discredit the whole procedure.

There were, however, more solid criticisms, cogently expressed by Mr Macleod. Most of them had been pointed out by various Select Committees on Procedure and in the debates referred to above. Mr Macleod, however, was able to argue that these objections had now been sustained as a result of the experiment. Basically, the ground of complaint rested upon the simple fact that only 50 Members—28 Labour, 21 Conservative and one Liberal—had been members of the Standing Committee. The rest had been largely excluded from serious discussion. The Recommittal stage, intended primarily to give an opportunity to non-members of the Committee, was unsatisfactory. Many amendments then moved, though by different M.P.s, were on matters already discussed upstairs. Moreover, the Report stage is 'largely a propaganda exercise since the Lords do not amend the Bill'. The only possible answer is that all should share in the Committee stage. Mr Macleod also condemned the tying-up of Members upstairs, particularly when important matters were being discussed on the Floor of the House. He was clearly disturbed by the lack of publicity for the proceedings. In Committee, he considered that the debates in general took far too long, largely due to the high calibre of the members. He made the somewhat curious remark that in similar circumstances he 'would select a somewhat weaker side'. Too little distinction, he thought, was made between important and less important discussions; a substantial number of members was kept in order to ensure a quorum, and these were therefore drawn into the discussions. Finally, and from the Opposition point of view most important, it is 'doubtful if the exercise of persuasion in relation to the really important amendments is anything like as effective as it can be on the floor of the House'. On time-tabling, Mr Macleod pointed out that for a long and controversial Budget the time allowed had been only the same as for the 'standstill' Budgets of 1964 and 1967. He reiterated his refusal to make agreements under the threat of a guillotine on which only two hours' debate was allowed.

Even the most ardent supporters of the experiment must have some misgivings, though to what extent they arise from the peculiar circumstances of 1968 it is difficult to say. Mr John Mackintosh considered that the Government gained something from the extra time available on the Floor of the House but that the House of Commons also gained because Treasury Ministers had not merely to read out a prepared brief but win an argument. His conclusion was not that the experiment should be abandoned but that a new Finance and Taxation Specialist Committee should be established; this would provide the nucleus of the Finance Bill Committee. For the 1969 Finance Bill, however, the Government—having tried a time-table procedure and a standing committee for the whole Bill—decided to adopt the third procedure discussed by the Select Committee on Procedure, 1966–67, that of dividing the Committee stage of the Finance Bill into two parts; important issues, Mr Peart stated on 24 April 1969, like S.E.T., the Corporation Tax and Purchase Tax, would be taken on the floor of the House, while 'minutiae'—at that stage undefined—would go upstairs to a standing committee.

On 6 May 1969, the Chancellor of the Exchequer moved that Clauses 7, 8, 36, 38, 43, and 44 and Schedule 6 of the Finances Bill be committed to a Committee of the Whole House and that the remainder of the Bill be committed to a standing committee. When the provisions of the Bill considered thus were reported to the House, the Bill would be proceeded with as if it had been reported as a whole to the House from the standing committee.

This is being written before the conclusion of this session's discussions of the Finance Bill. The guess may be hazarded, however, that the division of the Bill will save little time; all the evidence before Select Committees, not least that of the

Treasury, points to this conclusion. It is possible that in the future the failure of the various experiments will matter less. If the new presentation of government spending proposed in the Green Paper of April 1969 leads to a different kind of debate on public expenditure, the Budget and the Finance Bill may be demoted from what has been called the 'theatrical pinnacle'. Debate in the House may be supplemented by consideration in a new kind of Finance and Taxation Committee. These changes 'open up the prospect of restoring to Parliament the ability to perform its proper function in this critical sector', provided the Select Committee on Procedure proposes parliamentary reforms in line with these changes.

Whatever changes may be made in the procedures of standing committees it appears that the foundation for effective reform must be the achievement of a high degree of predictability so far as the time required is concerned. If this demand for predictability is defeated by a desire to retain large opportunities for the delay and even disruption of Government business, then the efforts to save time on the floor of the House might just as well be abandoned. Indeed, the suggestions for changes in standing committee procedure, such as that of assimilating it to Select Committee procedure, rests upon the assumption that the House desires more effective and more constructive attention to detail at the committee stage rather than a continuance of 'confrontation'.

Predictability appears to involve the regular time-tabling of Bills,—which, as we have seen, proved unworkable for the Finance Bill in 1967. Mr Bowden, then Opposition Chief Whip, suggested such time-tabling to the Select Committee on Procedure, 1963–64. In its Third Report, the Committee merely outlined the proposals, pointing out that further evidence and thorough discussion were not possible so near the end of the Session.

Mr Bowden proposed a select committee, appointed by Standing Order, to consist of a number of members of the Chairman's panel and some experienced backbench Members. Immediately after the second reading of any Bill, or at any time during subsequent proceedings, any Member could move that the Bill be referred to this committee. The motion would be decided without amendment or debate; if agreed to, the select committee would draw up a time-table for the remaining stages of the Bill, after hearing representatives of the Government and the Opposition and any other Members the committee might wish. The motion to agree with the committee would be open to amendment and debate. The Government could thus seek to reduce an allocation of time which they considered excessive.

The principal function of this procedure 'would obviously be to prepare time-tables for the more contentious Government bills'. Mr Bowden's two main objects were to reduce the antagonism on the part of the Opposition which is normally aroused when a time-table is introduced by the Government, to save the time of the House and of standing committees and thereby assist the Government in planning its programme of legislation, by ensuring that time tables could be in force from the beginning of the committee stage.

The Select Committee on Procedure, 1966–67, in its Sixth Report returned to the question of time-tabling. If it were possible to make an objective assessment of the time needed for the consideration of a Bill, which could be adjusted if necessary from time to time, and if this programme could be observed, then there would be general advantages in the more even examination of legislation; increased opportunities for Government supporters; and advantages for Governments in knowing how long a bill was likely to take. Both the Leader of the House and the Opposition Chief Whip, however, wanted to preserve the opportunities open to the Opposition to impose delay, 'so attenuating a Government's programme'.

The Committee, therefore, made no further proposals for sanctions in case of failure to reach voluntary agreements, beyond those in their Fourth Report on the Finance Bill, which we examined above. They suggested a steering committee which, *if unanimous*, would report recommendations about time-tabling after Second Reading. 'The fact that agreements were published, and known to have been reached unanimously, would assist in building up acceptance of them.' If an agreement were not being respected, the Government would table a motion to achieve the objects of the steering committee.

There must remain considerable doubt as to the number of

occasions upon which unanimous agreement would be reached. We return to our fundamental point. Unless there is agreement about the *functions* of the Committee stage, neither time-tabling nor reform of procedure is likely to be achieved. Some observers, notably Mr Ronald Butt in *The Times*, 8 May 1969, believe that the House will only be able to exercise a really effective influence on policy if fundamental changes are made in our constitutional arrangements. But discussion of changes in the right of the Prime Minister to demand dissolution, or of proposals to end the 'convention of confidence attached to every bill' (except the Finance Bill), lie outside the scope of this chapter. No Government, no Opposition expecting to achieve office, is likely to contemplate such fundamental alterations in the constitution.

In a Memorandum to the Select Committee on Procedure, 1959, Professor A. H. Hanson and the present writer, in advocating greater use of committees by the House, stated: 'We are convinced that the time has come when "committee" proposals should be considered strictly on their merits, and that this will not be possible unless they are clearly dissociated from the other wider and less generally acceptable proposals for political reform with which they have become fortuitously linked ... We do not favour proportional representation, coalition governments, minority governments, or weak Cabinets.' The author would extend these remarks to include the 'fundamental' reforms referred to above.

Chapter 10

The New Specialised Committees

H. Victor Wiseman

In the effort to provide for more effective scrutiny of the Executive by the House of Commons and a more positive and constructive role for backbench M.P.s, no remedy has been more continually pressed nor more belatedly adopted than that of specialised committees. The early history of attempts to persuade Parliament to accept what was for long rejected as a 'radical constitutional innovation' and an undesirable importation from abroad—doing things '*à l'Américaine*' as Mr Butler once put it, neatly killing two foreign birds with one stone—has been amply discussed elsewhere.[1] This chapter concentrates largely on developments from 1964–65 onwards.

The Select Committee on Procedure of 1958–59 (92–I, 1959) discussed the question of specialised committees almost exclusively in terms of a proposed Colonial Affairs Committee, which it rejected. A memorandum submitted by Professor A. H. Hanson and the author was acknowledged but not even printed in the Minutes of Evidence. The change of climate is well illustrated by the fact that they, with Professor Bromhead, were invited to give evidence on the subject to the subsequent Procedure Committee, primarily as representatives of the Study of Parliament Group, whose recommendations included one for specialised committees. This Committee also considered a memorandum from the Clerk Assistant, Mr D. W. S. Lidderdale.[2]

The latter suggested developing the Estimates Committee with new terms of reference—'to examine how departments of state carry out their responsibilities and to consider their

1. cf. *Parliamentary Reform* (London: Cassell for the Hansard Society), 2nd edn, 1967, pp. 45–60; A. H. Hanson and H. V. Wiseman, 'Use of Committees by the House of Commons', *Public Law*, August 1959; *Reforming the House of Commons* (London: P.E.P. for the Study of Parliament Group, 1965).
2. Fourth Report, 29 July 1965, 303.

Estimates of Expenditure and Reports'. Specialised sub-committees to cover the social services (health, national insurance, welfare services); housing, education and sport; trade, agriculture, power, science, labour; transport and aviation; home and colonial affairs; defence and foreign affairs, would be set up.

On whether Ministers should appear before such committees there was less agreement between witnesses. Sir Laurence Helsby, Head of the Civil Service, thought that it would be 'a drastic constitutional change to put Ministers before the Committee'. If the field were enlarged to include policy—the new terms of reference seemed to him to suggest this—civil servants could not answer. He agreed that, in principle, it might be possible for a Minister and a civil servant to decide who should give evidence on any point, but doubted the workability of such proposal. Mr Herbert Bowden was against Ministers appearing and against examining civil servants, especially below the level of the Permanent Secretary, on policy. Mr William Hamilton, Chairman of the Estimates Committee, was in favour of Ministers appearing, but he admitted that Sub-Committee A of his Committee was not.

The Study of Parliament Group's written evidence agreed that the terms of reference of the Estimates Committee were wide enough to embrace all aspects of the efficient conduct of administration. But the Group considered that specialised committees of advice and scrutiny should eventually cover the whole field. Five should be set up as an initial experiment —(1) scientific development, (2) prevention and punishment of crime, (3) machinery of national, regional and local government and administration, (4) housing, building and land use and (5) the social services. As such committees were set up, the Estimates Committee would devolve relevant functions to them. They might also eventually provide at least the nucleus for standing committees and function as 'pre-legislation committees', if such were considered desirable. The initial terms of reference for specialised committees might be: 'To examine the assumptions on which policy decisions have been made and to report on the implementation of policy in the field of . . .' The Group emphasised that there would still be a role for the Estimates Committee and for the Select Committee on Statutory Instruments, though specialised committees might watch the actual operation of such Instruments.

In oral evidence the Group's representatives expressed doubt as to whether the Estimates Committee could effectively perform all the functions envisaged for the specialised committees without a widening of its terms of reference so great that it would cease to be an *estimates committee*. The Group's witnesses had not, of course, seen the Clerk Assistant's Memorandum and, as was subsequently admitted, the Group had 'been slow to catch up with the cumulative effect of the changes' in the scope and methods of the Estimates Committee. The ultimate decision to use the Estimates Committee as a starting point was accepted as 'much the same thing in the end (as specialised committees) and probably a politically more realistic way of getting there'.

The Group's witnesses also argued strongly that matters of policy should not be rigidly excluded. Civil Servants were skilled in discerning when such matters were involved and ready to indicate that a particular question should be directed to the Minister rather than to themselves. The Association of First Division Civil Servants, indeed, told the Fulton Committee that civil servants were 'excused from answering questions on matters of policy', but that this did not, 'in practice, exclude very much'. The Group's witnesses considered that Ministers might be asked to appear before Committees, although without prejudice to their right to refuse to do so. It was pointed out that since the Government would always have a majority on each committee, this could effectively prevent an invitation to the Minister if so desired. To quote from a subsequent debate, there would be no question of 'hauling a Minister before a committee'.

The Report of the Select Committee on Procedure expressed its appreciation of this evidence. Yet the Committee refused to accept a proposal by one of its members that further information about the working of specialised committees be sought from overseas, and especially from Canada, and also a recommendation for the setting-up of an *ad hoc* select committee to examine further the possibility of specialised committees. Its own recommendations were based entirely on the proposals contained in the Clerk Assistant's memorandum. The terms of reference of the Estimates Committee were to be widened, and its sub-committees were to become 'specialised'. Justifying these proposals, the Procedure Committee said that it was 'anxious to retain the experience and method of work' of the Estimates Committee and to preserve the 'close working relationship' between the Committee and the Departments. It also pointed to the 'danger if the range of investigations got beyond that which could properly be replied to by civil servants', and emphasised the undesirability of the Estimates Committee becoming involved in matters of political controversy. Finally, to enable it to conduct its work more effectively, it should be given the services of two Clerks and one full-time Clerk for each of the sub-committees, and should be empowered to employ temporary technical and scientific assistance and permitted to hold sittings abroad.

The Study of Parliament Group, despite the rejection of some of the most important suggestions contained in its Memorandum, considered that the Report of the Procedure Committee 'could prove far-reaching in its consequences'.[3] Yet the debate on 27 October 1965 was disappointing to supporters of radical reform. Mr Herbert Bowden recommended that there be no change in the terms of reference of the Estimates Committee, and the House did not press for such change. Specialisation, he said, was entirely a matter for the Committee itself, while the staffing proposals would be referred to the House of Commons Services Committee. At one point he seemed almost to revert to the standard objections to Specialist Committees —did 'we want to develop a system of Specialist Committees not exactly like but something akin to American Congressional Committees and those in Europe?'—despite Sir Martin Redmayne's reminder that the Select Committee had actually rejected the American pattern. Sir Richard Nugent, Chairman of the Select Committee on the Nationalised Industries, also disappointed the reformers. In presenting the work of his Committee as not impinging on ministerial responsibility, as avoiding trespass on policy matters, and as striving to reach unanimous conclusions, he implied that Specialist Committees would be unable to avoid these pitfalls. (This,

3. *Reforming the Commons*, p. 287.

it may be noted, was before the Nationalised Industries Committee reported, in September 1968, on the whole question of ministerial control, relations with Boards, the role of civil servants, and many other 'policy' matters.) The debate as a whole revealed profound differences of opinion about specialised committees and the sole result was a relatively minor change in the working of the Estimates Committee.

It is convenient to complete the story of the latter before resuming the chronological account of further developments. In the sessions 1965–66 and 1966–67 the Estimates Committee set up Sub-Committees for Social Affairs; Economic Affairs; Technological and Scientific Affairs; Defence and Overseas Affairs; Building and Natural Resources. In the 1967–68 session, however, this specialisation was abandoned.[4] As a result of the establishment first of two and later of three specialised Committees, the Estimates Committee was reduced in size from 43 to 36 Members and the number of sub-committees from six to five. The Estimates Committee wished to avoid overlapping with the specialised committees and, indeed, 'any appearance of duplication'. Thus, although sub-committees would not be debarred from conducting interrelated enquiries in successive sessions, there would be a return to sub-committees 'lettered' A, B, etc. as a means of recapturing the 'greater element of flexibility . . . which should ensure that no subject of particular interest or topical importance is overlooked and that every Sub-Committee has an equal chance of having such a subject allotted to them'. The Committee also decided to make 'a limited experiment' by arranging that Sub-Committee B (Estimates relating to Mental Hospitals for Prisoners) should 'hear evidence in public . . . whenever they consider it practicable to do so'. By this time, specialised committees were in operation and had already taken evidence in public. To their history we now return.

On 21 April 1966, during the Debate on the Queen's Speech, the Prime Minister himself suggested 'an experiment to extend the committee system over a wider field'. He envisaged one or two new committees. He was not convinced of the

4. First Special Report, 29 Nov. 1967, 28.

desirability of committees on major questions of foreign policy and defence but thought that such Departments as the Home Office (where 'light could be thrown both on future legislation and day-to-day administration'), Education, and Housing and Local Government were eligible candidates. Ministers, including Junior Ministers, as well as senior officials would be available for questioning. He also envisaged the possibility of regional all-party committees—of which nothing further had been heard at the time of writing.[5]

Mr Crossman, Leader of the House, was doubtless delighted at this green light. But there was inevitable delay while a decision was made as to which departments or subjects might be selected as guinea-pigs. We may speculate that such factors as the willingness of Ministers (and/or their top civil servants) to co-operate; the difficult question as to which Ministers might put up a good (or bad) show before committees; the urgency or topicality, as well as the political implications of matters which might be investigated, and many other factors were being taken into consideration. Not until 14 December, 1966, was the setting up of two Select Specialised Committees, on Agriculture and on Science and Technology, announced in the House.

By 19 April 1967, it was clear, as Mr Crossman told the House, that some difficulties had emerged. He had doubts about extending the number of specialised committees and sub-committees unless they could be sure of recruiting more Clerks. There was also the problem of overlapping with the Estimates Committee. There was need for a Steering Committee of the Chairmen of the Public Accounts Committee, the Estimates Committee and the specialised committees and also for some co-ordination of practice in relation to the use of outside experts and travel abroad. Mr Selwyn Lloyd thought that there were too many committees and sub-committees chased by too few Members, and recalled Sir Edward Fellowes' suggestion that one whole day each week might be devoted to Committees. He also suggested that the specialised committees were not specialised enough, since their remit was too wide; but Mr Palmer, Chairman of the Science and

5. cf. G. H. Jones, Brian Smith and H. V. Wiseman, 'Regionalism and Parliament'. *Political Quarterly*, Vol. 38, No. 4, Oct.-Dec. 1967.

Technology Committee, emphasised the virtue of wide terms of reference as giving greater scope and flexibility.

However, when the House next debated Procedure on 14 November, 6 and 12 December 1967, the two Specialised Committees had reported, though their Reports had not yet been debated, and the atmosphere had somewhat changed. Mr Crossman opened with the remark that 'one is fascinated to observe how rapidly a radical innovation is absorbed into our customs and practice'. A year ago, for instance, the proposal that select committees should sit in public had been regarded as quite adventurous, and the idea that Ministers should submit themselves to cross-examination had sent shivers of apprehension through wide areas of Whitehall. There had been problems, of course, such as those of paying experts and arranging for foreign travel, and 'quite a number of difficulties, misunderstandings and even an occasional explosion of wrath'. But each Committee had evolved such a strong corporate will and personality that already—the academic in Mr Crossman must from time to time appear!—one chapter of Mr Ronald Butt's book[6] had become outdated.

Despite earlier misgivings Mr Crossman was now ready to argue that the specialised committees should be still further strengthened. The two existing ones would be renewed. He thought that the Science and Technology Committee was especially important. He then, however, made a statement which later caused much questioning and which seemed to many to misrepresent the whole purpose of specialised committees. Expressing doubts about the Agriculture Committee, he declared that the 'original intention was that a Departmental Committee should spend one Session on each Department and then move on.' Nevertheless, because of 'delays and disputes' the Agriculture Committee would carry on for a second year. Moreover, a third specialised committee, related to the Department of Education and Science and the Scottish Education Department, would be set up to deal with all relevant matters not already covered by the Science and Technology Committee. Finally, Mr Crossman suggested

6. *The Power of Parliament* (London, 1967). Chapter 13 discusses the role of committees and is generally sceptical about extending their role.

A second edition, however, appeared in 1969, *editors*.

that *ad hoc* committees might study and report on specific topics of possible legislation referred to them. One topic was already under consideration and he hoped to report 'very shortly'. Nothing further had been heard of this by the time of writing.

We now turn to a more detailed account of the first Session's work of the first two specialised committees. The Agriculture Committee issued its full Report on 27 July 1967,[7] and it was debated on 14 May 1968, together with the Departmental Observations.[8] The Science and Technology Committee reported on 25 October 1967,[9] and the Report was debated on 23 May 1968.

Both Committees had rather similar 'miscellaneous grumbles'. The Agriculture Committee complained of shortage of time; it was instructed to report by the end of the session, which effectively meant the end of July. The Science and Technology Committee was also pressed for time, especially in view of the sudden request to deal with the problem of oil pollution: the Sub-Committee appointed to consider this did not have its Report ready by October 1967, and hence had to be set up again in the following session. Both Committees complained of the long delay in debating their Reports—especially serious 'if the objective is to help formulate policy'—and of the inadequate time allotted to the debates. The Agriculture Debate had to take place in the absence of the Committee's chairman; that on Science and Technology came on without a Government Reply and at 7.45 p.m., after an all-night sitting which had terminated at 7.30 a.m. The Agriculture Committee also complained of procrastination in setting it up again and at the alleged 'coercion' of nine additional Members, in order to increase its size from 16 to 25.

Both Committees were aware that they were engaged in an important experiment in procedure. The Agriculture Committee regarded itself as a 'pioneer' in devising 'proper procedures for specialist committees.' It had held its meetings in public (without objection from any witness) and had taken oral evidence from the Minister. The Science and Technology

7. 378–XVII.   8. Cmnd. 3479.   9. 381–XVII.

Committee reported that it had been concerned 'to show that the decision to appoint Specialist Committees was of real value in contributing to the information available to the House of Commons'. Careful consideration had been given to the possible matters for investigation. Seeking a subject 'concerning events taking place rather than those already decided', it had embarked on an examination of the structure and activities of the Ministry before investigating the scope and adequacy of inquiries concerning the effects of entry into the European Economic Community on agriculture, fisheries and food. Such a subject, as Dr Dunwoody admitted in the Debate, was deliberately chosen as being to some extent 'provocative and in the mainstream of politics'. The Report, however, stressed that the Committee was not concerned as to whether entry into the E.E.C. would be beneficial. The Science and Technology Committee had as its main object to examine national scientific and technological expenditure and skills, and the use of manpower resources in both public and private sectors, in order to discover whether full value for money was being obtained and whether appropriate priorities were being observed. It decided to examine first the Nuclear Reactor Programme and then the Defence Research Establishments. These were subjects 'of prime national importance, involving large sums of public money'.

Both Committees had difficulties. The Agriculture Committee expressed satisfaction with the Ministry of Agriculture, which provided more than 30 memoranda, although some took a long time to arrive, five of them only just before the final meeting on the draft report. The Science and Technology Committee recorded 'one serious lapse by the Ministry of Power', which had promised a paper on costs on 22 June and had not delivered it until mid-October after 'the Committee had brought into play in full the powers given to it by the House of Commons'. In the Debate one Member stated that a certain paper was in existence but the Committee was not told about it. But these difficulties pale into insignificance in comparison with the problems posed by the Foreign Office.

The Agriculture Committee requested from the Foreign Office copies of some official correspondence about the staffing of the British Delegation to the E.E.C. in Brussels.

Although the Ministry of Agriculture had claimed that there were 'sufficient staff', the head of the Delegation had applied six months earlier for an assistant to the agricultural attaché. On 26 April the Committee asked for the correspondence. On 14 June the matter was raised informally with a Foreign Office Minister. On 26 June the Foreign Secretary stated that as constitutional issues were involved he could not disclose the correspondence; but he offered a further paper on staffing. The papers were again requested or, alternatively, reasons for the refusal. On 26 July the Foreign Secretary again refused to produce them, stating that this was 'a confidential matter relating to the internal administration of the Department'. In Debate, Mr John Mackintosh retorted that it was 'precisely the internal administration of a Department which we were set up to investigate'. The Committee, he said, should be able to find out the arguments going on in the Government and the priorities set by officials, to 'get behind the façade of ministerial unanimity and responsibility which is normally maintained. This is the constitutional innovation attempted by such committees.'

Both Committees experienced difficulties over foreign travel. The Agriculture Committee decided to visit Brussels; in March the Foreign Office was informed and the Commission of the E.E.C. asked if it was prepared to receive a visit. Two months later no reply had been received. On 31 May informal discussions were held with the Minister of State at the Foreign Office, who suggested that a 'formal visit would be embarrassing to the Government'. The alternative was a visit to the British Delegation but informal discussions only with the Commission. Two weeks later a new Minister of State saw no objection to the original proposal but on 21 June the Government expressed strong objections. Discussions were held with the Leader of the House—the Chairman, Mr Tudor Watkins, is alleged to have declared that he had never been spoken to like that before in his life! Finally, a Motion was tabled requesting leave to hold sittings in Brussels. But on 6 July, the Chairman not being present, it was not called. At last on 10 July, after an all-night sitting, the Chairman moved the Motion at 6.15 a.m. It was agreed without discussion. Ironically, similar permission was given to the Science and

Technology Committee even though its Chairman was not present. Not surprisingly, in the Debate, reference was made to 'unreasonable difficulties'. Scathing comment was also made on the revelation that a Foreign Office Minister had telephoned the Clerk to the Committee and instructed him not to reveal the conversation to the Committee!

The Science and Technology Committee experienced similar difficulties over proposed visits to the U.S. and Europe. For two months the Government was unable to find time for the necessary Motions and only 'after the strongest representation to Ministers by the Chairman' were they eventually agreed to on 5 and 10 July; but the Foreign Office made no progress with the arrangements and hence the work of the Committee had to be deferred and revised. On 18 July the Foreign Office stated that no sanction had yet been received to arrange the visits through ambassadorial channels. On 20 July, after the Chairman's intervention, the arrangements were made and excellent results were achieved. To the Committee and its Chairman, Mr Palmer, 'the apparent fears and apprehensions aroused in London by the intended visits' seemed, after the event, 'even more meaningless than ever'. In the same debate Mr Palmer remarked that 'Government Departments must accustom themselves to the various novel constitutional situations that Specialist Committees will create from time to time'. With some apparent justification, Sir H. Legge-Bourke opined that there were 'too many people throughout the Departments and, in particular, in the Treasury, who resent our existence and are determined if they possibly can to diminish our importance'.

A final complaint was of inadequate staffing. The Agriculture Committee was given only one Senior Clerk who was able to devote less than half his time to its work and was not available for all sittings. There was virtually no supporting staff and the Committee said it needed two full-time Clerks, especially if use were made of sub-committees. It was emphasised that staff should not be civil servants but persons directly responsible to the House. Staff were needed, among other things, for research and to annotate documents and help prepare questions. The Committee also considered that the Library was inadequately staffed. The Science and Technology

Committee considered that at least there should be additional scientific and technical assistance for collating background information. Both Committees, however, made effective use of specialist assistants appointed for the appropriate period.

The problem of staff was a serious one and in 1968 it was raised in somewhat dramatic fashion by Sir Barnett Cocks, Clerk to the House of Commons, before the sub-committee of the Science and Technology Committee which was investigating coastal pollution. Evidence published on 25 June disclosed that he accused the Treasury, through the presence of the Chancellor of the Exchequer on the House of Commons Offices Commission, of dominating decisions about staff made by the latter body. Dr David Owen considered it to be 'an intolerable situation whereby we can have a Government Department in effect limiting the scope and power and effectiveness of any select committee that might be established'.

Brief reference must be made to the conclusions and recommendations of the Specialised Committees. The Agriculture Committee was satisfied that the Ministry of Agriculture had done its work thoroughly and had made a solid assessment of the position. It wondered, however, whether the Ministry had sufficient information about the flexibility of Common Market agricultural policy in practice. The Minister, in debate, replied that no statement could be made about the Government's negotiating objectives in relation to the flexibility of application of policy; if officials had ventured opinions about the extent of such flexibility they would have been pre-judging not only the statement of the Government's objectives but also the outcome of the negotiations. This would seem to provide an apt example of the point at which probing must stop short of policy, at least with respect to matters still under consideration. The only other substantial complaint was that of inadequate consultations with other interested bodies in the United Kingdom. The Minister replied that the bodies concerned, such as the National Farmers Union, had expressed satisfaction with the degree of consultation.

The Science and Technology Committee had more substantive recommendations to make. We shall concern ourselves with only the more important. At the time of the Report there were four bodies concerned with nuclear power: three commercial consortia, each able to design and construct complete power stations, and the Atomic Energy Authority, which designed the reactors around which the stations were built and licensed the consortia to use its designs. The Committee recommended the phasing out of the consortium system of tendering and the putting together of the whole design function into one group—probably to be dominated or eventually absorbed by the A.E.A. The Minister of Technology, however, adopted what was in effect a minority and largely Conservative recommendation, namely two reactor design groups. The Committee's recommendation for a new British publicly-owned company for fuel supply and manufacturing was, however, accepted. In addition, something akin to another proposal of the Committee was accepted, in the form of an Atomic Energy Board, including the A.E.A., the design companies, the fuel company and the generating boards, responsible for research and development, export promotion, etc. On the more 'political' side, the Minister refused to accept, at least for the time being, either a technical assessment unit to advise the Government on the merits and prospects of particular projects, or a body like the U.S. Joint Congressional Committee with expert staff to deal with all matters of energy policy: these would infringe the responsibility of the Minister of Power.

We are not concerned with the technical aspects of these differences of opinion. But a point raised in *The Times* on 23 July 1968 is important. 'It would surely be intolerable', a leading article suggested, 'if Ministers were to be rigidly bound by [the] recommendations of Select Committees.' The Committee was overruled, the article continued, because it had not given sufficient weight to the evidence in favour of competition. It is difficult to dissent from the view that the Government must reserve the right of final decision. Yet, if specialist committees are to feel that their work is worthwhile, it might also be argued that they should be given all the evidence on which the final decision is taken and also the reasons for the rejection of any recommendation—preferably before the decision is announced in the House. In the context of the above problem, it may be suggested that the Minister might have met the Committee again after he had taken further advice.

One important aspect of this affair is that the Committee divided on party lines. True, the Chairman considered that the Press had exaggerated the extent of such division; he pointed out that even on the division about future structure one Labour M.P. had abstained and one Liberal had voted with the majority. Overall, he claimed, there had been a high degree of agreement. The Minister of Technology commented that a Committee ought not to be frightened of having a division if disagreements about policy arose in discussion. The Study of Parliament Group witnesses to the Select Committee on Procedure had expressed the opinion that a committee which divided on party lines might lack influence. In *Reforming the Commons*, however, the Group pointed out that even a divided committee sifts and publishes evidence and that the record of the examination of witnesses may sometimes be of more value than a 'committee view'. Did the Committee's Report lose influence because of a division on this matter? Even if it did, was its work worthwhile because of the facts and opinions which it elicited? A tentative answer to the first question is 'no'; to the second, a rather firmer 'yes'.

The Reports and Debates provide some interesting views on the role of Specialised Committees. Mr Wedgwood Benn's comment during the Science and Technology Debate emphasised one important aspect. To have a debate, he said, where one knew that almost every Member who wished to speak had engaged in serious study and had contributed his thought and knowledge to the publication of a basic document on which the House could debate these matters was quite unparalleled in parliamentary history. Rejecting the charge that Ministers had compelled the Committee to choose a particular subject, he emphasised that the work of the Committee had been of enormous help to Ministers and was not merely an opportunity for Ministers to influence Parliament through a Committee. M.P.s had discovered what was going on and the Report had contributed a great deal to changing the atmosphere of discussions.

211

The Agriculture Committee pointed out that Government Departments had published nothing on possible entry to the E.E.C. except a paper about its legal implications. 'It is perhaps doubtful', the Report stated, 'whether (the publication of its effects on agriculture, food and fisheries) would have happened if they had not been appointed.' In the Debate, Mr John Mackintosh asserted that the Committee had provided 'a method of opening up a discussion on policy'. 'These Committees,' he said, 'are the one effective agency out of the whole gamut of Parliamentary Reform left to back benchers.'

In the Science and Technology Debate Mr Palmer, Chairman, asserted that it was definitely the business of the Committee to help in the formulation of public policy. 'This system of detailed parliamentary enquiry will be extended in future, I believe, by the House as part of the whole business of modernising Parliament and providing more effective public accountability.' 'People said that the House of Commons was now so thin because too many people were investigating too many things or debating too many Committee stages upstairs,' remarked Sir I. Orr-Ewing: but 'How else would Parliament provide the checks and balances on programmes of this importance?' Mr Brian Parkyn added that for any satisfactory type of accountability, the House must have specialised committees to probe in depth. Mr Airey Neave considered that the work so far done had been a vindication of the specialised committee system. Finally, Mr Stephen Hastings thought that the Committees would be more effective in proportion to the extent that they concerned themselves with current policy and with future achievement rather than with what had happened in the past.

The two Committees were reappointed for the Session 1967–68. The Agriculture Committee decided to enquire into the Ministry's assessment of food requirements over the next few years; into how far it would be both practicable and in the national interest to increase the proportion of production from home sources; and into the methods of ascertaining costs of production, returns to producers, and all matters relevant thereto.[10] The Science and Technology Committee

10. First Special Report, 1967–68. 31 Jan. 1968, 110.

decided to enquire into the system for the proper and effective use of qualified scientists and engineers and of resources for (a) defence needs, (b) defence procurement, and (c) the broader needs of the national economy.[11] A third Committee, on Education and Science, decided to enquire into H.M. Inspectorate.[12] Compared with the subjects chosen by the other two Committees, this was a cautious choice, partly dictated by the late setting-up of this Committee. Only one general criticism of the Department emerged: it had failed sufficiently to appreciate the effect upon H.M. Inspectorate of the growth of the local inspectorates, the development of the Schools Council, and the enhanced status of the teaching profession. At the time of writing the Report has not been debated.

In November 1968, the Education and Science Committee decided to investigate a much more controversial subject, staff-student relations in universities and other institutions of higher education; and the Science and Technology Committee was re-appointed to continue its work. The Agriculture Committee, however, continued to be a subject of controversy. At the beginning of the 1968–69 session an attempt was made to wind it up by 31 December 1968, on the grounds that Members wished to examine other Departments and that it was impossible to retain 'Agriculture' while manning additional committees. In the event the Committee was allowed to continue until the end of February 1969; its main Report was published on 5 March 1969. A further set-back to the idea of continuity occurred on 17 December 1968 when the Education Committee was informed that its life too would be limited. On this occasion Mr Peart distinguished between subject committees, which might be continuous, and departmental committees, whose work should be brief so that as many Departments as possible could be covered. To succeed the Agriculture Committee he later announced the appointment of a Committee on Overseas Aid and Development. In addition, a Committee on Scottish Affairs was set up.

Another interesting committee is that on Race Relations and Immigration. Although it is too early to comment in

11. Second Special Report, 1967–68. 14 Feb. 1968, 124.
12. First Special Report, 1967–68. 27 Feb. 1968, 142; and Report 400–1, 24 July 1968.

detail on its work, three particular features may be mentioned. Firstly, it was set up on departmental initiative by the Home Secretary and therefore had at least initial ministerial good-will to help it on its way. So far, Departments appear to have been very co-operative. Secondly, the Committee is specifically enjoined to review *policy* with regard to race relations and immigration. Thirdly—and here the Education and Science Committee behaved similarly—in its first enquiry into 'the problems of coloured school leavers' the Committee took a great deal of direct evidence at local level from teachers, employers, trade unionists, local authorities and above all from coloured parents and youngsters.

It is convenient at this point to refer to a new and perhaps unexpected centre of disquiet about the activities of specialised committees. The local authority associations expressed alarm at the way in which the Education and Science Committee made enquiries on the spot about students and their relationship with institutions run by local education authorities, and especially about the holding of public sittings. They also directed criticism, on similar grounds, at the local activities of the Committee on Race Relations and Immigration. The *Municipal Review* (March 1969) suggested that 'where then Parliament stands, particularly in the way of creating for Members with no Departmental responsibility opportunities to enquire into the activities of individual local authorities, is far from clear. Constitutionally, until now, it always seems to have been clear enough but . . . concern . . . has been aroused and the activities and procedures of Select Committees are seen to be matters needing clarification and consideration.'

There are a number of points arising from an examination of the first two years' working of specialised committees to be considered before attempting to assess their likely future. Clearly, the problem of manning is a key factor. The average attendance at three selected Royal Commissions was 78, 74 and 68 per cent respectively. Average attendance at the Agriculture Committee has been 50 per cent, at the Education Committee 66 per cent and at the Science and Technology Committee 70 per cent. (Average attendance in the same sessions for the Estimates Committee was 36 per cent—and lower for its sub-committees.) There have been difficulties in getting and keeping a quorum. One reason for this is the very large increase in the number of committee sittings: for standing committees from 234 in 1964 to 327 in 1968; for select committees from 240 to 539. One possible remedy is smaller committees: perhaps from 10 to 12 members would be sufficient. They should certainly sit on Mondays and Fridays, even if the more drastic remedy of adjourning the House on one or two days a week is at present unlikely to commend itself.

The fact has to be faced that more than 100 Government Members and over 40 Opposition frontbench Members do not serve on specialist committees. This leaves nearly 500 Members, of which not more than 300 appear to make themselves available. Figures relating to standing committees show that in 1966–67 550 M.P.s, including Ministers, were summoned to such committees. 187 of these attended between 0 and 5 meetings; 88 between 6 and 10. The *Economist* commented: 'These figures suggest that the real cause of the trouble is the old one—that less than half the House carries the main parliamentary work burden of the whole.'

It has been suggested that since on the Government side over 100 of the most able men become Ministers, it has been difficult to find good Chairmen. Perhaps, following the example of the Public Accounts Committee, it may not be necessary always to have a Government backbench Chairman. Moreover, it would seem unnecessary to insist that Chairmen should always have had many years' experience of the House. Good men might make able Chairmen after only two years' experience.

The argument over the continuance of the Agriculture Committee and of the Education Committee raises an important point of principle. Members wished to examine other Departments, it was asserted, and it was impossible to man additional committees. Yet it seems desirable to plan ahead; given a short life, a committee is likely to bite off more than it can chew and to proliferate sub-committees dealing with different subjects. Perhaps nine or ten committees, with no sub-committees, would be preferable. There are strong arguments, also, for making these permanent, not sessional committees. Their reports tend to come at the same time and therefore to make less impact on the House. The subject-matter of their enquiries does not always fit into one session. There is also a waste of time at the beginning of the session before the committee is set up. This also means delay in calling for reports from Departments.

Relations with Departments are an important key to future success. Some civil servants may still suspect specialised committees. Yet more help is needed from the Departments—on which specialised committees already impose a large additional burden of work. At times, information has been extracted only with difficulty and seldom are possible alternative policies or decisions which may have been considered by Departments disclosed. There is some feeling that Ministers' contributions are not much more illuminating.

Subject committees, it has been suggested, might create less bad feeling on the part of Departments; narrow issues would be avoided and the burden of work spread. But it would seem a pity to abandon the departmental basis altogether, important though 'across the board' investigations may also be.

Finally, what validity is there in the argument that committees keep the House better informed? If we judge purely by debates in the House, the answer would appear to be 'not much'. Attendance is low when Reports are debated. On 25 May 1968, the Science and Technology Report was discussed by 17 M.P.s of whom 11 were Committee Members, 2 Ministers, and only 4 'outsiders'. (On an Estimates Committee Report, debate 'collapsed' at 9.30 p.m. and on a P.A.C. Report at 8.30 p.m.!) However, the fact that the Reports are available for reading and debate in the House is not the only measure of their significance. Indeed, some evidence has been used effectively both by Ministers and Members in other than 'set-piece' debates on the Reports themselves. Moreover, with greater specialisation on the part of M.P.s there will inevitably be less general interest in the House. The case for or against specialised committees closely hinges on this very point.

To reach a final verdict on the future of specialised committees at the end of two sessions is impossible. Firstly, the experiment has been under way for less than three years and in a limited fashion. Even if there were agreement that the first committees had worked well, there would still remain the broader problem as to whether the system can be extended so as to cover the whole field of administration, as advocated by the Study of Parliament Group. This is particularly important with regard to, for example, Defence and Foreign Affairs where, unless the present tendency to 'spill over into policy' is accepted, the exercise might be sterile. A second difficulty arises from the fact that criticism of the new Committees is inextricably bound up with criticism of other procedural novelties. Most critics regard the creation of specialised committees as part of a package deal which includes, among its other unpleasant features, morning sittings, taking the Finance Bill upstairs, and the proliferation of standing committees.

Among informed commentators, however, there appears to be general agreement that the experiment with specialised committees should be continued and, indeed, extended. Mr David Wood reported that none of the M.P.s involved in the new Committees wanted the innovation to suffer. Their criticism is not that the Executive set them a pointless job to keep them out of mischief but that, having allowed back-benchers to get more closely to grips with departmental policy and policy-makers, it has provided them with no opportunity to put their work to use—a reference to the long delay in debating the Reports. Mr Trethowan has repeated the 'simple case' for specialised committees: the Floor of the House no longer provides adequate opportunity for detailed investigation, since government action covers too wide an area and the issues are too complex. The first two specialised committees, in his view, had done useful work, but the whole experiment was 'at the cross-roads'. Clearly, they should cover every area of policy but without further reform this would pose 'intolerable strain'.

To relieve this, two suggestions have been made. The first is that the Committees deal also with legislation and thus enable standing committees to be abolished. This requires detailed research into the proper procedure for the Committee stage of Bills. The Study of Parliament Group suggested that the specialised committees might form the nucleus of standing committees, but this would not go so far to relieve the strain on Members. The second suggestion is that the House as such should not meet on one day a week. S.O. No. 10 already provides for this; Sir Edward Fellowes suggested it and the author wholeheartedly agrees. A further suggestion, from the *Economist*, is that investigating committees should be Joint Committees of both Houses. This must clearly await reform of the House of Lords.

Mr John Mackintosh has used *The Times* to repeat his arguments in the House in favour of specialist committees. He argued the case for a Finance and Taxation Specialised Committee, which would form the nucleus of the Finance Bill Committee. He would also add committees on foreign affairs and economic policy, arguing also that such committees would be immediately oversubscribed. And, he considers that the threat to close down existing committees and substitute others would defeat the original purpose of ensuring that continuity which would permit the acquisition of knowledge of a particular Department.

The Agriculture Committee in a special Report (HC 138 Session 1968–69) strongly condemned the decision to abolish it. There was no evidence, the Report complained, that the Government considered the Committee's opinions nor that it was aware of points of view other than those of the Ministry and the producers' organisations. On procedure, it suggested that specialised committees might be used as the core of standing committees on appropriate bills and might also play a role in examining the background to proposed new legislation and delegated legislation. Above all, specialised committees should have a measure of permanence; to wind them up after a session or two was destructive of the purpose of gaining a body of expertise, while the uncertainty inhibited any rational planning. *The Times* (13 March 1969) commented that the reasons for treating the Agriculture Committee the way it was treated were so unconvincing as to nourish the suspicion that the Committee was being put down because it was doing its investigatory job too well. In such conditions the 'conscious attempt to revive back-benchers' powers of surveillance over government administration and to enlarge their influence in the forming of policy' could not succeed.

In an investigation conducted on behalf of the Study of Parliament Group it was revealed that just over two-thirds of a sample of 111 M.P.s approved of the new specialist committees, though whereas two-fifths favoured a general extension to all Government Departments, between one-quarter and one-third favoured only a limited extension. The latter appear to be worried about the effective manning of committees and thought that a check on the administration would be closer if confined to relatively small areas. The same study reveals that in general there is greater support among Labour than among Conservative M.P.s and that the former are also more likely to favour a general extension of the committee system. Not surprisingly, among all M.P.s there is greater support from those with less than 13 years' service than from those with 13 years or more. Significantly, no frontbench spokesman in the sample was strongly against specialist committees. The authors of the review are probably right in their opinion that the movement in favour of such committees is far more likely to founder because the various supporters do not agree on what form they should take than because of a numerically large opposition to them.

Assuming that the system continues, it seems clear that while the specialised committees must deal with detailed matters of administration, they must also not be too chary of 'spilling over' into policy. The Fulton Committee had some interesting comments to make on this. The Committee 'noted the potential significance of the development of the new specialised Parliamentary Committees' and hoped that these would 'enable M.P.s to be more closely associated with the major business of government and administration ... We hope, too,' it continued, 'that their consultations with departments will increasingly include civil servants below the level of Permanent Secretary. It would be deeply regrettable, however, if these committees became an additional brake on the administrative process. We hope, therefore, that in developing this closer association with departments, Parliament will concentrate on matters of real substance, and take fully into account the cumulative cost (not only in time but in the quality of administration) that the raising of minutiae imposes upon them.'[13] Perhaps most significant were the views of a group of Members of the First Division of the Civil Service.[14] They

13. Vol. I, para. 281.
14. Vol. 5(2), Memo No. 128, pp. 906 et seq.

praised the current development of parliamentary select committees as a step in the direction of providing more information and knowledge of the way in which it was analysed by the Government. They would also provide safeguards against abuses in the execution of policy.

But will the political lead in this direction be forthcoming? Two widely different interpretations of current progress and future prospects have been offered by Alfred Morris M.P.[15] and John Mackintosh M.P.,[16] and these merit some consideration. The former is optimistic. He mentions the strengthening of the role of the Nationalised Industries Committee, the establishment of an Overseas Aid and Development Committee and of a Scottish Affairs Committee, together with the Committee on Race Relations and Immigration and that on the Parliamentary Commissioner—in addition to the Committees discussed in detail in this chapter. 'This record is surely not at all bad for a Government most of whose members are alleged to have wanted to continue their work unfettered by any increase in parliamentary scrutiny.' He appears to approve Mr Crossman's view that departmental probes were intended to last for only one parliamentary session, though he makes no reference to Mackintosh's report that in discussions with Labour M.P.s interested in parliamentary reform, Mr Crossman explained that 'he hoped to set up two more departmental committees each year until all domestic policy was subject to scrutiny and the last and most difficult hurdle was reached, the creation of foreign affairs and defence committees'. He rejects suggestions that 'certain Ministers' were hostile to committees and that Mr Peart had tried to 'pack' the Agriculture Committee. Nor does he accept that civil servants are hostile to the idea of committees.

Mackintosh, on the other hand, regards the winding-up of various committees as denoting a changed attitude to parliamentary reform. The Scottish Affairs Committee is 'simply to give the Government something to point to when attacked by Nationalists', while Overseas Aid is 'in Whitehall terms a peripheral and quite unimportant department'. The Committees on Race Relations and on the Parliamentary Com-

15. *Sunday Times*, 16 Feb. 1969.
16. *The Times*, 13 March 1969.

missioner 'are not performing the main task of scrutinising sections of Whitehall'. The result is that 'instead of ending this Parliament with an established range of investigatory committees covering the key sectors of internal administration and with a solid body of Labour and Conservative M.P.s convinced by experience of the value of this work, an incoming government will inherit a run-down experiment which, if its leaders so desire, can be quietly dropped'. The House of Commons, it appears, cannot reform itself, 'since the Cabinet can set up or sack committees and decide who will or will not be members'.

Those concerned to see continuous reform of parliamentary procedure and, in particular, to develop effective specialist committees must to some extent share Mackintosh's disappointment, without necessarily endorsing all his opinions or his deductions from facts which are clearly in dispute between him and at least one other M.P. Nevertheless, some progress has been made in the face of considerable practical difficulties.

Less than three years' experience of specialist committees, then, would seem to suggest that the experiment, if not as bold as many hoped, has not been insignificant. Given the attitude of large numbers of M.P.s, both frontbench and backbench, of civil servants, of academics and of journalists, it does not appear likely that the whole machinery will be abandoned. Certainly this is not the impression to be gained from some ministerial remarks made during the debate on the Consolidated Fund (No. 2) Bill on 25 March 1969.

On this occasion the case for a Select Committee on Defence was presented by Mr Julian Ridsdale and supported by others. In reply, Mr John Silkin made some general observations of real importance. He reviewed the history of such committees and took credit for the establishment of seven new Select Committees in under three years. 'When one considers the request . . . for a Select Committee on Defence', he said, 'the Government must also take into account requests for other Select Committees.' Suggestions had been made for Welsh affairs, economic affairs, trade and industry, the status and development of Her Majesty's Government's Dependencies Overseas, pre-legislation, statute law repeal, Members' outside interests, the rights and obligations of women in a free society—and 16 specific short-term committees on information leaks!

Mr Silkin pointed out that not every M.P. was convinced that the select committee was the best way of considering our affairs. But even if it were accepted that the right evolution was towards a greater number of such committees, it was to be done 'in the correct manner'. He referred again to problems of staffing, both by M.P.s and by Clerks. He mentioned complaints about overwork on committees, including standing committees. Finally, 'the time has come for the Government to take stock of this whole experiment, for experiment it was, of Select Committees. I hope that the House will never abandon Select Committees. Indeed, I doubt whether it ever could. This idea has gripped the consciousness and general fibre of Parliament today, and Parliament would be a very much poorer institution without Select Committees. But the House must consider . . . the experiment as a whole . . .'

What is the likely outcome of such consideration?

Addendum

Since this chapter was written the Select Committee on Procedure has reported on *Scrutiny of Public Expenditure and Administration* (1968–69, 23 July 1969, 410). Reference is made to this Report elsewhere in the book. But it is important to examine briefly the possible consequences of its implementation for existing and future specialised committees. The Report notes that these committees can conduct extensive enquiries into a Department or subject, but 'do not appear to have attempted to scrutinise the process of Government expenditure'; further, they have depleted the membership of the Estimates Committee and reduced the scope of its examination of departmental spending. The conclusion is that 'the existing system of select committees for scrutinising policy and its execution is at present inadequate for the functions set out' in the Report. Specifically, a committee investigating the activities of a particular Department is inhibited from pursuing enquiries into activities of Departments other than that to which its order of reference restricts it. There is also uncertainty as to the length of life of specialised committees.

Little objection can be taken to the specific proposals of the Procedure Committee for a Select Committee on Expenditure, operating through a general sub-committee and eight functional sub-committees. But the proposed terms of reference suggest that much of what is being done by specialised committees might be lost if they ceased to exist, or if the terms of reference of the functional sub-committees were not extended. These latter would 'consider the activities of Departments of State concerned with (a functional field of administration) and the Estimates of their expenditure presented to this House; and examine the efficiency with which they are administered'.

As to the specialised committees, the Report recommends that 'the House should decide on their future in the light of this Report and as the occasion arises'. It is to be hoped that the House will realise the importance of the 'forays' made into policy by these committees from time to time and of the public examination of Ministers and civil servants, as well as of the proposed 'pre-legislation' function of such committees. Control of expenditure is vital. Influence over policy, however, seems to this writer to be a *prior* consideration. If it be argued that the two cannot be separated, the case for wider terms of reference is the stronger.

Chapter 11

Select Committees as Tools of Parliamentary Reform

Nevil Johnson

The discussion of parliamentary reform which got under way in the early 'sixties had two main facets. One was concerned with how to modernise procedure so that certain kinds of business—predominantly Government business as it later proved to be might be dealt with more expeditiously. The other was concerned with how to strengthen the House of Commons in relation to the Government of the day. In this part of the argument it was the select committee which got most attention. Similarly, it was the select committee which stood out most prominently in the programme of reforms which the present Government began to implement in 1966–67, though this is certainly not to say that the Government itself attached most importance to this particular element in its package deal. But in a manner which is comparatively rare it seemed that those who had long argued the theory of parliamentary reform by regeneration of the committee system had at last won over the practising politicians: here was a chance to see whether the theory would work.

The aim of these remarks is twofold. First, I want to outline the main features of select committee development since 1966; second, I want to consider why the changes have had such a modest impact, so modest that it is no exaggeration to say that the effort to strengthen and diversify select committee scrutiny now shows signs of petering out. But before coming to these matters it is worth looking back to the terms in which the argument for parliamentary reform was cast, at any rate insofar as it affected committees.

For many a long year those concerned with the position of Parliament had talked in terms of the declining power of

Parliament. They feared 'the passing of Parliament',[1] protested against the impotence of the Commons and bewailed the relentless advance of the administrative state. Admittedly when the current phase of the reform argument got going some tried to escape from the equation of power. Professor Crick, for example, denied that Parliament had ever in modern times had much 'power', and based his plea for a new structure of committees of administrative scrutiny on the argument that control of the activities of the Executive can only mean influence through access to public opinion.[2] No doubt this justification for extending the activity of committees of mainly administrative inquiry has to be seen in relation to his wider argument that in the present state of party politics in this country the House of Commons should no longer be seen as an institution directly affecting the position or fate of Governments: it has become an instrument through which a continuous (and necessarily discordant) appeal is made to the sovereign electorate. This is not the place to examine the validity of this view of the role of the House of Commons as a platform for an unending electoral campaign. What is relevant here is that this theory of the uses of select committees can be sustained only if it is backed by a more convincing anatomy of 'public opinion' in present-day society than either Crick or other exponents of the case have so far provided, and by some explanation of the network of communication and response inside and outside of Government through which the presumed influence of investigating committees secures particular results. Public opinion is an elusive concept: an analysis of it might, for example, lead us to the conclusion that there are numerous and competing 'public opinions', and that the diverse interests expressed by them are in no way related either to the pattern or functions of existing select committees.[3]

1. *The Passing of Parliament* was the title of a book by Professor G. W. Keeton, published in London in 1952.
2. Bernard Crick, *The Reform of Parliament* (1st Edn, London, 1964). See particularly pp. 77 and 199.
3. Public opinion has often been invoked in the discussion of the role of Parliament. This is reasonable, but is unfortunate that the concept has so rarely been analysed. For some of the difficulties in a foreign context, see Jürgen Habemas, *Struckturwandel der Offentlichkeit* (3rd Edn. Luchterhand, 1968).

C.T.—H

In the end those who argued that more select committees = more access to public opinion = more control of the Executive by Parliament could offer little more than an act of faith in support of this contention. They had to postulate that Ministers and Departments as well as other types of public agency would gradually recognise that their interest lay in co-operating more closely with the new and specialised committees of scrutiny because those bodies gained strength from accessibility to and perhaps even an appeal to 'public opinion'.

There are, however, other questions to be raised when assessing the recent developments in select committees. The case just outlined for more committees assumed without question the need of Members of Parliament for more information if they are to scrutinise effectively the affairs of Government. It has been widely accepted that the power of the Executive has increased not just because of the growing number of issues on which the Government is expected to take decisions, but because the processes of decision-making have become too inaccessible to parliamentarians. The superiority of information possessed by the Executive and its ability to withhold this information from Parliament means that Members can neither accurately foresee what issues are coming up for decision, nor make known in reasoned terms their own opinions and preferences before decisions are taken. A strengthening of select committees was intended to help remedy this situation. Thus a primary function of such committees was seen to be that of inquiry, eliciting information upon which reasoned criticism and recommendations might be based. This approach was not, of course, new. The rationale of the Public Accounts Committee, the Estimates Committee and the Nationalised Industries Committee is to some extent simply that they make information available which would otherwise not be there. What stands out in the re-assertion of the value of information as the justification for major extensions of select committee scrutiny is that the whole matter was seen so abstractly. Very few attempts were made to work out how additional flows of information might be related to parliamentary functions or powers, still less to specific stages of governmental activity. (After all the Public Accounts Committee and the Estimates Committee have some link, even if tenuous, with certain events in the cycle of Government business.) Instead the production of more information was seen almost as an end in itself: information was good and would change the environment in which the Executive operates, would somehow or other render Ministers more sensitive to Members' views and enable the latter to interpose their opinions' more frequently before decisions were taken.

Two other aspects of the case for more select committees deserve special mention. One was the argument that they would facilitate more specialisation amongst Members: small groups would become more knowledgeable and, again it was supposed, more influential in virtue of this fact. Second, it was hoped that the committees would be allowed to range more freely and to raise in a manner previously denied to them 'questions of policy'. This was to be reflected in the orders of reference of the new committees.

It follows from all this that, in looking at the extension of select committee activity during the last few years, we do need to consider whether there is much evidence that it has at least initiated a greater degree of specialisation amongst Members. Equally one has to ask whether the broader terms of reference have really opened the door to more challenging or more penetrating inquiries than are practicable, for example, for the Estimates and Public Accounts Committees with their formal exclusion from the area of policy. Finally—and this is an issue to which I will return towards the end of these remarks—we need to consider whether recent experience of select committees does lend support to this argument about the persuasive and cumulative influence of information on the decisions of Government. Perhaps the connection between more information and more influence or even power is far less direct than some have assumed.

Let us now consider briefly how in the past three years the select committee system has been modified and what select committees have been doing. It seems convenient to distinguish four main areas of activity and development. First, the experiment with a subject committee; second, the development of departmental committees; third, thee mergence of two new committees linked with specific institutional and legal developments outside Parliament; and finally the continuing work of the older, well-established select committees.

When the original decisions to introduce new and more specialised committees were taken the distinction between subject and departmental committees was shadowy. Indeed many participants in the debates about committees obviously did not appreciate that such a distinction could be made. In logical terms the distinction remains shadowy, but it has assumed a certain pragmatic clarity as well as practical importance in the Government's approach to the future pattern of committee activity. A subject committee seems now to be regarded as a body which may specialise permanently in examining activities whose common characteristics are defined in terms of method rather than purpose or function. The one example so far of such a committee is that on Science and Technology which is entitled to examine any matters involving a large measure of scientific and technical research and development.[4] The curious thing is that it is not easy to envisage other examples of subject committees in this peculiar sense of the term. Could one seriously imagine a committee for social science, or for law? The fact is that Science and Technology as a subject designation has no coherent logical basis. But it does satisfy the widespread belief that Government and Parliament should pay more attention to activities in which scientific and technical factors are dominant, it seems to require from Members a degree of subject specialisation which need not be linked too closely with concentration on any particular functions of Government, and it beckons towards looking at activities which prima facie can be examined without too close an involvement in controversial party political arguments.

4. The Science and Technology Committee was set up on 14 December 1966, its order of reference being simply 'to consider Science and Technology and to report thereon'. In the Second Special Report, 1966–67 (H.C. 351) the Committee interpreted its order of reference to mean that it should examine scientific and technological expenditure, together with skilled manpower involved in both the public and private sectors, examine the relative merits of priorities and discover whether value for money is obtained. There seems to be a close resemblance in this gloss to the order of reference of the Estimates Committee as that is in practice interpreted.

On performance so far the Science and Technology committee has shown itself to be reasonably successful. Its membership has been stable and a fairly high proportion of its 20 Members have experience of scientific and technical problems. Equally important has been the care and discretion which the committee has shown in selecting subjects for enquiry. Whilst it has not shied away from important topics, it has shown a preference for weightiness and substance before political glamour. Thus its first major theme was the Nuclear Reactor Programme[5] and its second defence research.[6] In addition the committee has at the request of the Government inquired into coastal pollution (following the Torrey Canyon disaster), reporting late in the 1967–68 session,[7] and on its own initiative enquired briefly into the development of carbon fibres early in 1969.

It is still too early to reach firm conclusions on the success or otherwise of this one experiment with a subject committee. The first major report from the committee was a valuable contribution to the analysis of the problems of the nuclear power industry and its programme, though some of the principal proposals relative to the organisational pattern of the industry were not in the end accepted by the Government. Generally the quality of the committee's published findings has been high, resembling in style and tone the reports of the Nationalised Industries and the Estimates Committee. The Committee appears too to have been successful in avoiding serious conflicts with the Departments which helps to explain the assumption, which the Government has not challenged, that this subject Committee will be 'permanent'. And as far as specialisation goes there is no doubt that this Committee has both encouraged and facilitated specialisation

5. Report on the United Kingdom Nuclear Reactor Programme, 1966–67. H.C. 381–XVII. See also especially for this Report, R. Williams, 'The Select Committee on Science and Technology'. *Public Administration*, Autumn 1968.

6. The Report of the Science and Technology Committee on Defence Research (1968–69: H.C. 213) came out after this paper had been written. Unfortunately it has not been possible to take account of this, though it appears that the character of this inquiry and report lends support to the evaluation of this Committee offered here.

7. Report on Coastal Pollution, 1967–68. H.C. 421.

by a group of Members who are seriously interested in scientific questions.

When we turn to the departmental committees the position is different. Though there is some reason to believe that the then Leader of the House of Commons, Mr R. H. S. Crossman, regarded these as both 'departmental' and 'subject' committees,[8] it is the former attribute which has steadily received more emphasis, and in a special sense. A departmental committee is to be defined in terms of its concentration on the functions of a particular department, but also, and perhaps more importantly, in terms of its 'non-permanence'. It has come to be considered as a committee concerned with a particular area of activity, broadly identified with the responsibilities of a Department of State, which after a short life ceases to exist and is replaced by another similar committee dedicated to another departmental field. The first of such departmental committees was that on Agriculture (in England and Wales) which was brought to an end in February 1969 after operating for barely two years. The second departmental committee was on Education and Science, that is to say on the work of the department of the same name. This too is now expected to vanish at the end of the 1968–69 session despite the fact that it has protested against its relegation to the departmental category.[9] To replace these Committees a group on Scottish affairs was set up (which for special reasons may hope for a modest degree of 'permanence'[10]) and one on Overseas Aid (a topic recently examined competently by the Estimates Committee[11]) has been promised.

Clearly these experiments have been somewhat confusing and disappointing. Committees of such short duration cannot

8. When the Education and Science Committee was set up Mr Crossman suggested that it was both departmental and subject. He also showed a preference for subject committees, remarking that 'it is arguable that subject committees are on the whole better and easier to work'. This enigmatic remark was not amplified. H.C. Debates, 22 Feb. 1968 Col. 791.

9. See Third Special Report, 1968–69: H.C. 103, for the Committee's reaction to its classification as a temporary departmental committee.

10. For order of reference see First Special Report of Select Committee on Scottish Affairs, 1968–69. H.C. 178.

11. Seventh Report of the Estimates Committee, 1967–68. H.C. 442.

facilitate any serious specialisation on the part of Members, and they are hardly likely to reach a stage of development at which the relevant Departments will regard them as more than minor irritants. Nor has the actual output so far of these departmental committees been such as to inspire confidence. The Agriculture committee (which was rapidly expanded to 25 members, thus making it an unwieldy body) started off with a somewhat imprudent choice of subject, the effectiveness of the Ministry of Agriculture's analysis of the implications for British agriculture of going into the E.E.C. The findings,[12] whilst voluminous, were anodyne, and, as events turned out, had no practical significance. Its next choice was also on a rather grand scale, the Ministry of Agriculture's assessment of food requirements for the next few years, with particular reference to the practicability of increasing home production. Working with two sub-committees the Committee produced a modest report on Horticulture and a slender note on Fisheries.[13] The work on Horticulture was in any case duplicating to some extent work carried out by the Economic Development Council for the industry, which reported in detail in 1968 on agriculture's import-saving role. The rest of the inquiry had to be hastened to a conclusion so that a report could be produced before the Committee was dissolved.[14] This came out strongly in favour of policies designed to raise agricultural output to a level which would permit import substitution rather than merely keep pace with the rise in home demand.

The Education and Science Committee started off more modestly, devoting its attention to the Inspectorate of Schools in England and Wales, and in Scotland. Very little came out of these enquiries—there was perhaps little to discover—and the Committee then turned to student–staff relations in institutions of higher education. It hopes too to examine the provision for the training of teachers, if spared long enough. Though the Committee has not so far reported on staff–

12. H.C. 378, 1966–67.
13. H.C. 445, 1967–68 on Horticulture, and on Fisheries: third Special Report of the Agriculture Committee, 1967–68. H.C. 309.
14. The Agriculture Committee's final substantive Report, 1968–69, no title, is contained in H.C. 137, and its parting protest at dissolution in the Special Report, H.C. 138.

student relations, the published reports of its open hearings clearly indicate the pitfalls of such a topic. The broader and more 'political' the theme, the greater is the risk that a committee simply becomes involved in general talk: it lacks the focus and the discipline which are present when the subject of inquiry is a specific departmental activity on which those actually responsible must deliver detailed evidence. It might also be thought surprising that a parliamentary committee should devote so much effort to matters for which the Government so far acknowledges no responsibility, as indeed was circuitously explained to the Committee by the permanent head of the Department of Education and Science when the proceedings opened.[15]

The reasons for the difficulties which have affected departmental committees and led to this concept of the short term transitory departmental committees are both narrowly practical, and political. Foremost amongst the practical difficulties are those of staffing. It was discovered that the staff resources of the Committee Office of the House of Commons, the availability of rooms, and even the purely technical services needed for processing committee work, were not adequate for a wide range of departmental committees, given the other new developments already in train. In short the plan for a whole bevy of specialised departmental committees which many reformers cherished, was simply not practicable without quite radical changes in staffing methods and accommodation. As early as 22 February 1968 Mr Crossman sounded a note of warning on staffing problems: these warnings were repeated a year later by his successor. Consequently the Government were faced with the choice either of giving some qualified permanence to the two first experiments with departmental committees, thus disappointing those Members who wanted to see committees on other areas of departmental activity, or of accepting overtly this doctrine of the temporary nature of departmental committees. Here no doubt political reasons combined with the practical ones in favour of the second conclusion. The departmental committee had turned out to be rather disappointing, occasionally

15. H.C. 45 (i)–(iv). Minutes of Evidence of the Education and Science Committee, 26 Nov. 1968.

troublesome as when the Agriculture Committee insisted on going to take evidence in Brussels, time-consuming, and to some extent duplicating work being done in other official bodies. To set up a new cycle of committees would effectively nip in the bud any pretensions to specialised departmental surveillance which the two first committees of this kind might have had, as well as allowing the Government to claim that it was meeting the wishes of other groups of Members. So genuine problems of servicing combined with political expediency to give the experiment with departmental committees a character which it was probably never intended to have, even by those who had always viewed it with reserve.

We now come to the third aspect of select committee development, the committees which owe their existence to extra-parliamentary innovations. There are two examples here, first the Select Committee on the Parliamentary Commissioner for Administration, and second the Committee on Race Relations and Immigration. The former follows quite clearly the precedent of the Public Accounts Committee. It receives the reports of the Parliamentary Commissioner for Administration who is an officer of Parliament, and then, guided by him, examines further such issues of importance as may arise out of his reports. Though it is too early to judge the success of either the P.C.A. or of this committee, there are grounds for assuming that the committee's most likely role will be similar to that of the Public Accounts Committee, namely to add its authority to the work of a permanent official and his staff. In one important respect, however, there is the possibility that the committee may remain in a weaker position than the P.A.C. In the second report of 1967–68 it appeared to accept that it would in general be undesirable for it to re-open and re-examine specific cases dealt with by the P.C.A.[16] It seemed to see its main task as being to enquire into remedial action taken by departments and into limitations of competence affecting the P.C.A. himself. In contrast the P.A.C. has as one of its main functions to probe further into issues already opened up and commented on by the Comptroller and Auditor General. Thus it is in a position to build on the work done by its agent and to develop further in a

16. H.C. 350, 1967–68—especially paragraph 29 of the Report.

dialogue with those actually responsible, the points of criticism which may have been suggested. It would appear that the scope for the Select Committee on the P.C.A. to operate in a similar manner is more limited, particularly as the P.C.A. has so far paid more attention in his reports to the facts of the cases examined by his office than to analysis of the grounds, legal or administrative, for the decisions complained of. There may, therefore, be a risk that the committee will find it hard to discover topics for its own hearings other than those of a narrowly procedural nature. But admittedly all this is tentative: a few more cases like that of the Sachsenhausen prisoners could push both the P.C.A. and the Select Committee in a different direction.

In some ways the Committee on Race Relations and Immigration represents a genuine innovation. Here is a committee required to review policies arising out of the operation of a specific Act of Parliament, The Race Relations Act of 1968, with particular reference to the work of the Race Relations Board and the Community Relations Commission, and to keep under review the admission of Commonwealth immigrants and aliens into the United Kingdom.[17] Potentially at any rate this is a precedent for associating future select committees with the implementation of major legislative acts. One can, however, easily see why the precedent may not prove to be compelling. Race relations is a subject which is acknowledged to be above party, or rather to raise issues on which the leaderships of the parties wish to avoid sharp controversy. For this reason there is some attraction in the scheme for having a select committee watch over the treatment of the associated problems. But in most areas of Government action and legislation the lines of party controversy are clearly drawn and it is more difficult to imagine circumstances in which a select committee would be deemed an appropriate body to review on a regular basis the implementation of specific government policies embodied in legislation.

This experiment has then a special interest because it falls outside any established categories of select committee activity. But there is as yet no basis for evaluating it, since the Committee has only recently embarked on its first inquiry. The

17. The Committee was set up in November 1968 with 16 members.

subject chosen, after taking evidence from the Home Office, was the problems of coloured school-leavers. Judging from the manner in which the Committee has so far proceeded, it appears to be pursuing the usual kind of discursive select committee inquiry. Certainly the fact that it is required to review the implementation of an Act of Parliament does not seem to have made any big difference to the technique of inquiry. Assuming that the committee survives, one can expect that it will develop as a subject committee sui generis, but will not in any significant way be different from other committees. Logically, of course, it could equally well be classified as a multi-departmental committee, geared chiefly to Home Office responsibilities, but also to the work of other departments concerned with immigrant problems.

Finally we need to pay some attention to the three main established committees.[18] On the face of the record they have continued to operate much as before. The Public Accounts Committee has issued substantial annual reports on the findings of the Comptroller and Auditor General, together with occasional special reports such as those in 1966–67 on Bristol Siddeley Engines[19] and on the extension of the C. & A.G.'s scrutiny to universities.[20] The latter resulted in a considerable extension in the range of both the C. & A.G. and of the committee. Unlike nearly all other select committees the Public Accounts Committee has declined to hold public sittings. (Perhaps its members are even mindful of the additional printing costs entailed by this procedure.) The Nationalised Industries Committee, now usually operating in two sub-committees, has maintained a steady flow of reports, amongst them the really major study of Ministerial Control of Nationalised Industries, published in the autumn of 1968.[21] The Estimates Committee has, more than the other two established committees, suffered from the competition of the new com-

18. I have deliberately excluded here the Statutory Instruments Committee on the grounds that the scrutiny it performs is of a technical kind.

19. Report on British Siddeley Engines Ltd, 1966–67, H.C. 571.

20. Report on Parliament and the Control of University Expenditure, 1966–67. H.C. 260.

21. First Report from the Select Committee on Nationalised Industries, 1967–68. H.C. 371–I.

mittees both for members and for staff. First reduced from 43 members to 36, it found its membership reduced to 33 at the beginning of the 1968–69 session. This meant that it could set up only four investigating sub-committees instead of five, and had to abandon regular consideration of Spring Supplementary Estimates. Nevertheless the output of the Committee in this period of experiment has remained impressive—fourteen reports in 1966–67 (including some carry-over from before the 1966 election), eight reports in 1967–68 and six topics under review in 1968–69. Moreover many of the topics examined have been of major importance—the European Space Vehicle Launcher Development Organisation and Space Research and Development, Government Statistical Services, The Movement of Defence Personnel and Stores, Manpower Training for Industry, the Promotion of Exports and Overseas Aid.

In quantitative as well as qualitative terms the bulk of administrative scrutiny is still being carried out by these older committees. And though they may be tied more closely to expenditure and accounts than the new committees, there is little in the outcome to show that they are significantly more restricted in the questions they raise than those committees which have been given orders of reference which are prima facie much broader. But undoubtedly the older committees all face an increasingly heavy burden, not only because other committees compete for supporting resources, but more importantly because the range of activities which prima facie might be examined has been growing at an alarming rate. As the level of expenditure has risen, so has the volume of potential audit queries; as the machinery of government has been changed and expanded to take on new functions, so there are more areas for the Estimates Committee to examine; and as the public sector of industry has grown, so has the task of the Nationalised Industries Committee become heavier. Perhaps the most interesting aspect of the latter Committee's attempt in early 1969 to bring several more state-controlled commercial bodies within its scope was not the hostility shown by the Government towards such claims,[22] but the

22. See the debate on the motion to set up the Nationalised Industries Committee. H.C. Debates, 11 Feb. 1969.

apparent reluctance of the Committee and the House to notice how the whole public sector of industry and commerce is rapidly becoming too extensive for any single committee of the House to keep watch on by traditional means. In this respect at least it is doubtful whether the Nationalised Industries Committee's proposals in their original form were best calculated to make its task any more manageable.

So much for an impressionistic survey of the main features of select committee development and activity over the past three years or so. Before turning to an assessment of the success of these experiments there are some general points about the manner in which select committees have worked and modified their procedures which need to be made. First, there can be little doubt that one of the most striking innovations carried out by nearly all committees has been the introduction of open sittings. It is important to be clear what this means: it does not mean that evidence is now published which was previously withheld.[23] It means simply that hearings are often open and a record of proceedings is published immediately rather than appearing several months later along with the report. In practice this means that there is a very modest amount of press comment on what is currently happening at committee sittings which was previously impossible. In terms of information made available, open hearings make no difference. But they may have some psychological and even political importance both for the committees and for witnesses. They suggest an effort on the part of committees to tell the world what they are doing, and for witnesses they mean that it may be more necessary to pay attention to what earlier witnesses have said (though again, it has long been normal for witnesses to be given beforehand a transcript of relevant earlier hearings). The significance of the change will emerge more clearly in the long-term. Traditionally committee sittings have been occasions for the examination in private of expert witnesses with executive responsibility (i.e. mainly

23. It is of minor interest that in its report on the effects of entering the E.E.C. the Agriculture Committee criticised the need for always having a verbatim record of hearings, and its Horticulture Sub-Committee also took evidence in private and did not report it. In the bad old days of private hearings select committees were always very punctilious about publishing a full record of their proceedings with witnesses.

officials concerned with the subject-matter of the enquiry). This has been very much a judicial procedure. The open hearing may turn into an opportunity for those who think they have something to say to come along to say it. This is more likely if committees issue open invitations asking people who have evidence to get into touch with them. If there is a transition from the judicial-style cross-examination of executive witnesses to the open hearing of interested parties who want primarily to air their views, then at the very least it is doubtful whether such a change will assist committees in the collection of accurate and relevant information. And if this happens it is bound gradually to undermine one of the few major claims which it has been possible to make on behalf of select committees, namely that they have dealt only in fully reliable information. Such authority as they have has depended to a large extent on this characteristic of their work.

Fortunately the strength of this trend must not be exaggerated. The Estimates Committee and the Nationalised Industries Committee have continued to show care in the selection of witnesses, relying primarily on those who are executively responsible. The same goes for Science and Technology. It is principally Education and Science and Race Relations and Immigration which have shown signs of moving in this direction of general public hearings at which people are present to offer opinions rather than facts.[24] Here the subjects have encouraged such a move: student relations obviously tempted the Education and Science Committee to visit universities and colleges in order to hear a wide range of witnesses; Race Relations and Immigration decided that it could look properly at the problems of coloured school-leavers only if it held hearings in particular local authorities.

Linked with the move to open hearings is the practice of

24. One consequence of public hearings by peripatetic sub-committees which nobody foresaw has been the interruption of proceedings by witnesses or spectators determined to turn the occasion into a political demonstration, as happened at Essex University on 24 April 1969 and at the London School of Economics and Political Science on 30 April. Unless the House is prepared to assert its authority to protect itself, the generalisation of this behaviour can only lead to the abandonment of public hearings, at any rate outside the Palace of Westminster.

summoning Ministers to give evidence. This has been adopted by the new committees and by the Nationalised Industries Committee. It is difficult to determine whether this step has brought substantial benefits. Theoretically it can be justified by the inclusion of policy questions in the order of reference of several committees. But in so far as policy refers to future decisions it is doubtful whether Ministers are any more willing to commit themselves than officials. And in practice policy refers more often than not to the justification of existing courses of action, and here the official has usually been no more inhibited than his political master. As against all this it can be held that the status of select committees is enhanced by the appearance before them of Ministers, and in some instances, such as the enquiry into ministerial control of nationalised industries, there can be no doubt about the practical advantages of taking evidence from Ministers.

Second, there has been a modest move by several committees towards the use of part-time specialist advisers. But valuable though this has been (e.g. in relation to the Nationalised Industries Committee's report on the Ministerial Control of Nationalised Industries) it has not led to any radical change in the manner in which committees are staffed and serviced. Essentially they have continued to depend on the overstretched resources of the Committee Office, on the competent generalists who will very often combine the secretaryship of a select committee with other duties. And on the whole there is little evidence of serious discontent by Members with this situation. This reflects the fact that it is still as hard as ever to discern what kind of specialist staffs for committees might be needed and how they would be related to the existing staffs of the House of Commons. In addition the concept of temporary departmental committees makes it even harder to envisage the direct employment by committees of persons specially qualified in their fields of investigation.

Thirdly, there is the factor of additional work imposed on Government departments and other public agencies by this expansion of committee work. Before 1964, allowing for sub-committees, there were usually about eight investigating groups at work. At the beginning of 1969 there were at least fourteen, though in some cases one could not be certain how effectively sub-committees were operating. It is impossible without prolonged research to determine quantitatively how much the sheer demand on departmental time both for oral hearings and for the preparation of papers has increased in recent years. That it has, there can be no doubt. It is usual to brush this factor aside as the price willingly to be paid for increased parliamentary scrutiny. At the same time we cannot overlook the extent to which the tasks of administration have increased, quite independently of the growth in committee activity in the House of Commons. This in turn has increased the burdens on the administrative apparatus and has complicated the problem of maintaining operational efficiency. The additional demands made by parliamentary committees— even assuming that these have no other inhibiting effects on the decision-making processes in departments—add still further to the strains imposed on an already overburdened central administration. It is true that administrative scrutiny may make a positive contribution to greater efficiency by high-lighting unsatisfactory procedures or by suggesting modifications in existing policies. But on balance the demands of committees in terms of time and effort must outweigh the gains looked at narrowly in terms of operational efficiency. At a time when we are more acutely aware than before of questions of efficiency in administration perhaps more thought needs to be given to measuring the costs of parliamentary accountability.

Finally it does not seem that the growth of committees has altered significantly the average pattern of backbench activity. Certainly the increase in committees of all kinds has increased the number of Members who are occupied upstairs,[25] and has made it steadily more difficult to man all types of committee adequately. But equally there has been no cut-back in

25. At the beginning of 1969 eight select committees of enquiry claimed 152 members (though this was not a net figure owing to a small amount of double membership). Standing Committees may require at least 200 Members at any one time; and in addition there are a number of domestic and special-purpose committees. In March 1968, for example, standing and select committees, together with one second reading committee, required 532 Members. Whether the House of Commons has adapted the programme of work on the Floor of the House to this situation is, to say the least, questionable.

the plenary sittings of the House, there are no signs of a decline in Questions and of the other means by which Members seek to pin down Ministers individually, and there are no grounds for believing that for most Members their role as a constituency grievance-man has been modified in favour of that of committee specialist. In short most Members involved in the new committee development are simply endeavouring to superimpose the extra work on to their existing roles as Members of the House. And indeed this points to a peculiar feature of the whole select committee experience, the manner in which this has always been seen as something additional to the existing workload of the House, never as at least in partial substitution for other activities which might be modified or restricted.

The reform of Parliament movement must be seen against the wider background of the critique of our institutions which has preoccupied the political and administrative world in Britain for the past five years or longer. How one judges this phase of introspective analysis and the institutional adaptation which it has inspired, depends largely on how one judges the causes of the malaise which provoked it all. If one suspects that these causes lie deep in the social and economic structure of the country, one will be correspondingly sceptical of the significance of tampering with the political and administrative superstructure. But be that as it may, it can hardly be denied that the adaptation and reform of our political institutions has been marked by a restless passion for experiment: nowhere has this been more evident than in the House of Commons. It was in keeping with this mood of experiment that, when Mr Crossman began to put through a programme of procedural innovation, the purposes of some of the proposed changes, and indeed their exact procedural shape, were not at all clearly defined. What mattered, so it seemed, was the commitment to experiment, the willingness to try various devices, and to find out by experience what they might yield (or might not yield). Not surprisingly this approach left open the possibility of continued retrospective reinterpretation by the Government of its intentions when introducing changes, and at the same time permitted Members to preserve their own varied ideas of the rationale of what was being done.

Nowhere was this lack of definition, and uncertainty, greater than in respect of select committee developments.

Though only a short time has passed since the initiation of changes under discussion here, it is perhaps long enough to justify the conclusion that the results have been meagre. Only a little has been gained in terms of the subject specialisation of Members. It remains very doubtful whether the granting to some committees of wide and untrammelled terms of reference has had a definable impact on the type of questions they can probe and more particularly on the initiatives they can take in their recommendations. We cannot seriously claim that the control or checking of the Executive by the House of Commons has been significantly strengthened. For those who saw select committees as a means of giving some power to the House, the battle has been lost yet again.[26] The Science and Technology Committee can be judged a useful and perhaps stable addition to the House's traditional means of disseminating information and opening up areas of executive activity to more informed discussion. The departmental committees have so far been a failure and if they are now to be conceived as essentially temporary and *ad hoc*, it is difficult to see how they can be taken seriously either by Departments or by Members. Of the other new committees that for the P.C.A. will in the long run stand or fall with the institution of the P.C.A. itself, whilst the Race Relations and Immigration Committee will need to tread carefully if it is to avoid introducing new elements of controversy into a field where the major political interests wish to keep the temperature down. Above all the

26. When these matters are debated in Parliament there is no doubt that many Members do cling to the belief that the crucial issue is to strengthen Parliament, to give it more powers of control. As recently as February 1969 in the debate on the motion to set up the Select Committee on Nationalised Industries—when there was a sharp clash on the scope of this Committee's investigations—we find as a persistent undercurrent the belief that select committees were there to strengthen Parliament against the executive, no less a person than the Leader of the House of Commons confessing that he spoke as, 'a consistent advocate of the need to extend Parliament's control over the executive'. It seems clear that speakers in this debate, as in others, were not thinking just in terms of some undefined influence via public opinion. They were hoping that select committees could in some concrete manner affect the actions of Government in the here and now.

House finds itself saddled with an odd patchwork of committees of scrutiny. At least in the case of the three older committees there were certain unifying themes in their orders of reference and in the manner in which they interpreted these in practice—financial accountability, the economic management of resources, sound organisation and so on. But there is no such coherence under the new dispensation, with a pattern of committees determined largely by political expediency and with the terms of reference so vague as to exclude in some cases any possibility of defining the functions of the committees with tolerable precision.

How can this rather cheerless outcome be explained? In part it is the inevitable consequence of a superficial diagnosis of the potentialities of select committees, and of an exaggerated faith in the operative effects of disseminating more information both on those who produce it and on those to whom its lessons are directed. It was simply naïve to assume that the House of Commons could be strengthened vis-à-vis the Executive just by improving its possibilities for scrutinising the activity of government and for making information available. This is not to contest the value of scrutiny by select committee in general terms, nor to dispute the importance of information as a condition for encouraging responsiveness on the part of Governments. But it is to question whether the extension of scrutiny beyond the quite respectable level which it had already reached before 1965 can, without changes in the formal powers of committees and in party behaviour, add anything very substantial either to the influence of Members in relation to particular activities of the Executive or to their impact on the overall environment of government.

There are many reasons why this is so. Let us first consider some of the more technical reasons. The House's committees work slowly, and to a time-scale different from that of Government Departments; it is, therefore, difficult to relate what they are doing to the current activities of government. The interests of select committees are often diffuse and badly-defined: they lack the focus which those in executive positions must necessarily have. The House remains chiefly a debating stage and a legislative machine; no way has yet been found of linking intimately what select committees do with the work of the

House. (The idea that the House would be keen to debate reports of more specialised committees was always suspect and has turned out in practice to be unfounded.) It follows that the efforts of committees must always have a certain academic quality, removing them from the day to day press of business. Another problem, which perhaps deserves more attention than it has had, lies in the multiplication of official agencies and official committees of enquiry which are themselves doing many of the things which select committees purport to do, but with the advantage that they are more coherently geared to the preparation of policies and the making of decisions. To this extent a select committee may merely be duplicating in an inadequate way what is already being done elsewhere, a point which has had some relevance, for example, to the investigations of the Agriculture Committee.

There is another factor which should not be overlooked, what might be called the probability of diminishing returns from scrutiny. It has been too easily assumed that more scrutiny can only be beneficial, both to those scrutinised and to the House of Commons. Yet in comparison with most other parliamentary systems, the amount of enquiry of this kind in Britain was already in 1965 remarkably large: we know (or could know) more about the operations of government and administration than many cared to admit. It is impossible to define what is an optimum level of scrutiny, whether in terms of the impact on administration, or of improving parliamentary accountability, or of providing an occupation for backbenchers. But judging the matter negatively with regard, for example, to the reactions of departments to select committee recommendation, the extent to which Parliament, Press and public pay attention to select committee findings, and the willingness of Members to serve on committees, it is plausible to argue that the House has already pushed the quantity of scrutiny in its present form beyond the point at which diminishing returns set in. If this is so, it means that scrutiny becomes more a means of keeping backbenchers out of mischief than of performing functions which are demonstrably useful within the system of government.

Lest these criticisms appear too pessimistic, let us consider two possibilities which have been neglected in the development of select committees. If serious thought had been given to how the techniques of the select committee might have been harnessed to specific purposes, where decisions are involved and not just recommendation, it might have been recognised that they could have been applied to the legislative process. Few dispute the unsatisfactory nature of standing committee scrutiny of Bills, nor the complexity and the imperfections of much of the public law which is passed through Parliament. This is undoubtedly due in some measure to the failure of the House of Commons to develop any means of examining Bills in detail other than debating them. Yet here is an area of activity in which it is reasonably clear that to proceed by something like select committee enquiry would permit a more thorough analysis of proposals and perhaps a major contribution to their clarification and improvement. This is not to suggest that the whole of the committee stage of legislation could be dealt with in this way: rather that major parts of proposed legislation could be better examined in this way. In practice this would mean relatively permanent and, therefore, specialised standing committees, empowered to use both standing and select committee methods. It is easy to see the objections here: the risks of slowing down the passage of some Bills and of increasing the opportunities of Members to alter or amend the Government's proposals. This brings us up against a dilemma which will be touched on later. The point at issue is, however, essentially simple. If select committee methods could be related to the legislative process, Parliament would have discovered (or perhaps rediscovered) a new function for select committees. This could be a meaningful and challenging reform.

The other possibility which unfortunately has been lost sight of is that of developing rather further the three older committees, two of them being primarily financial and the other concerned with public industry.[27] In particular not enough thought has been given to the improvement of the factual basis on which these committees work. All of them have developed a major interest in questions of efficiency and

27. Some of the possibilities inherent in strengthening the Estimates Committee were underlined by the Select Committee on Procedure 1964–65 in their Fourth Report, 1964–65. H.C. 303.

organisation. None of them, not even the Public Accounts Committee, is supplied regularly with the kind of evidence which might permit a more searching scrutiny of the performance of public administration and industry, and from the point of view of the committees a scrutiny which might be more economical in terms of time and effort. The technique of essentially discursive and often repetitive enquiry has persisted. This problem could be overcome only by the development of some kind of state efficiency audit, serving both the Departments and Parliament. In short, we may have overestimated seriously the capacities of select committees, old as well as new, to perform unaided the kind of tasks which they should be tackling. But the solution of these difficulties does not lie solely in the hands of committees or in Parliament itself: it has to be found equally within the executive apparatus.

The recent phase of committee experiment was started under a banner which proclaimed the crucial importance of scrutiny as a means of disseminating more information about the activities of government. It was believed by many that this of itself would in some way strengthen Parliament. But in essentials this case rests upon peculiarly academic assumptions about important elements in the political process. Of course, the persuasiveness of the argument about information and enlightenment is understandable in the British context: we do maintain an unusually strong atmosphere of personal accountability around Ministers and we do pay a lot of attention to publicising, often in great detail, the deeds and misdeeds of governments. But we should not conclude from the general proposition that information is a crucial element in the maintenance of an environment favourable to responsive government, that those who share significantly in the dissemination of information necessarily gain any specific influence at all in the formulation of public policies or in the making of particular decisions. For the capacity to make or share in the making of decisions depends both on the formal allocation of powers as well as on the political means available to the participants to sustain their preferences. The British parliamentary system confers nearly all formal powers of decision-making on Ministers, and as is well known Members of Parliament viewed as participants in the making of decisions normally have few political resources at their disposal which might enable them to assert successfully their preferences. The diffusion of information by and to Members cannot be expected to alter significantly this situation. The right to enquire and to enlighten confers no formal right to share in decisions, nor does it constitute an increment of political power in the absence of other conditions being met which enable those concerned to insist that their views and interests are taken account of at the right time. In short, the case for extending select committees so that more information is available and enlightenment increased may be plausible in relation to the overall environment of government, but it cannot be assumed that it will have any specific effects on the roles of the main actors in the process of government. It was perhaps a misunderstanding of this basic kind which encouraged expectations of the growth of select committee activity which are now seen to have been pitched too high.

In the last resort there is no escape from the permanent dilemma of parliamentary reform in so far as it is directed to strengthening the House of Commons vis-à-vis the Executive. Fundamentally the Executive does not want this, and it could take place only if there were important changes in the structure and behaviour of the political parties. It follows that any schemes for reform—such as those for select committees which have been discussed here—find their limits whenever they show signs of disturbing the balance of power to the disadvantage of the Executive. Nor do we find a way out of this impasse when we cease to talk in terms of 'restoring' power to Parliament and talk instead of giving powers to Parliament without diminishing those of the Executive. (Such is the mode of argument of those who at the end of the day always confess their faith in the virtues of strong government.) For giving powers to Members of Parliament still means that potentially we set up positions of influence which will necessarily limit the discretion of the Executive. 'Seul le pouvoir arrête le pouvoir': the price to be paid for effective parliamentary reform in the sense predicated of the current experiments with select committees must be an interference with and some diminution of the prerogatives of party leadership and of the Executive. The disappointing results of the select committee developments flow from the refusal to acknowledge this dilemma and from the obstinate belief that desirable results can be secured in politics without paying a price for them. But this again reflects an academic view of the dynamics of political life. Political activity means choice, if it is to achieve anything at all, and every choice means the sacrifice of an alternative. The House of Commons stands in this period of transition where it has so often stood before in this century. It can go on being roughly what it has become in the era of a highly disciplined two-party system when the only effective sanction of government is the ability of the electors to turn it out—that is to say, a place where political issues are dramatised and simplified before the public, and a place where Ministers are required to answer for a surprisingly wide range of their actions. Or it can seek to become something else, that is to say a representative body conscious of its quasi-separation from government and of its right to share in some of the decisions of government. But in the latter event we must be clear that it means changing significantly our system of government. And if we do not want that, then it may be wiser to pause before depriving our existing parliamentary procedures and methods of such coherence as they have so far possessed.

Chapter 12

Whither Parliamentary Reform?

Bernard Crick

I believe that there are three questions by which the working of the House of Commons can be tested, both today and for future change: First, is the legislative process designed to enable policies to be translated into law at the speed required by the tempo of modern industrial change? Secondly, can our time-table . . . leave room for debating the great issues and especially for the topical debates on matters of current controversy which provide the main political education of a democracy? Thirdly, while accepting that legislation and administration must be firmly in the hands of the Government, does the House of Commons provide a continuous and detailed check on the work of the Executive and an effective defence of the individual against bureaucratic injustice and incompetence. It is by these three tests, I suggest, that we should try out both our existing procedures and the proposals for modifying them put forward by the various schools of parliamentary reform.
R. H. S. Crossman in the debate on procedure of 14 December 1966

If one accepts these three tests, let it be clear that one may have sensible criteria to judge how well the House of Commons is working, but not to judge how important is the House, indeed Parliament as a whole, in the whole pattern of British government and politics. Sometimes both reformers and House-traditionalists have claimed too much for the power or influence of Parliament.

The Wider Context
Take Mr Crossman's criteria in turn. The speed of legislation, on even the most superficial level, is as much a product of the organisation, attitudes and behaviour of Whitehall as of Westminster—and to speak of 'the executive' is only to provide a verbal link between two machines and cultures which at times have remarkably little mutual knowledge and interaction; and, on a more profound level, we are still on very dark and slippery ground, on the evidence of the Five Year

249

Plan and the annual economic forecasts, in thinking that 'the tempo of modern industrial change' can be speedily 'translated into law'. Rarely are we sure which is cause and which is effect. So much basic statistical knowledge is still lacking that much legislation is still a stab in the dark—and hence so much amendment.[1] But we should have learned at least that many such laws depend far more on their acceptance and on the way in which they are administered than on their hatching in 'the Cabinet', their drafting in Whitehall and their promulgation in Westminster—to allude delicately to incomes policy and the aborted Industrial Relations Bill. The question should at least arise of what do we mean by legislation? The intention, the statutes, or the effect?

Take Crossman's second point too. It is at least plain that Parliament has effective rivals in the business of raising 'current controversy' as 'the main political education of democracy'. When Bagehot used the terse phrase 'political education' to describe the main function of Parliament, which Crossman eloquently echoed, he was writing before the cheap popular press, radio and television and a universal educational system up to the threshold of manhood. All these now have their place, and it is extremely hard—no political scientists have even attempted to measure it—to see the precise nature of the primacy that Parliament may have among them either in shaping or expressing public opinion, let alone public behaviour. It is not so long ago that Parliament attempted to insist that radio and television should not discuss matters of current controversy while they were before the House. And when a 'Politics Association' was recently formed by teachers, at a large conference in London, to raise the standard of civic education, which was generally agreed to mean getting more realism and somewhat less 'constitution' into syllabuses, *The Times* did not think it worthy of mention nor the Ministry of support. Changes in the press and changes in schools could

1. See Malcolm Joel Barnett, *The Politics of Legislation: the Rent Act 1957* (London, 1969) for a rare case-study which shows how an important change of law intended to achieve certain precise targets of decontrol, drew these targets from ministerial speeches based on no real feasibility studies; and how, stuck with these targets, the Ministry made no attempt to predict the consequences of varying levels of decontrol. Such things never happen now, of course.

well have more effect on the general 'political education' of the public than any changes that are likely to come out of Parliament, but they are perhaps even more difficult to realise than changes in Parliament.

And for the former Leader of the House's third point, it is all too obvious that it both is and should be the case that press, radio and television can both rival or complement Parliament's activities in 'defending the individual against bureaucracy'. How well either do it is a different question; but neither could do it alone. Politicians and journalists quarrel like husband and wife.

Now I am not criticising Mr Crossman. I doubt if he would disagree. I only wish to point to the general context of politics in which Parliament may, perhaps, play the dominant or the primary part, but not the omnipotent or the only part. The greatest importance of Parliament is as a centre of political communication, and a two-way process. Thus while Mr Crossman's criteria should give a sense of direction to the methods of the House, they do not define its scope or relative importance. The inference I wish to draw is simply that the House should act with an outward-looking rather than an inward-looking eye. The future of parliamentary reform lies in such a direction. Many things can be done as Crossman pointed out in the same speech quoted above, to modernise the House and to increase the ease and convenience of Members, which may have little to do with enabling Parliament to have any great influence on the social and economic problems of British society.

So here I am primarily concerned with the role of Parliament as an agent of reform or, in Crossman's words, as 'an effective institution for furthering and criticising Government policy and the conduct of public affairs', not with its own internal modernisation. There are obvious connections between the two: an inefficient Parliament can delay and frustrate policy, above all it can fail to act as an important device for actually changing public opinion on particular issues;[2] but the most streamlined and well-equipped assembly in the world cannot rise above an ineffective Government or an

2. As I argue at length in Chapter 11, 'Parliament and the Matter of Britain' of my *The Reform of Parliament* (2nd Edn., London, 1968).

inert or hostile population. Someone who believes somewhat less than I do in the need for basic economic and social reforms has put the essential matter well:

No constitution, written or unwritten, is worth more than the political temper of the community allows it to be worth. The best of paper constitutions is worthless if applied to an unstable, divided or intolerant community. The worst of paper constitutions can evolve into something better in the right political atmosphere ... a narrow institutional view of Parliament can be a distorted one. It can give the impression that our political attitudes have been entirely created by Parliament whereas (although Parliament has fostered their growth) it might be equally true to say that our political attitudes have created Parliament.[3]

And Mr Butt goes on to quote the doleful remark of Sir Kenneth Pickthorn that 'procedure is all the Constitution the poor Briton has'.

Above all, parliamentary reform should not seek to 'take the politics out of politics' or to leave it elsewhere, but to make Parliament a more effective political forum. Parliamentary reform is itself a political issue, albeit one that cuts right across party lines. Some resist it because they see it as a threat to their Government—even to all government; some applaud it because they see it as a way of limiting all Governments and parties; while some see it as the need to assert something like Crossman's three criteria in a particular epoch when too many of the cards are in the hands of Governments. There is never a 'balance', but there can come about a gross inequality in the fight. This does not mean, however, that parliamentary reform automatically favours the Opposition over the Government; it can well strengthen opposition within the governing party (which is what many Ministers have against it: they can look after the Opposition, it is their own friends who worry them); and it can, on occasion, strengthen the collective ability of the House to influence, not just weakly mirror, public opinion. There is at times a terrible shyness in admitting that communication is a two-way process, and that politics is much more lumpy a business than pure smooth government or pure smooth democracy— if ever either existed alone.

3. Ronald Butt, *The Power of Parliament* (London, 1967), p. 2.

Where Do We Stand Today?

Certainly some progress has been made during the period of
the two Labour Governments since 1964, and stirrings were
abroad before that—as in the late 1950s when many began to
consider the problems of Parliament under a long period of
one-party rule and as, surprisingly quickly afterwards, some
Conservatives came to consider—a little more pressingly—
the problems of opposition.[4] But when anything in politics
gets even mildly near to improvement, it becomes a bore to
the press and the public. The press was full of parliamentary
reform from 1964–67, but when 'the Crossman reforms' went
through in the winter of 1967–68 there was little notice taken
and less enthusiasm; the Bill to reform the Lords of 1969 was
almost universally unpopular in the press, being actually
attacked for its 'political' character (in that it represented an
agreed compromise between the two front benches), and all
sorts of politically unrealistic, constitutional bright-ideas
were peddled in editorials; and, recently, the most important
report for many years of the Select Committee on Procedure,
on 'Scrutiny of Public Expenditure and Administration', got
extraordinarily little coverage in the press, and it appeared to
defeat television altogether. Perhaps basic political issues have
reasserted themselves over exaggerated hopes for reforms of
procedure? Somehow one doubts. Perhaps these matters are
just too difficult and given to the press with too little time to
digest (48 hours to be precise) before they become yesterday's
—the great god—'news'. Or perhaps Parliament simply has
to be judged by results, not by good intentions? And it can
hardly grumble at that. For we are all, after all—and politicians
must forgive us for it—usually more worried at being mis-
governed than grateful for being governed so relatively well.

4. I do not imply that nothing happened under the Conservative
Government. If the Report of the Select Committee on Procedure, 1959
was largely ignored, the debate began and the Procedure Committee
was established as a hardy annual in April 1962—though mostly dealing
with small things. Selwyn Lloyd was the most forthcoming Chancellor
of recent years, starting the White Papers on Public Investment and on
Government Lending to Public Bodies, and Maudling published the
first 'forward look' on public expenditure in 1963. Many Conservatives,
like Selwyn Lloyd, become highly interested in Parliamentary reform,
like Airey Neave's *Change or Decay* (London, 1963) group of M.P.s.
But by then political change was in the air.

Only in autocracies do people celebrate the routine competence of their rulers. In political democracies, as the great Mr Dooley, the Aristotle of the Chicago Irish, once remarked, we build our triumphal arches of bricks, not of stones, so they can be quickly torn down and hurled after the departing heroes—even a Churchill. The chairman of the Select Committee on Procedure is as inherently unlikely to be hoisted on the shoulders of the workers and the students as he is to be stoned. Most people have not heard of him—which is the position, if he is wise, that he should prefer.

Perhaps it is a good sign that parliamentary reform has become a bore; but then bores must justify themselves by looking backwards. It amounts to this: since 1964, when a really effective and continuing Select Committee on Procedure was set up on the somewhat tentative 1962 model and since the heady two years when Mr Crossman was Leader of the House, more deliberate changes in parliamentary procedure have taken place than at any recent period of the House's history—for anything like it one must go back to Balfour's reforms of the 1900s or Gladstone's of the 1870s. And if they have contained large elements of streamlining the business for the good of the Government (like the Morrison 'reforms' of 1945–46), yet they have also been deliberately balanced (unlike the Morrison 'reforms') with reforms in the interest of Parliament as a whole to improve the quality and relevance of debate or of the critical scrutiny af the administration.

The continued reappointment each session of the Procedure Committee is no small innovation and achievement. From being an occasional and spasmodic *ad hoc* creation (there were only three important reports of such a committee between 1918 and 1964, those of 1932, 1946 and 1959), it has become in the last six or eight years firmly established as a senior committee of the House and seemingly now almost as much a permanent and prestigious institution as the Public Accounts, the Estimates and the Nationalised Industries Committees. This alone is no small change. At least Westminster, if not Whitehall, is now under a continuous scrutiny and investigation. The Committee has done much good work, perhaps not enough, but certainly it has changed much of the familiar geography of parliamentary procedure. A lot of the 'parliamentary mumbo-jumbo' has gone (as other essays in this volume show): notably the end of pretending to debate Supply on Supply days so that they are now quite simply Opposition Days, and will be so called; and the Mace will remain steady on the table, as will the Speaker in the chair (or as a school essay I have just been shown puts it—'Black Bob now only comes knocking at the door when sent for at the end of each term').

At least the textbooks are now out of date, and they will have to remain so. There is now obviously going to be continual change, adjustment and experiment in details of procedure: accounts of the House, even or particularly for school children, can now no longer be sensibly written in terms of 'good old traditional procedure', but rather in terms of the basic political forces and parliamentary needs which give rise to changes of procedure—and policy! They will now be driven to explain the 'why?' and the 'what for?', not just the 'how?' of Parliament. The bulk of the Finance Bill will now probably settle down upstairs, for instance, but it would be ludicrous to write even the most simple account of Parliament which did not attempt to show what kind of items from the Bill the Opposition now pick for the three days on the Floor. The famous Three Readings *tout simple* of a Bill can now no longer be taught; the greater use of Second Reading Committees will have to be mentioned, but it is still not clear how the moving pattern will settle down, if ever it settles down like before. The Report Stage, for instance, plainly needs tidying up: it tends to be a regurgitation of the Committee Stage by the same Members who spoke at that stage, but now addressing a largely empty House. But, anyway, clear knowledge of this kind of detail never mattered as much as the textbooks implied, so it is as well that their authors may be driven to look at the contents a bit more than the vessel and to see them both as parts of a political process. The sweet fixity of procedure, which enabled so many schoolteachers and a good many Members to take refuge from policy in procedure, has now gone forever.

On the other hand, there is room for genuine disappointment. Some of it, of course, arises because all this procedural change (dare one say 'superficial'?), all the brave and vague words spoken by Ministers (of which the Prime Minister's Stowmarket speech of 3 July 1964 was the classic example) and the gentle rain of reports from the Procedure Committee itself, have all aroused quite false expectations. And on top of this must be mentioned, once again, the more professional attitudes of the new intake of Members on both sides in 1964 and 1966, their undoubted commitment to free politics, but their lesser respect for the traditions of the House and their, at times, not very great understanding of its difficulties. But some of the disappointment is more genuine. When the first round of new specialised committees were set up in 1967, as Professor Wiseman has shown, it was assumed that they would be reappointed annually. But after the Select Committee on Agriculture had had its famous dispute with the Foreign Office over visiting Brussels, Crossman tolerantly announced that it would be allowed one more session, since its work had been somewhat delayed, but that 'our original intention was that a departmental committee should spend one Session on each department and then move on'. As has been unkindly said, this 'original intention' was one of the best kept secrets with which the then Leader of the House was ever associated.

Mr John Mackintosh, himself a member of the Procedure Committee as well as the Agriculture Committee, did not share the evident satisfaction of some of his colleagues with, as it were, 'steady progress made' and 'the new status of the committee itself.' He wrote a *Times* turnover article in angry or exasperated vein:

In a special report published yesterday the (now defunct) House of Commons Select Committee on Agriculture forcefully criticises the Government's decision to end its existence. A few weeks ago the Committee on Education formally protested against the announcement that it too will be closed down at the end of the Session, while on February 11, the protracted struggle by the Nationalised Industries Committee to extend its terms of reference was finally lost. These events show that while the committees wish to continue with and even expand their work, the Government has lost any enthusiasm for this experiment. . . .

The Agriculture Committee has been replaced by a committee on the Scottish Office, which is simply to give the Government something to point to when attacked by the Nationalists; while Education is to be replaced by a committee on Overseas Aid—in Whitehall terms a peripheral and quite unimportant department. There remain committees watching over certain Acts (race relations) and institutions (the Parliamentary Commissioner) but they are not performing the main task of scrutinising sections of Whitehall. Thus instead of ending this Parliament with an established range of investigatory committees covering the key sectors on internal administration and with a solid body of Labour and Conservative M.P.s convinced by experience of the value of this work, an incoming government will inherit a run-down experiment which, if its leaders desire, can be quietly dropped.[5]

And one must remember that Mackintosh must have been writing this with at least the broad outlines in mind of the radical proposals (as we will see) of the Procedure Committee for expanding the Estimates Committee to obtain a *general and comprehensive* scrutiny of the effectiveness and efficiency of administration.[6] But all that could be seen as pie in the sky. So opinions obviously vary both as to the value of what has been done and as to the probable consequences.

What Has Been Done?

So let me try to survey briefly what has been done since 1964 either by way of changes in procedure or changes in the practices of Parliament which affect the way procedure is used,[7] limiting myself in both cases to changes which could have some real affect on the products of the whole parliamentary process and not repeating in detail matters dealt with in other essays in this book.

(i) *Salaries*. The increase of basic salary from £1,750 to £3,250 which followed the Lawrence Committee Report of November 1964 for the first time put salaries on a half-way decent level which was an essential condition for enabling

5. John P. Mackintosh, 'Dwindling Hopes of Commons Reforms'. *The Times*, 13 March 1969.

6. 'Scrutiny of Public Expenditure and Administration': First Report from the Select Committee on Procedure. 1968–69, H.C. 410, published in July.

7. A very useful more detailed and deliberately less interpretative account of the former is Clifford Boulton's 'Recent Developments in House of Commons Procedure'. *Parliamentary Affairs*, Winter 1970, pp. 61–71..

more 'young professionals' to stay in politics and for replacing a fair number of old lay-abouts (who all, of course, admirably represented the average citizen). But the basic nonsense remained that M.P.s had to meet most of the expenses of their job from their own basic salary—thus penalising the active and over-rewarding the idle.[8] Only last year did a committee of the House firmly insist on linking the question of salary to that of services and facilities available.

(ii) *Services.* The *Sixth Report* from the Select Committee on House of Commons (Services)[9] began: 'Many Members have made representations to Your Committee that their present salaries are not sufficient to enable them, in addition to paying their living costs, to meet out of their own pockets expenses necessarily incurred in the discharge of their duties.' The most important of their recommendations (on which no decision has yet been made) is that 'provision should be made at public expense for secretarial assistance or an allowance to meet the cost up to a maximum of one full-time secretary per Member'. Free trunk calls were also proposed, a more generous photocopying service and free postage on all official business both in Session and in the recess (that is to include correspondence between Members and on all parliamentary business, not just letters to Government Departments and other official bodies).[10] And they kept up their by now often

8. See my *Reform of Parliament*, pp. 62–6 for an account of the disputes about money.

9. 'Services and Facilities for Members'. Sixth Report from the Select Committee on House of Commons (Services), 1968–69. H.C. 374.

10. The kind of thing they are up against can be seen by the following paragraph from their Report,:

'14. Your Committee recommend two other small concessions which have been agreed to by the Treasury [i.e. that's as far as the Treasury would go]. These are: (i) That Members should be allowed a free supply of stationery up to the value of £25 instead of £20. (ii) That Members should be entitled to a free supply of 100 file pockets for their filing-cabinets instead of the existing 25.'

Quis custodiet custodes?, indeed. While as a tax-payer I am, of course, delighted at such strict Treasury control of the watchdogs themselves, yet as a man of average common sense I find it hard to believe that without such tight restrictions M.P.s would start to use official stationery on a vast scale for commercial, literary, social or amatory purposes, or to start selling file pockets for filing cabinets.

repeated demand for an office for each Member and his secretary—which everyone recognises to entail a new building. Their only omission was not to link the question of increasing the staff of the Commons, both on the Clerks and the Library side, to services and facilities. But quite apart from specific reports, the very existence of this committee, first set up in 1965, has given the House much more initiative and control over its own facilities than ever in the ramshackle division of authorities in the past. Perhaps quite as important as the Services Committee's advocacy on accommodation and individual facilities[11] has been the work of its sub-committee on the Library—particularly in relation to the expansion of the Research Division.

(iii) *The Library.* The Research Division in particular and the information services of the Library in general have been considerably expanded, adding scientists and more statisticians to their staff (the first statistician arrived in 1946). The House has now, in fact (although I am not sure if Mr Geoffrey Lock would agree with this description), a Legislative Reference Service such as would grace an average size American State Legislature.[12] I do not mean this ironically, for the comparison with the Legislative Reference Service of the Library of Congress (itself the national library) would be absurdly out of scale. But the Library is now just about coping with a greatly increased demand from Members, is beginning to anticipate demand (perhaps even, dangerous to say, to create it in small ways) and is plainly going to be a key institution in a reformed or still reforming Parliament. It stands at the heart of the whole communications process. And in theory there is no reason (if not in immediate practice because of staff and cost) why many of the background papers, reference sheets and

11. Strange to relate there is no clear and definitive account of what facilities M.P.s can use and are entitled to in all aspects of their work; a sub-committee of the Study of Parliament Group hopes shortly to remedy this odd omission.
12. As well as G. F. Lock, pp. 130–151 above, see David Menhennet, 'The Library of the House of Commons'. *Political Quarterly*, July–Sept. 1965, and David Menhennet and J. B. Poole, 'The Information Services of the Commons Library', *New Scientist*, 7 Sept. 1967.

bibliographies it provides for Members should not reach the public.[13]

(iv) *The Ombudsman* has been dealt with well in these essays. If his powers and his facilities are not enough, at least the foot is in the door. And it is worth remembering that the existence of the office is the result of a timely bright idea, a press campaign, and pressure from lawyers outside the House.[14] It is now only amusing to remember all those metaphysical objections about 'ministerial responsibility' and the like which evidently so worried such intensely practical men as Mr Harold MacMillan as Prime Minister and Lord Dilhorne as Lord Chancellor. Perhaps it has not really made all that much difference, but that was not what these weighty opponents prognosticated: their fears were greater than the hopes of the reformers. And the institution has been sensibly linked, after some initial fears to the contrary, to a Select Committee of the House who consider the Parliamentary Commissioner's reports and make recommendations (a linkage much on the lines that the Study of Parliament Group proposed in a privately circulated but widely reported memorandum at a time when the matter was in doubt.[15]

13. See J. B. Poole, 'Information Services for the Commons: A Computer Experiment', *Parliamentary Affairs*, Spring 1969, which described the Library's role in the experimental *Current Literature Bulletin* sponsored by the Office for Scientific and Technical Information (O.S.T.I.)—aimed at extending to civil servants, Local Government officers, libraries and social scientists bibliographical references already available to M.P.s.

Also see Antony Barker and Michael Rush, *The MP and His Information* (London, 1970), the result of research jointly sponsored by Political and Economic Planning (P.E.P.) and the Study of Parliament Group.

14. For which Mr Louis Blom-Cooper may first claim credit, in an article in *The Observer* of 31 May 1959, which newspaper then kept up the advocacy and discussion on many occasions—notably 7 June 1959; 10 and 31 January and 11 December 1960, and 12 June 1961. Other notable blows were *The Citizen and the Administration*, the unofficial report published by the lawyers' organisation, Justice (usually known as the 'Whyatt Report'); John Griffith, 'The Council and the Chalk Pit Case', *Public Administration*, Winter 1961, and the three articles he published and his own editorial in *Public Law*, Spring 1962; and Geoffrey Marshall's influential, 'Should Britain Have an Ombudsman', *The Times*, 23 April 1963.

15. See *Guardian* report under Home News, 6 Dec. 1965.

(v) *The New Committees*. Again, a mixed record both of creation and achievement, as Professor Wiseman has well shown, but a foot in the door: a general acceptance of their benefits even if continued scepticism by many M.P.s about their extent. Agriculture was shut down after considering horticulture, fisheries, the formation of agricultural policy generally and the sensitive question of agricultural prices in relation to possible entry into the Common Market; and Education was put in jeopardy after considering the school inspectorate and staff–student relations. Here the myth was born and sustained that the object of the 'Crossman reforms' of the committee system was to have departmental committees, usually no more than two, tackling one department a session but then moving on; but that there were also to be 'across-the-board' or functional committees which might enjoy a longer life—a sort of 'Ulster right' tenancy based on custom but no legal right, and the real risk of being expropriated if they improved the property. So Science and Technology continues from 1967, and in 1968 a Select Committee on Race Relations and Immigration was set up with a wide and potentially powerful remit—powerful in the sense that it is operating in a field where the leaders of both major parties will, for political reasons all too obvious, welcome not merely cross-bench support but also cross-bench initiative.[16] Perhaps the new and permanent Welsh Grand Committee comes into this category too, although at the moment it is only a debating and not a report-producing committee. And in place of axed Agriculture and Education, committees on the Ministry of Overseas Development and on Scottish Affairs—on which John Mackintosh's sardonic comments seem fully justified.

16. Their remit is 'to review policies but not individual cases in relation to—(a) the operation of the Race Relations Act 1968 with particular reference to the work of the Race Relations Board and the Community Relations Commission, and (b) the admission into the United Kingdom of Commonwealth citizens and foreign nationals for settlement'.

Their first report was on 'The Problems of Coloured School Leavers" 1968–69. H.C. 413—thus playing themselves in gently, avoiding for the beginning the most contentious issues, but a report, none-the-less, of first class importance and at the heart of the matter of race relations.

(vi) *New Developments in Committees.* The Nationalised Industries was the first since the 1930s to meet in public[17] and was the second (after the Estimates sub-committee on Government Services) since the 1920s to be allowed to employ a temporary but expert outside consultant. Generally since 1964 slow but steady progress has been made in allowing Select Committees to hear evidence but not to deliberate in public, to recruit specialist assistance up to two days a week and to meet in the field and even to travel abroad; but staffing on an adequate scale could soon become a problem, and in some ways a more acute one than that of finding enough Members to man an expanded committee system: for the House has learned that far smaller committees than in the past can be trusted and can do the work well or even better. The Nationalised Industries Committee did not fight shy of issues of major policy, as its First Report of the Session 1967–68 showed on Ministerial Control of Nationalised Industries which followed long hearings, mostly in public, of evidence from heads of the Nationalised Boards as well as Ministers, senior officials and independent experts. It has moved a long way from its early reluctance to get involved in issues of major policy even when those issues were not partisan. But, on the negative side, its wish to do a broad study of the Bank of England was disallowed,[18] after an extraordinary delay the following Session in setting up the committee at all, a delay due to civil service opposition and dispute about its proposals for new terms of reference.[19] Also on the negative side was the brief experiment in 1965–67 of allowing the sub-committees of

17. And I was the first—and very lonely—member of the public, other than officials and journalists, to attend.

18. Select Committee on Nationalised Industries, Special Report, 1967–68, H.C. 298, proposed to widen their scope to cover the Bank of England, British Petroleum, Cable and Wireless, the Independent Television Authority and some smaller bodies. It was reappointed only in February of the following Session with terms of reference allowing them to look at I.T.A., Cable and Wireless, and activities of the Bank *other than* monetary policy, management of the money market and exchange control etc.—Hamlet without the King and the Queen at least. (See H.C. Debates, 777, cols. 1181–1274, 11 Feb. 1969).

19. See Early Day Motion 81, 1968–69, tabled in December 1968 by Mr Ian Mikardo and others protesting at the delay in setting up the committee.

the Estimates Committee to specialise—following the famous Fourth Report of the Select Committee on Procedure, 1964–65 (H.C. 303).[20] But in November 1967 the size of the committee was cut down, and with the appointment of the first two specialised committees they were persuaded to give up specialisation;[21] and in the next session they suffered still further cuts in size. The new committees were won at perhaps too great a price, particularly when some of them proved so transitory—as the Procedure Committee has now come to see.[22]

(vii) *Privilege*. A Select Committee reported that much archaic matter should be swept away, that reporting of Parliament should be not even technically a breach of privilege and generally that the House should take a more pragmatic view of alleged 'contempts'.[23] But as yet the Government has taken no action on the report—it rests in limbo. The reason for including it in this list, however, is that one suspects that its logic will prove irresistible and that it will have to be acted upon if M.P.s do not abide by its advice or ever come again to embroil themselves and the press in any new round of technical, touchy and factious privilege cases—such as led to the setting up of this select committee in the first place. While the committee did not consider that the House should surrender its penal jurisdiction to the courts, it did argue that: 'In the future exercise of its penal jurisdiction the House should follow the general rule that it should be exercised (a) in any event as sparingly as possible and (b) only when the House is satisfied that to exercise it is essential in order to provide reasonable protection for the House, its Members or officers, from such improper obstruction ... as is causing, or is likely to cause, substantial interference with their respective functions.'

(viii) *Discipline in the Governing Party*. Procedure has to be seen, as we have said, in a wide and ultimately political con-

20. Select Committee on Estimates, First Special Report, 1965–66. H.C. 21.
21. Select Committee on Estimates, First Special Report, 1967–68. H.C. 28.
22. See below, pp. 267–69.
23. Report from the Select Committee on Parliamentary Privilege, 1967–68. H.C. 34.

text. Therefore, quite as important as many of the strictly procedural reforms, has been the greater easing of discipline within the Parliamentary Labour Party than in the Attlee administration. Amid trials and tribulations, mistakes and provocations from on high as well as from the depths, Crossman and Silkin, while Leader of the House and Chief Whip, went far to establish a new style of 'firm but tolerant' leadership which has allowed far more open opposition from within the governing party itself. The dropping of the proposed Industrial Relations Bill in 1969 and of the Parliament (No. 2) Bill showed the strength of the backbenchers and, for once, of the Parliamentary Labour Party, particularly when its chairman read the balance and intensity of opinion somewhat differently from the Prime Minister. And Mr Douglas Houghton has claimed that a new, or greatly revived and expanded, pattern of consultation between the Government and its Backbenchers has emerged in the last two years, born of political necessity but admirably conformable with reason.[24]

(ix) *Lords Reform.* The great frustration? A sensible and extremely well presented compromise, agreed by both frontbenches, thrown out by a strange alliance of those who thought it went too far and those who thought it stopped short of the knife. But if the dropping of the Bill, to clear the decks for the Industrial Relations Bill, also withdrawn, was either a first-class piece of mismanagement by the Government or a rather second-class vindication of the power of the backbenches, depending on how one chooses to look at it, the logic of the White Paper and the Bill can hardly be avoided whenever the matter comes up again: a nominated chamber still but with a not-too gradual weeding out of hereditary right; and with a strong and independent committee to review the kind of nominations made.[25] And one most important note for the future was struck in Appendix II of the White Paper on 'Possible Changes in Functions and Procedure': 'The proposed reform of the composition and powers

24. See Douglas Houghton, 'The Labour Back-Bencher'. *Political Quarterly*, Oct.–Dec. 1969, pp. 454–63.
25. House of Lords Reform. Cmnd. 3799.

of the House of Lords would open the way to a review of the functions and procedure of the two Houses of Parliament.'

(x) *The Finance Bill.* The 'Mumbo-Jumbo' has been taken out of Supply procedure for the voting of money and the Supply days are now in effect 29 Opposition Days which can be scattered more widely throughout the Session, taken in half-days even and, of considerable importance, subjects can be raised at 48 hours' notice—a formidable potential increase in the topicality of major debates in the House. As for the Finance Bill itself, it was eventually decided, after successive Procedure Committees had almost despaired of the Government and the House ever making up their minds,[26] that the committee stage should be taken upstairs rather than on the Floor. In the memorable committee stage of 1967–68 the Opposition made its dislike effective, proving by deliberate obstruction that it is politically impossible to thrust on the House major changes in procedure with which substantial numbers of Members simply will not co-operate. So in 1968–69 a compromise was struck which shows signs of sticking: that the bulk of the Bill goes upstairs, but that the Opposition select two or three juicy issues and can hold the floor on them for three days. The Government gets its business through more quickly, the House is less cluttered with detail, but the Opposition get the best lines and the largest audience —which is about as it should be.[27]

(xi) *Streamlining the Legislative Process.* The phrase was Mr Crossman's and this streamlining was supposed to be part of the famous 'package deal' of 1967 by which the House allowed the Government to get major legislation through with greater speed and control of the time-table in return for some concessions to the Opposition in particular and Private Members in general. Its main features were a simplification

26. The Select Committee on Procedure's Fourt Report, 1966–67, H.C. 283, had set out all possible alternatives and told the House to make up its mind.
27. Although some backbenchers with specialised or particular constituency points now count themselves losers that they cannot bring them to a standing committee which has more time than the Floor.

of the stages of most Bills—the Third Reading is now ordinarily taken without debate (S.O. 55, 14 Nov. 1967), some Bills can now be taken in committee for their Second Reading (S.O. 60, 14 Nov. 1967) and even on Report (S.O. 62, 14 Nov. 1967). Also the Guillotine can now be put after only two hours' debate. And, of course, the new arrangements for the Finance Bill. One part of the alleged streamlining broke down completely—morning sessions. These had been authorised in December 1966[28] but were soon abandoned since they provoked determined obstruction from the Opposition and had little support from the Government's backbenchers. All that was left was a provision to suspend debates until the following morning if the 'midnight hags' attempted to ride too often—which has been useful and apparently successful.[29] The concessions for this streamlining were, specifically, the changing of S.O. No. 9 to allow more urgent and topical debates,[30] the widening of the Statutory Instruments Committee's terms of reference, and the granting of half-days and motions at 48 hours' notice for Supply (now Opposition) Days; and, more generally, a noticeably more relaxed attitude by the business managers of the House towards Private Members' rights—so as not to put the new arrangements under strain.[31] But procedure on legislation is still a patch-work quilt with remarkably little shape or pattern. No such conceptual breakthrough has been made as, even on the level of reports if not of implementation, appears to be the case for financial control.

28. See the motion moved and the debate, H.C. Debates, 738, 14 Dec. 1966, cols. 70–610.

29. See Sessional Order of 12 Dec. 1967 and S.O. of 12 Nov. 1968.

30. Select Committee on Procedure, Second Report, 1966–67. H.C. 282. This could become important and perhaps deserves singling out. For about five debates a Session of this kind have taken place since all the old precedents were swept away and the Speaker given complete discretion. They take place the day after being raised and at 3.30 p.m. —hence they get great publicity.

31. Mr Douglas Houghton has recently argued that backbench pressure 'has persuaded the Labour Government to end the hypocrisies and the frustrations of the traditional procedure on Private Members' Bills'. With some obvious pride and justification he points to the number of important Bills on moral issues which have passed in recent Sessions—the Government no longer allowing any small group of Members to filibuster them out of existence. See his 'The Labour Back-Bencher', op. cit.

The House is still hypnotised by legislation actually before it, and spends far too much time on Bills that are going to pass anyway, but too little time (and what time there is, far too haphazardly) on the 'pre-legislative' stage of legislation and on subsequent detailed and systematic scrutiny of what happens to the law-as-voted-upon when it becomes the law-as-acted-upon—or not, as the case may be.

(xii) *Estimates and Public Expenditure.* Most radical of all have been proposals by the Procedure Committee to gain greater 'control' or influence over public expenditure by devising procedure to look at public expenditure as a whole—not just of individual services on an unreal year to year basis, but the implications of each authorisation for future expenditure over several years, and also whether it is giving value for money or proving cost-effective. The committee made two main recommendations: (1) That the proposed new annual White Paper on Expenditure should be the occasion of a major debate on the Floor, and that it should both furnish detailed reasons for variations in estimates and make a five-year projection, based on the first three years for which the Government will have taken decisions, of the whole pattern of public expenditure and income.[32] (2) That the Estimates Committee should be reconstituted as the Select Committee on Expenditure. It would then divide into eight sub-committees each specialising in a broad field in such a way as to cover all activities of government and the nationalised industries and public corporations. Each of these sub-committees would have a three-fold task:

(a) It should, first, study the expenditure projections for the Department or Departments in its field, compare them with those of previous years, and report on any major variations or important changes of policy and on the progress made by the Departments towards clarifying their general

32. Which proposals were foreshadowed in Michael Ryle's 'Parliamentary Control of Expenditure and Taxation', *Political Quarterly*, Oct.–Dec. 1967. But Ryle put the case for a new Economic Affairs Committee to prepare the ground and to look in detail at the assumptions made in such projections. To follow his argument would suggest that the proposed new committee structure might have too many disparate tasks foisted upon it.

objectives and priorities. (b) It should examine in as much detail as possible the implications in terms of public expenditure of the policy objectives chosen by Ministers and assess the success of Departments in attaining them. (c) It should enquire, on the lines of the present Estimates Sub-Committees, into Departmental administration, including effectiveness of management.[33]

In other words, that the House should shift from its attempts at querying changes in Estimates, on the one hand, and piece-meal and sporadic investigations of particular subjects, on the other, into attempting to discover the assumptions on which policies and economic projections are made; and generally to see financial control as concerned with the whole efficiency of a department, with getting value for money, in relation to the policies of a department. And the committee's proposals would involve winding up the ad hoc new specialised committees, but putting all hands and extra staff into a greatly expanded and specialised Estimates or Expenditure Committee.[34] For once it is not misleading to report good intentions as progress: to establish the correct concepts is more than half the battle. For the first time a senior committee of the House has grasped fully the indissoluble link between public administration and public finance (not helped by the almost complete divorce of these two activities when taught as subjects in the academic syllabuses and textbooks).

If one thinks, as I do, that the whole parliamentary reform movement of the last six years has been concerned simply to match the new machinery of the executive with new machinery in Parliament, the responses have been piece-meal and opportunistic, assessable and even mildly heartening in quantity rather than in quality, until this last report of the Procedure Committee. But this last report attempts to match qualitatively the stress on accountable-management and cost-efficiency analysis that runs all through the Plowden Report on Control of Public Expenditure and the Fulton Report. The new Estimates

33. First Report from the Select Committee on Procedure, 1968–69. 'Scrutiny of Public Expenditure and Administration'. H.C. 410.

34. As was generally argued for in the Study of Parliament Group's evidence to the Select Committee on Procedure of 1964–65, republished in *Reforming the Commons*, the Oct. 1965 issue of P.E.P.'s serial, *Planning*.

sub-committee would be equipped to follow these developments, to scrutinise them intelligently, even to stimulate them further. At last it has been seen that financial control is meaningless in terms of book-keeping and pounds, shillings and pence unless it can comprehend and control the efficiency or inefficiency of the management of resources. Expenditure is a function of management. The only doubt, however, is that beyond management there is still policy. In governmen, management is ultimately a function of policy: what different patterns of expenditure can be created and rendered more compatible, self and mutually sustaining; but also, far beyond and above that, what patterns of priorities *should* be instituted? Political ends need better technical means, and Whitehall is now reaching and Westminster could reach far in those directions; but techniques do not determine ends, or if they do then 'we', in any possible sense (politicians, voters or simply mankind) have lost control indeed or, more likely, cannot understand the unconscious assumptions and moral goals on which we are in fact basing our techniques.

What Still Needs to be Done?

To be brief and not to repeat what is elsewhere.[35] Oh like Bentham that one could go on for ever plagiarising oneself in ever new words, sometimes jargon and sometimes sprightly, all as if newly invented!

Parliament should not and does not threaten the ability of a Government to govern. But it still needs, in the most general terms, to make sure that more and more of that government is 'opened up' to the light of publicity and that controversies can take place at a time early enough to affect a Government's thinking, not when matters are cut and dried into the Bill as printed for the First Reading or the Order in Council or other Statutory Instrument. This should be done, briefly, for three reasons: because it ought to be done as a matter of principle (democracy has far more to do with openness, communication and publicity than it has to do with direct participation);[36] because it is likely to prove educative

35. See Chapters 10 and 11 of my *Reform of Parliament*.
36. See my ' "Them and Us": Public Impotence and Government Power', being the University of Nottingham's Gaitskell Memorial Lecture for 1967. *Public Law*, Spring 1968.

to the public if it is so done; and because if so done it is likely (or more likely than any other way) both to mobilise more energy and support behind the Government's economic policies and to stop a Government in time before it attempts the impossible in terms of public opinion or expert support. The functions of Parliament in 'mobilising consent' (in Professor Samuel Beer's phrase) and in 'mirroring opinion' (John Stuart Mill's) are equally important and are a fully complementary relationship. Where major Bills have had to be withdrawn, as in the salutary lesson of Lords reform and industrial relations in 1969, it has been precisely because of a double failure of the Government to build up support in public opinion first and among its own backbenchers— themselves usually the best missionaries.

Perhaps we can now begin to apply, in this light, Mr Crossman's three tests[37] quoted at the head of this essay: the efficiency of the legislative process, the effectiveness of the House in airing great issues topically, and the quality of its defence of the individual against the bureaucracy. And to see them in the light of four likely tendencies of future development. I see as overwhelmingly likely that (i) the House of Commons will spend less time in consideration of legislation already before the House (which is going to pass anyway, by virtue of parties fighting elections with programmes) and more time in looking at the before and after of legislation thus narrowly conceived: it will both 'get into the act earlier' and stay with it longer. (ii) The House will create more facilities to enable individual M.P.s and committees to participate in these processes more fully and to be more fully informed—a general increase in staff, particularly in the Research division of the Library, but also a general application of Fulton doctrines on the Clerks' side too. (iii) The eventual reform of the House of Lords will lead to a rationalisation of

37. Just to pause to say, 'Damn all those authors and M.P.'s who deliberately or in unguarded moments talk (*o mea culpa!*) about '*the* function of Parliament', and then worry, as does Mr Michael Foot. for instance, that 'the vital function of debate' gets neglected if everyone runs to earth in committees. Parliament does and should fulfil many functions and, with all those M.P.s can give a fair crack of the whip to them all if it thinks in relative and proportional, rather than absolute, terms.

functions between it and the Commons, so that it will develop more into an Upper Chamber of committees to the Commons, a House of Scrutiny which will do those things which the busy Commons leave undone rather than to presume to censure those things which it ought not to have done. And (iv) the way of working of Parliament will be profoundly affected by both the opening-up and the greater degree of professionalism in the new Civil Service and by the increasing degree of occupational mobility in British professional life as a whole—there will be more people around with experience of different sectors of the economy and the national life as a whole, and this will help to take away the mystery from each: the precise political effect will be more resignations among senior M.P.s and Ministers and fewer slavishly loyal and over-reliable hangers-on.

These things will emerge as a consequence both of decisions already taken in the narrow field of parliamentary procedure and of changes more basic by far in British society, particularly in the social structure and educational experience of the professions. But how well they will work is quite another matter. Here certain things need to be done or to be seen correctly which are by no means as highly probable.

The Legislative Process. It may seem odd to say, but the primacy of the political needs to be asserted if we are not to turn into an unreflective technocracy only concerned with identifying trends and delaying them or accelerating them. Consider again the Procedure Committee's excellent report on 'the Scrutiny of Public Expenditure and Administration.' It moves the House forward into the post-Fulton world of accountable management. But, as we have said, the management function cannot provide goals any more than the accountancy function can, and if the goals are wrong or self-contradictory, neither the economy nor the quality of life can be rewarding. To come down to brass tacks: would the proposed net-work of sub-committees of the Expenditures Committee sweep away the existing and hard-won specialised committees? Their report leaves this profoundly unclear. Several of these committees have, quite apart from financial control, raised issues of policy, not always but often, well.

This should not be lost. Policy cannot simply be reduced to cost-effectiveness. Cost-effectiveness of what and for what? The House must do both tasks: scrutinise the real effectiveness of the administration and question the assumptions behind its policies, but also float new policies, form an alternative source of policy advice and influence to . . . one wonders what even to name? Both tasks need doing. If the objection is numbers, the answer is simple: the kind of things the Procedure Committee wishes a new Expenditure Committee to do can be done, in the sub-committees, by very few people indeed *if* they have sufficient clerical, administrative and expert help. But select committees like the Race Relations Committee and the Education Committee need more members, adequately to mirror sections of opinion within the House, because they are—and should be—dabbling in policy.

The Sixth Report of the Procedure Committee for 1966–67, on Public Bill Procedure, needs to be kept in mind: their argument for pre-legislative committees. The danger of this is, of course, that it would simply add another stage: the pretence of consultation at 'an early stage' can be more galling than the cut and dried commands. The idea is right, but the means are far less likely to be yet new committees, than the uncovering of areas of administration or public concern which need new legislation or amendments to statutes as a result of increased select committee activity. The House will get in first by getting in first, helping to create the climate of opinion which makes legislation appear necessary—not by asking to be told a little earlier what the Government intends to do. There may be a case for both, but the latter without the former would be a Pyrrhic victory.

The traditional concept of control of legislation is that the House is primarily concerned only with the stages of a Bill before it, but this concept is really relevant only to those Bills which emerge directly from the party programmes. But there are at least two other major sources of legislation: inconsistencies and contradictions between previous laws discovered in administrative practice, or else quite simply the lack of powers to carry out already agreed public policy or the plain public interest; and the need to react to unexpected events. The committees of the House are wise to keep clear of the first, but with the other two they should reach a point where they discover the administrative problems at about the same time as the department does (if all functions were covered by permanent and specialised committees), and can speedily hold inquiries into the nature of unexpected events which affect the public interest.

In general on legislation I cannot do better than to quote the words of my colleague, Mr Stuart Walkland:

> The legislative process in Britain is first and foremost an executive process, and this it will, and should, remain. Parliament has many virtues and many capacities, particularly those associated with a wide and varied membership, an ability to reflect electoral fears and wishes, and to represent to a government 'the state of the nation'. Its capacity for detailed work of a specialist kind is, however, necessarily limited by the capacity and experience of its members; it is far greater than most Ministers and civil servants would credit it with, and rather less than some parliamentary reformers wish to believe. But policy needs to be developed and legitimised by the activity of an informed and representative assembly. To advocate changes that would ensure this is not to advocate parliamentary dominance of what is and should be an executive function. It is, however, an attempt to add a realistic and powerful political dimension to the work of government. That is what Parliament exists for; that is what it often finds difficult to do at present.[38]

We are getting nearer the time when backbench M.P.s will realise that what is actually in the Bill as it advances to the Second Reading, whether upstairs, downstairs or in my lady's chamber, can often be very much a product of the degree of scrutiny that a department has been subject to and to the evaluation that has been put, by both Westminster and Whitehall on how the previous legislation in the particular field worked out in practice.

Airing the Great Matters. Again, no wish to underestimate the importance of procedure—providing more time for Opposition Days, adjournment debates and emergency debates etcetera; but these must be seen in the whole context of communications. No one has even begun to study the actual

38. S. A. Walkland, *The Legislative Process in Great Britain* (London, 1968), pp. 103–4.

effectiveness of Parliament as a communicating device with the public, nor yet how well the Press does this part of its job. The working of the lobby and lobby correspondents are, unfortunately, arcane if fascinating trivialities compared with gaining a better knowledge of how much opinion filters up, and how much filters down. Two things are fairly clear: that the House still has many absurd restrictions on the working of journalists, but also that few, if any, papers have staff remotely large enough to cover properly and to digest adequately either parliamentary proceedings or parliamentary and government publications. The Press is very touchy on this score. The meanness of proprietors goes hand-in-glove with an ingrained and rather charming old-fashioned amateurism in the style of operation of most political and lobby correspondents.

Debates are vitally important, but they are only one part of a total flow of information—a flow so great that it threatens at times to defeat its own objects and to drown us in milk and honey. Digesting becomes of vital importance. And still more so journals or periodicals of record—which would simply record what has been done in Westminster and Whitehall, knowledge which otherwise vanishes in the day to day reporting and the worship of the great Moloch, 'Instant News'. As many people feel that the future of the press, if it is to resist television as news, lies in developing better features and background material, so the effectiveness of Parliament in the future may lie less in picking out and sharpening 'great debates', but in continuing itself to develop—and to release to others, above all to journalists—digests of what has happened over reasonably long periods of time. If the Library of the House of Commons moves this way, there is no real reason—and there would be much public benefit—why it should not ultimately become a centre of service not merely to Members, but to journalists and academics as well: part always, of course, for the urgent needs of Members; but a new and larger part as a centre that studied and disseminated information about what has happened in Parliament to all who need to know. It is an odd thought that 'the Mother of Parliaments' has no publication like *The Congressional Quarterly*—and a still odder thought that few readers will know what I am talking about. Look and see. Trivial or academic? I think not. The character of any organisation is much affected by reading well-informed and intelligently critical accounts of what it has been doing—far more so than by the always expected, hence always discountable, brick-bats, laurel wreaths and ordinary wreaths of the daily press.

Individual Rights. Again the importance of the House cannot be underestimated. But alone it is not enough. It is beginning, ever so slowly, to sink in that even Parliament plus Parliamentary Commissioner and our good old courts still leave some odd gaps. It is now over 40 years since William Robson published his *Justice and Administrative Law*. Rumours are rife, among a few, that Ministers have actually asked for and read papers arguing the case for a new administrative jurisdiction, and that some civil servants now have a fairly clear idea that countries can be governed which have a Conseil d'Etat.[39] Again, this idea is not opposed to the growth of specialised committees, but rather complements it; and perhaps a direction in which a section, at least, of a reformed and de-politicised Upper Chamber might move.

Above all, however, a point not covered in Mr Crossman's three tests: the degree to which Parliament is the centre of our national life. After all these criticisms, I hold—and dare to presume that most of my fellow essayists do—to a somewhat old-fashioned but true view of things: that as much as one needs to specialise and distinguish, something has to pull all threads together and look at all things that affect each other as part of one system. And in our national life that is Parliament. Ultimately knowledge and information, to be used as well as gained, depend upon the contact of acting and thinking men in different fields, professions, vocations— classes and regions even. Anything that is important, and anyone who has anything to say that is important, should somehow pass before or through Parliament at some time.[40]

39. See especially J. D. B. Mitchell, 'Administrative Law and Parliamentary Control'. *Political Quarterly*, Oct.–Dec. 1967.
40. But this is not to imply that Parliament need be in one place all the time. I see no overwhelming reason against, and much advantage

M.P.s can sometimes be as strangely isolated on an island as can civil servants in a ministry or the management or workers of a great industry—not to mention Fleet Street, despite its pride to the contrary. This is the ultimate point and test of select committee procedure and 'opening up' the civil service; that all those who have problems in common should meet, and that meeting place is Parliament. When people of real or believed importance think that Parliament can be by-passed, be they Ministers, industrialists, trade union leaders, it is up to Parliament to prove that they are wrong. The power of Parliament was never great, so cannot be restored; but its authority influence and prestige was once greater, and should be greater again—but in a very different manner.

---

for, those aspects of parliamentary control which affect Scotland and Wales, particularly or peculiarly, being exercised in Scotland and Wales. The devolution of Parliament is a more realistic speculation than the setting up of new parliaments.

Index

Index

Fontana Philosophy Classics

This series of texts and anthologies, with substantial introductions, was originated by G. J. Warnock and is being continued under the editorship of A. M. Quinton.

The Principles of Human Knowledge and
Three Dialogues Between Hylas and Philonous
George Berkeley   *Edited by* G. J. Warnock   **40p**

An Essay Concerning Human Understanding
John Locke   *Edited by* A. D. Woozley   **50p**

Leviathan
Thomas Hobbes   *Edited by* John Plamenatz   **45p**

A Treatise of Human Nature
David Hume **Book I**   *Edited by* D. G. C. Macnabb   **50p**
Books II and III   *Edited by* P. S. Ardal   **60p**

Hume on Religion
Edited by Richard Wollheim   **45p**

Russell's Logical Atomism
Edited by David Pears   **50p**

A Guide to the British Moralists
Edited by D. H. Monro   **75p**

Utilitarianism
Edited by Mary Warnock   **40p**